The Politics of Succession

The Politics of Succession

Forging Stable Monarchies in Europe, AD 1000–1800

ANDREJ KOKKONEN
JØRGEN MØLLER
ANDERS SUNDELL

OXFORD
UNIVERSITY PRESS

Great Clarendon Street, Oxford, OX2 6DP,
United Kingdom

Oxford University Press is a department of the University of Oxford.
It furthers the University's objective of excellence in research, scholarship,
and education by publishing worldwide. Oxford is a registered trade mark of
Oxford University Press in the UK and in certain other countries

© Andrej Kokkonen, Jørgen Møller, and Anders Sundell 2022

The moral rights of the authors have been asserted

Impression: 2

All rights reserved. No part of this publication may be reproduced, stored in
a retrieval system, or transmitted, in any form or by any means, without the
prior permission in writing of Oxford University Press, or as expressly permitted
by law, by licence or under terms agreed with the appropriate reprographics
rights organization. Enquiries concerning reproduction outside the scope of the
above should be sent to the Rights Department, Oxford University Press, at the
address above

You must not circulate this work in any other form
and you must impose this same condition on any acquirer

Published in the United States of America by Oxford University Press
198 Madison Avenue, New York, NY 10016, United States of America

British Library Cataloguing in Publication Data
Data available

Library of Congress Control Number: 2021952609

ISBN 978-0-19-289751-0

DOI: 10.1093/oso/ 9780192897510.001.0001

Printed and bound by
CPI Group (UK) Ltd, Croydon, CR0 4YY

Links to third party websites are provided by Oxford in good faith and
for information only. Oxford disclaims any responsibility for the materials
contained in any third party website referenced in this work.

We dedicate this book to our children; Andrej's daughter Siri; Jørgen's sons Erik, Bjørn, and Bror; Anders's daughter Linn and his son Harry. May they inherit a world of political stability.

Preface

'In this world, nothing is certain, except death and taxes,' wrote American Founding Father Benjamin Franklin. For social scientists working on state-building and political stability, the latter issue—taxation—has received sustained attention but the same cannot be said of the former of Franklin's two certainties, death. This is surprising, considering that leader transitions have been a daunting challenge in most historical societies. It continues to be a test that modern authoritarian regimes regularly face and often fail.

An autocratic system where political power is vested in one person will almost automatically struggle when it comes to passing that power on. In the past, the fate of entire kingdoms could be decided by a ruler being childless, or by vague rules of succession in cases where several members of a royal family laid claim to the throne. This book investigates how European monarchies struggled to overcome this succession problem.

To do so, it hones in on the institution of primogeniture (eldest son taking the bulk of the inheritance), which has been at the receiving end of a lot of criticism by social scientists in the period since the American Revolutionary War and the French Revolution. The abolition of primogeniture was one of the few reforms of social institutions that the English cleric and scholar Thomas Robert Malthus acknowledged as being able to mitigate the 'Malthusian Trap' of population growth outpacing increases in food production that he has famously given name to. According to Malthus, doing away with primogeniture would decrease human suffering by equalizing property and increasing the number of agrarian proprietors, and he singled out the absence of primogeniture in the United States as a key reason for its ability to sustain large increases in population (Winch 2013: 25, 30). This point was echoed by the French nobleman and political scientists Alexis de Tocqueville (1984[1835/1840]: I.i.3), who saw the lack of primogeniture as one reason for the equality of conditions that he found in the young American republic he visited during nine months in 1831–1832. Primogeniture has also been identified as an institution that has sustained the agrarian nobility—large landowners—that Barrington Moore (1991[1966]) saw as the enemy *par excellence* of modern representative democracy (Mahoney 2003: 364–5).

We do not dispute that primogeniture has been the cause of much evil well into modern times. But this book shows how long before that—in the period from AD 1000 up until the French Revolution—the development and spread of primogeniture hereditary monarchies stabilized political rule in Europe. The famous and often parodied saying 'The King is dead, long live the King' illustrates a power transfer mechanism that has provided for a remarkable political durability, in which there is no gap in political authority, no *interregnum*. As Fichtner (1989: 84) pointed out more than a generation ago, 'dynastic history is also part of the modernizing process.' What we term the 'politics of succession' therefore sheds light on important aspects of European state-formation. The main ambition of the book is to place this insight as a new and independent line of research.

The idea behind the book goes back to 2011, when Andrej Kokkonen and Anders Sundell started mapping succession practices and fates of European monarchs. Jørgen Møller had meanwhile stumbled upon the political importance of succession in a study of the development of medieval parliaments in the Iberian Crown of Aragon and therefore paid close attention when Andrej and Anders started publishing their work. The result was a gradual collaboration, eased by Andrej Kokkonen's two-year spell as associate professor at the Department of Political Science in Aarhus 2017–2018, which now culminates with this manuscript.

The data collection for the book has been funded by the Swedish Research Council, grant 2014-00604. Further support has come from the Danish Innovation Fund, grant 4110-00002B and from the Independent Research Fund Denmark, grant 1028-00011B. We would like to thank various publishers and journals for allowing us to reproduce material from previously published articles. An earlier version of Chapter 5 has been published as Andrej Kokkonen and Anders Sundell (2020), 'Leader Succession and Civil War', *Comparative Political Studies* 53(3–4): 434–68, reproduced with permission from Sage Publications. An earlier version of Chapter 6 has been published as Andrej Kokkonen and Anders Sundell (2014), 'Delivering Stability—Primogeniture and Autocratic Survival in European Monarchies 1000–1800', *American Political Science Review* 108(2): 438–53, reproduced with permission from Cambridge University Press. An earlier version of Chapter 7 has been published as Andrej Kokkonen and Jørgen Møller (2020), 'Succession, Power-sharing, and the Development of Representative Institutions in Medieval Europe', *European Journal of Political Research* 59(4): 954–75, reproduced with permission from John Wiley and Sons. An earlier version of Chapter 8 has been published as Andrej Kokkonen, Suthan Krishnarajan, Jørgen Møller, and Anders

Sundell (2021), 'Blood Is Thicker than Water: Family Size and Leader Deposition in Medieval and Early Modern Europe', *Journal of Politics* 83(4): 1246–59, reproduced with permission from University of Chicago Press. A special thanks goes to Suthan for his excellent contribution to this work.

We are also indebted to our editor at Oxford University Press, Dominic Byatt, who has supported the book wholeheartedly from the very first day we contacted him to present the idea and who organized an efficient and constructive review process. We have benefited much from the four reviews, over two rounds, that Dominic solicited and wish to thank these anonymous reviewers for taking their time to read and comment—so very usefully—on our work. Finally, we are indebted to the many other people who have provided inputs along the way. The Departments of Political Science at Aarhus and Gothenburg University, where we work, have offered academically as well as socially stimulating environments, at least until the Covid-19 closedown. Suthan Krishnarajan, Svend-Erik Skaaning, David Andersen, Tore Wig, Carl Henrik Knutsen, Agnes Cornell, Jonathan Stavnskær Doucette, Jakob Tolstrup, Carl Dahlström, Victor Lapuente, Andreas Bågenholm, Avidit Acharya, Alexander Lee, Anne Meng, Yuhua Wang, Jan Teorell, Johannes Lindvall, Scott Abramson, Mats Hallenberg, Lars Hermanson, Joakim Scherp, Wojtek Jezierski, Lisa Blaydes, Anna Grzymala-Busse, Leandro De Magalhaes, Magnus Bergli Rasmussen, John Gerring, Jacob Gerner Hariri, Bertel Teilfeldt Hansen, Oendrila Dube, Mikael Gilljam, Sören Holmberg, and many others have provided feedback and offered other kinds of help.

Contents

1. Introduction — 1
2. The Politics of Succession — 19
3. Conceptual Framework and Data — 44
4. The Origins and Spread of Primogeniture — 60
5. Civil War and International War — 88
6. Leader Depositions — 111
7. The Development of Parliaments — 134
8. Family and Dynasty — 158
9. The Politics of Succession in Comparative Perspective — 183
10. Conclusions — 205

Bibliography — 224
General Index — 240
Index of Names — 253

1
Introduction

In St. Peter's Basilica in Rome, on Christmas day in the year 800, Charles, King of the Franks and Lombards, was crowned Emperor of the Romans by Pope Leo III. At the time, Charles ruled a realm larger than any in the Occident since the fall of the Western Roman Empire, uniting modern-day France, the Netherlands, Belgium, Switzerland, Northern Spain, and large parts of Germany, Austria, Slovenia, and Italy under the rule of one man. He truly deserved the later epithet 'Charlemagne', Charles the Great. But only 43 years later, the empire he built split into three separate kingdoms.

While Charlemagne was able to conquer and incorporate vast territories, he was unable to lay the foundations for a polity that would last. His only surviving legitimate son, Louis the Pious, inherited the empire intact but gave three of his sons authority to rule different parts of the realm. When Louis died in 840, a civil war broke out between them. After three years of fighting, the Treaty of Verdun established the kingdoms of West, Middle, and East Francia, ruled by the three brothers. Western Europe would not be unified under one ruler again until the conquests of Napoleon almost 1000 years later, and then only briefly.

History contains numerous other examples of great realms that flourished under a particular ruler, only to collapse upon his[1] death. This was the case for two of the largest empires ever conquered by a single individual. In the wake of Alexander the Great's death in BC 323, his Macedonian empire was torn apart in wars between his generals. The Mongol Empire created by Genghis Khan 1500 years later splintered within the lifespan of his children and grandchildren.

But there are important counterexamples which show how power can be transferred from one ruler to the next without disruption or disintegration. The state of West Francia developed into France, which in the second half

---

[1] We use the masculine third-person pronoun to refer to a generic ruler as the overwhelming majority of rulers throughout the period we study in this book have been men.

The Politics of Succession. Andrej Kokkonen, Jørgen Møller, and Anders Sundell, Oxford University Press.
© Andrej Kokkonen, Jørgen Møller, and Anders Sundell (2022). DOI: 10.1093/oso/9780192897510.003.0001

of the seventeenth and in the early eighteenth century was ruled by another Louis, the Fourteenth (XIV). In a reign lasting 72 years, Louis centralized power and expanded France's influence abroad, earning him the epithet 'the Sun King', the star around which all planets orbit. When Louis died in 1715, power was handed down not to his son, nor even to his grandson, but to his five-year-old great-grandson. This happened in an entirely peaceful and orderly way, and when Louis XV came of age, he was in possession of one of the most powerful states of Europe, inherited intact from his great-grandfather. He would go on to rule for 59 years.

The stark difference in the way these successions played out does not simply reflect a secular trend of increased political stability. Less than two decades after the accession of Louis XV, the death of Augustus II of Poland sparked an international war of succession that drew in major powers such as France, Russia, and Austria. While the outcome of the war was that the eldest son of Augustus II eventually took the throne, the fighting over the Polish throne cost tens of thousands of lives and sowed the seeds of the Polish state's destruction towards the end of the century, when it was dismembered by its neighbours.

The explanation for why eighteenth-century France was able to cope with the transfer of power, whereas eighteenth-century Poland and ninth-century Carolingian Francia were not, lies in the principles of royal succession. At Louis the Pious's death in 840, the kingdom was treated as his personal property and divided up among his heirs. Eighteenth-century Poland was an elective monarchy, one of the last remaining in Europe, which meant that the claim of the dead king's eldest son could be challenged by other claimants. In contrast, eighteenth-century France had since long practiced *primogeniture*, hereditary succession in which the eldest son (or, if he has predeceased his father, his eldest son) inherits the entire kingdom.

In this book, we make two major claims. *First*, that the problem of succession has been a perennial driver of conflict, ruler depositions, and political instability in European history. To understand how European states formed, operated, and developed, we must therefore take succession into account, something much previous social science research has failed to do. *Second*, that the gradual adoption of primogeniture hereditary monarchy helped to mitigate the problems of succession, leading to greater political stability and allowing for the development of the modern European territorial states.

The book thus analyses European state-formation and ruler–elite relations in the period from AD 1000 up until the French Revolution through the lens of what we term 'the politics of succession'. In a series of empirical chapters, enlisting new data on succession, war, rulers and their relatives, and political institutions in Europe AD 1000–1800, we show how successions have regularly destabilized European states, but that primogeniture helped to counteract this instability, preventing coups and civil wars. We also show that fraught moments of succession increased the chance of parliaments being called to resolve disagreement and to facilitate bargaining between rulers and elite groups.

Although the empirical focus in this book is on the short-term effects of succession for political stability, they point to the importance of solving the issue of succession to create a favourable context for the more mundane state-building tasks of creating administrative, fiscal, and military structures and institutions. Primogeniture provided a solution to the problem of succession that was in the interest of both the ruler and the elite groups, and which therefore prolonged the time horizons of European state-builders. It was a revolutionary invention, which in Europe was made possible by a particular constellation of social factors, including weak state structures and an independent church.

Charles Tilly (1975; 1992) analysed the same historical process, which transformed Europe from a mosaic of petty lordships around AD 1000 to 25 territorial states around 1900, through the lens of warfare, showing how what he termed 'nation states' gradually won out over other forms of political organizations, including city states and empires. Others have singled out the importance of geographical and economic endowments, arguing that the uneven development of European states can be explained by different preconditions for agriculture and trade (Rokkan 1975; Boix 2015; Abramson 2017; Abramson and Boix 2019).

Both bodies of theory, which dominate the literature on European state-formation and which we review later, have a hard time explaining the puzzle that lies at the heart of the European development, namely why the hitherto backward region of north-western Europe would ultimately surpass the older civilization areas in the Eastern Mediterranean, the Middle East, on the Indian Subcontinent, and in Eastern Asia. After all, many of these areas also saw sustained warfare, and some of them had much denser urban populations, at least around AD 1000 where the European dynamism seems to have started (Bartlett 1993; Moore 2000; Bosker et al. 2013: 1424; Stasavage 2016: 152–3; Wickham 2016: 217; for broader overviews see Hall 1985; Mann 1986; Morris 2014; Boix 2015).

Our book complements these perspectives by highlighting how crucial the issue of succession has been for the temporal dimension of state-formation. In the short term, state-building is about controlling territory, vanquishing external enemies, neutralizing internal rivals, and raising revenue to finance the means of coercion. But in the long run, it requires institutions that transfer power from one ruler to another and sustain the state over time. Long-term state-building can only occur if a polity's destiny does not depend upon a particular individual.

To succeed, the state must become what Douglas North, John Wallis, and Barry Weingast (2009) has termed a 'perpetually lived organization'. In the European process of state-formation, polities that managed to achieve this transformation survived, while those that were repeatedly convulsed by the demise of their leaders did not, or at least did so much more infrequently. Unstable succession arrangements also directly affected the incentives of leaders and their elites during their reign. Mancur Olson (1993) famously attributed the origins of economic development to the change from 'roving bandits' to 'stationary bandits', that is, settled kings or princes ruling distinct territories. The roving bandit cares only about plunder, while the stationary bandit aims to maximize rents extracted from the populace in the long run, which allows for investment and security. Established and predictable principles of succession shift the time horizons of rulers and elites, making them more interested in the development of their kingdoms. 'If the king anticipates and values dynastic succession, that further lengthens the planning horizon and is good for his subjects', as Olson (1993: 571) puts it.

The problem of succession is not unique to medieval and early modern kingdoms in Europe. All political systems regularly face the problem of succession. Modern representative democracies address this problem by lowering the stakes of each power transfer, limiting the power of governments, and mandating recurrent elections. The peaceful transfer of power is in fact a defining character of what it means to be a democracy (Schumpeter 1974[1942]; Cheibub, Gandhi, and Vreeland 2010). Modern authoritarian systems have been less successful in this regard. Authoritarian leaders who do not hold elections are more likely to lose office violently than peacefully (Cox 2009), and among the dictators who are removed from power through non-constitutional means, most are deposed by regime insiders (Svolik 2012), indicating that elites often do not agree on how to uphold the regime.

It is hardly surprising that systems that concentrate power into the hands of a single individual have a hard time dealing with a change in authority. What is so fascinating about the primogeniture monarchies of medieval and early modern Europe is that they managed to combine centralization of power with durability and stability. North, Wallis, and Weingast (2009) argue that a hallmark of perpetually lived organizations is that they are 'impersonal'. However, hereditary monarchy is in its essence highly personal and biological. Power is perpetuated through biological reproduction, and legitimacy is conferred by virtue of royal blood (Bartlett 2020: 1). Nonetheless, when it works, it allows for continuous rule, over centuries. It is thus a paradox that has proved to be highly successful and lasting, and which has made an enormous imprint on European state-formation. And at the heart of monarchy lies the issue of succession.

The importance of political stability

The problem of succession has received surprisingly little attention in the modern literature on European state-formation, which has been dominated by the two approaches mentioned earlier: the 'bellicist' emphasis on warfare and the emphasis on geographical and economic endowments.

As the name says, war and war-making take centre stage in the 'bellicist' literature. Scholars such as Otto Hintze (1975[1906]) and Charles Tilly (1975; 1992) have argued that the fundamental threat posed by war constitutes the primary driver of state-building (see also Morris 2014). To survive, a state needs a strong army; to finance this army, it needs revenue; to raise revenue, bureaucracies are created; to secure the cooperation of elite groups, representative institutions may be called; to pave the way for conscription, broader civil rights are instituted; and so on and so forth. There are many different theories about how, more precisely, the pressure to survive in the context of geopolitical competition interacted with domestic factors such as the type of local government (Ertman 1997) or the structure of the economy (Tilly 1992; Downing 1992; Spruyt 1994), but the fundamental role of war-making is not questioned. Recent empirical contributions include studies on how mobilization for crusades affected institutional development (Blaydes and Paik 2016) and how battles promoted urbanization by forcing people to flee to cities (Dincecco and Onorato 2018). These developments arguably left an imprint on the nature of the state that can be seen even in our time, and according to recent scholarship, the dynamics of war-and-state-making still affect how states are built outside of Europe today (Herbst 2000; Centeno 2003).

The endowment literature instead stresses how initial economic factors, largely the product of geography and climate, interacted with technological developments to increase some European areas' capacity to sustain large populations, develop cities, and to cultivate the institutions these developments necessitated (Boix 2015). The seminal statement of this perspective is found in

Stein Rokkan's (1975) conceptual maps of Europe, with their heavy emphasis on the European city-belt organized around riverine trade routes (see also Tilly 1992; Spruyt 1994). More recently, Acemoglu, Johnson, and Robinson (2005) argue that it was Atlantic trade, enabled by already existing institutions which constrained the executive, that set Europe on a more prosperous path, in which trade itself promoted further institutional development and subsequent economic growth (see also Blaydes and Paik 2021). Boix (2015), Abramson (2017), and Abramson and Boix (2019) show that variations in climate led to uneven growth of city centres, and that vibrant cities enabled townsmen to place constraints on the executive and form the basis of independent states.

By focusing on the politics of succession, this book provides an important complement to both accounts. While warfare and economic and geographical factors are undoubtedly important, approaches that privilege these factors tend to have a very long-term—sometimes on the verge of deterministic—perspective. However, a closer look reveals considerable variation in the fortunes of states that had comparable endowments and were exposed to the same type of military competition. A famous example is the different trajectories—and ultimately different fortunes—of the Roman Empire of the German Nation (the Holy Roman Empire) and France and England, respectively.

Around AD 1000, the German emperor was by far the strongest ruler in the Latin west, both in economic and military terms, ruling a polity that had much higher levels of central capacity than neighbouring West Francia or France (Southern 1956: 19–20; Wickham 2009: 430, 523; 2016: 64, 77). Indeed, eleventh-century France was the sick man of that age, as the Capetian king's writ only ran effectively in a small area around Paris (Jordan 2001: 52–62; Wickham 2016: 102). Four centuries later, the Empire had become an empty shell; power had been transferred to its constituent units, including the Electorates of Brandenburg and Saxony, the Kingdom of Bohemia, and the Archduchy of Austria. Meanwhile, France and England were developing modern territorial states with a high degree of central capacity (Tilly 1992; Spruyt 1994).

This example also illustrates that the endowment literature and the bellicist approaches have a hard time accounting for European state-building patterns before AD 1200. It was only around 1200 that urban clusters became vibrant—Abramson and Boix (2019) therefore begin their analysis at this point in time—and it was also at this rather late date that warfare first intensified in medieval Europe (Ertman 1997: 25–8; Maddicott 2010: 106; Wickham 2016: 212). The explanation for the strengthening of France and weakening of the German

Empire, which mainly took place in the period 1050–1300, must lie elsewhere (Jordan 2001: 228–9; Wickham 2016: 103; see also Spruyt 1994).

To understand these reversals of fortune—or more generally why some states succeeded while others did not—it is necessary to account for short-term factors of political instability such as coups, civil wars, succession crises, and how different polities managed these challenges. For instance, the last straw for the German Empire was the great interregnum that followed the death of Emperor Frederick II in December 1250. Not until 1312 was a new emperor recognized by the Pope, and especially the period from Frederick's death until the crowning of Rudolf of Habsburg as German king in 1273 can be seen as one long succession conflict, as different claimants fought each other while the Empire's political and military infrastructure went to pieces. The 'Great Interregnum', as it is known in historiography, accelerated the breakdown of centralized public power that had already progressed rapidly in the previous 100 years (Jordan 2001). This state collapse is clearly reflected in the politics of succession. In the period 1254–1438, seven different dynasties held the German throne, and there is only one instance of a father-to-son succession (Bartlett 2020: 398).[2]

Another example is found on the Empire's western fringes. By the fifteenth century, the agglomeration of political entities controlled by the Duke of Burgundy had emerged as one of the major forces of Europe, but it fell apart when Charles the Bold was killed in 1477, leaving no male heir (Mann 1986). Large parts of the possessions were inherited by the Habsburgs via dynastic marriage, further propelling that dynasty to the pinnacles of power in Europe. These short-term developments, in combination with the institutions that moderated their impact, had long-term consequences for processes of state-formation.

Add to this that scholars have criticized the bellicist perspective for misrepresenting medieval and early modern Europe. At a closer look, this does not look like a Darwinian world where states would regularly conquer each other (Spruyt 2017; Gorski and Sharma 2017; Abramson 2017; Haldén 2020). Medieval wars were normally limited affairs that seldom resulted in one polity swallowing another, with a few notable exceptions such as the Norman Conquest of England in 1066. This does not mean that territorial agglomeration did not occur throughout the period we analyse. But it was more often a result of dynastic politics—inheritance of realms or realms uniting via marriage—than of conquest (Sharma 2015; Bartlett 2020).

---

[2] In contrast, '[b]etween the mid-tenth and the mid-thirteenth century, all German kings with sons ensured that they were acknowledged as king during their father's lifetime. There are eleven examples' (Bartlett 2020: 95).

Previous scholarship on succession

That succession is a crucial problem for states has been acknowledged by many political thinkers. Sixteenth-century French philosopher Jean Bodin (1575) noted that succession poses a challenge in monarchies even when the change is from a bad monarch to a good one, and that the problem is especially acute when the monarchy is elective:

> all elective monarchies are constantly menaced by the danger of a relapse into anarchy on the death of each king. The state is left without a ruler or regular government, and is in imminent danger of destruction, just as a ship without a master is liable to be wrecked by the first wind that blows.
> (Bodin 1967: 209)

According to Bodin, hereditary monarchy is therefore the best form of rule, specifically where the first-born son succeeds. Bodin thought that primogeniture could be regarded as a law of nature and has been observed among all peoples. Another influential proponent of hereditary monarchy was Thomas Hobbes. In *Leviathan* (1651), he discusses how political stability can be preserved through time, indefinitely, despite the mortality of man:

> Of all these forms of government, the matter being mortal, so that not only monarchs, but also whole assemblies die, it is necessary for the conservation of the peace of men that as there was order taken for an artificial man, so there be order also taken for an artificial eternity of life; without which men that are governed by an assembly should return into the condition of war in every age; and they that are governed by one man, as soon as their governor dieth. This artificial eternity is that which men call the right of succession.
> (Hobbes 1651: 119)

Sovereignty lives on, even though the individual monarch dies. Bodin (1967: 7) had used the metaphor of a ship that retains its identity even though all individual planks are replaced to describe how a people could never die. During the seventeenth century, this idea was taken one step further and applied to the monarch himself, to distinguish between the king's *body natural* and the *body politic* (Kantorowicz 1957). The natural body could die, but royal dignity was immediately transferred to the successor, so that there was no interruption in authority. The principle is summed up in the famous, but at first glance seemingly contradictory, cry 'the king is dead, long live the king.' When the king dies, he arises again immediately (given that there is a successor), without any interregnum.

Jean-Jacques Rousseau acknowledged in *The Social Contract* that monarchies have made the crown hereditary to avoid conflicts over the succession. But the cost, he argued, is worse selection of rulers; hereditary succession can result in the enthronement of 'children, monstrosities, or imbeciles' (Rousseau 1920: 75). The American revolutionary Thomas Paine noted that the strongest argument put forward in favour of monarchy is that it preserves a nation from civil wars. If this were the case, admits Paine, 'it would be weighty; whereas it is the most barefaced falsity ever imposed on mankind' (Paine 1986: 59). The evidence Paine marshals in support of this conclusion is the history of the Kingdom of England, which despite its hereditary monarchy had seen eight civil wars and nineteen rebellions, according to Paine's reckoning.

The issue of succession has thus been a recurrent feature of political thought. Most agree that it presents a serious problem; the vantage point determines the solution. Enlightenment thinkers such as Rousseau and Paine argued that the problem could be avoided entirely by eschewing the model of a single person being in charge, allowing for continuous replacement of the governing body. Those who saw the need for consolidated sovereignty and thus took monarchy as a given, e.g. Bodin and Hobbes, argued that hereditary succession avoided the pitfalls inherent in elective monarchy. As even Paine concedes, the normative argument for hereditary monarchy – and primogeniture in particular – is thus to a large extent empirical: it is desirable if it promotes stability. One of the purposes of this book is to put this claim to the test.

Modern historians also regularly take note of the way successions destabilized European monarchies in the period before the French Revolution (e.g. Kagay 1981; Procter 1980; O'Callaghan 1989; Helle 2003; Schück 2003; Wickham 2009; 2016; Maddicott 2010; Greengrass 2014; Bartlett 2020). As Jordan (2001: 77) observes, 'in all eleventh-century kingdoms and lesser principalities, it was the succession that would test the institutions and traditions of unity and cohesion.'

Historians such as Bartlett (1993) and Moore (2000) have more specifically pointed out that the ascendancy of primogeniture was part and parcel of the process that allowed the Frankish core of the Latin west to 'colonize' areas such as the British Islands, the lands east of the Elbe, the Iberian Peninsula, and Southern Italy in the period after AD 1000. Bartlett (1993: 49) associates the advent of primogeniture among Frankish nobles in the eleventh century with the expansionism that created, for instance, the Norman kingdom in Southern Italy and Sicily. His argument is that this expansionism—which gradually extended the frontiers of Latin Christendom during the high Middle Ages—was driven by disinherited younger sons of nobles and later on cadet sons of Capetian kings seeking their fortune abroad. Moore (2000) sees the introduction of primogeniture as a crucial aspect of what he terms the 'first European revolution', which took place in the eleventh and twelfth centuries, and which gradually radiated outwards from its areas of origins in the old Carolingian heartlands. According to Bartlett (1993) and Moore (2000), this process was ultimately what brought 'Europe' into being.

A separate historical literature argues that primogeniture was itself a consequence of changes in heirship practices and family structures implemented by the Catholic Church, beginning in late antiquity (Goody 1983; Hall 1985; Moore 2000; cf. Spruyt 1994: 72–3; Sharma 2015). By sundering the kinship relations among the Roman clans (*gens*) and the invading Germanic tribes, the Church made it easier for religious men and women to bequeath property to ecclesiastical institutions, possessions that would otherwise have remained in the possession of family or kin (Goody 1983). The principle of primogeniture was arguably the climax of this transformation of kin relations as it disinherited all but one family member, and it was inconceivable in the absence of the development of the European monogamous marriage and firm rules about which children were legitimate heirs—both sponsored by the Church (see also Henrich 2020).

A few modern social scientists also emphasize the historical importance of succession.[3] Gordon Tullock (1987) has presented the most elaborate theoretical argument for why hereditary succession is more conducive to stability than its alternatives. Kurrild-Klitgaard (2000) has applied this argument empirically in a case study of how de jure and de facto changes of the Danish monarchy's succession rules affected Danish monarchs' chances of surviving in office between AD 935 and 1849, finding that hereditary succession via primogeniture stabilized monarchical rule. More recently, in a statistical analysis of 812 European rulers in the period AD 1000–1500, Acharya and Lee (2019) show that a shortage of male heirs had long-term negative effects on state capacity in Europe; Wang (2018) similarly shows how an abundance of male heirs (due to polygyny) prolonged ruler tenures in imperial China in the period AD 1000–1800. A more general attempt to place the politics of succession at the heart of European state-formation has been made by Vivek Sharma

---

[3] We return to the scholarship on succession in modern authoritarian regimes in the concluding chapter.

in a string of articles and book chapters (e.g. Sharma 2015; 2017; Gorski and Sharma 2017). Sharma's general claim is that European state-formation processes were shaped by 'dynastic lordship', not by war. He further emphasizes how primogeniture conferred certain advantages in this world of dynastic politics.

The competitive edge of primogeniture also occasionally crops up in more general work by social scientists on European state-formation. When setting the stage for his analysis of the advent of the modern territorial state, Hendrik Spruyt (1994: 52) notes—without pursuing the point—that '[o]ne of the main factors contributing to the decline of the Carolingian Empire was the absence of primogeniture—inheritance by the eldest son alone.' Walter Scheidel observes the following about the Carolingian empire: '[d]ynastic feuding—fuelled by the lack of primogeniture in the royal succession—not only weakened rulers but invited intervention by aristocratic factions' (Scheidel 2019: 240).

Political thinkers, historians, and social scientists who mention the problem of succession thus all recognize its importance. Nonetheless, the politics of succession has not been given the central theoretical emphasis and systematic empirical scrutiny it deserves if we are to understand processes of state-formation and political stability, in and beyond Europe. For instance, in Francis Fukuyama's monumental *Political Order and Political Decay* (2014), succession is only mentioned in passing, in a discussion of how the Ottoman Empire was destabilized by its inability to deal with leader succession (a case we return to later). In their influential typology of different kinds of states, Douglas North, John Wallis, and Barry Weingast (2009) argue that rules of succession for the leader and the elites are an important feature that distinguish 'basic natural states' from the most primitive form of state organization, 'fragile natural states'. But they do not expand on how these rules should be designed, how they come about, or what the consequences of them are. Even Tullock (1987), in his public choice work on autocracy, fails to distinguish between different hereditary succession arrangements and only substantiates his argument with anecdotal evidence. Likewise, the historians who have emphasized the importance of succession and primogeniture have neither attempted to theorize the way the politics of succession affected European state-formation nor to apply their ideas about primogeniture in general comparative analysis (see e.g. Bartlett 2020)—and much the same can be said about the work of social scientists such as Sharma (2015; 2017). Finally, as argued earlier, the two dominant approaches to European state-formation—the bellicist and endowment literatures—completely slight the politics of succession. There is thus a need for both a more thorough theoretical treatment and a systematic empirical investigation of the issue.

The politics of succession

This book develops the scattered theoretical insights about the role of the politics of succession in European state-formation and it applies these arguments empirically. To do so, we have assembled a dataset of over 700 rulers in 27 European states between 1000 and 1799, with biographical information on the monarchs, their tenure, their marriages, their paternal aunts and uncles, their siblings, their offspring, and the end of their reign—be it a peaceful death, a violent overthrow, or an assassination. We combine this with a dataset of wars, both internal and external, as well as information about parliamentary meetings at the realm level. This allows us to paint a broad yet multi-faceted picture of the workings of European states and their rulers in a period when the foundations for the current territorial states and the current state-centred international system were laid. It also allows us to show how moments of succession often shook polities, and how the institution of primogeniture enabled elites and rulers to coordinate their efforts to uphold their regimes.

Our theoretical point of departure is the fundamental dilemma that succession creates. The main problem is designating an heir, and it is well captured by the quip, 'you can't live with them, you can't live without them.' To solidify his position, a ruler needs to convince the elite that his rule will be perpetuated. Otherwise, the elite will start making plans for the succession, and they will be tempted to carry out those plans before the ruler dies to avoid losing in the game of thrones that awaits them (Tullock 1987; Brownlee 2007). The best way to avoid such pre-emptive challenges is by designating an heir who can prolong the regime into the ruler's afterlife. However, this immediately creates what has been termed the 'crown prince problem' (Herz 1952). The heir apparent might not be willing to bide his time and is therefore a potential rallying point for opposition against the ruler.

This dilemma repeatedly politicized the succession. Historians have documented how in the historical context we analyse in this book—medieval and early modern Europe—bargaining between elite groups and rulers was most intense during successions (Kagay 1981; Bartlett 2000: 7; 2020; Jordan 2001; Bisson 2009: 102; Greengrass 2014). However, not only the rulers but also the elite groups feared succession conflicts. If they ended up on the losing side, they might forfeit their property and privileges, or even, in rare cases, their lives. As Svolik (2012: 95) puts it when describing leadership struggles in modern authoritarian states, the 'fear of joining the losing side outweighs any substantive preferences over who prevails.' Both nobles and high clergy would therefore normally prefer that a regime be perpetuated rather than risk a succession struggle that could wreak havoc and transform the composition of the elite (Brownlee 2007).

This means that both sides had an interest in solving the dilemma of succession. We argue that the hereditary principle of primogeniture, which was gradually introduced across Western and Central Europe in the high and late Middle Ages, offered such a solution. Primogeniture automatically provides the elite with a young heir who can bide his time in the knowledge that his father is a generation older and that his hereditary claim on power will make it very difficult for elite groups to side-line him or for his father to change the line of succession (Tullock 1987: 163–4). At the same time, the crown prince serves as a reminder to the elite that the regime is likely to be continued. To quote Jordan (2001: 245), '[d]ynastic stability was a *sine qua non* for getting aristocrats to see that it was to their advantage to hitch their destiny to that of the Crown.'

Primogeniture also ensured that a monarch's lands were not partitioned but left intact to a single heir, as opposed to the partible inheritance practiced under the Merovingians and Carolingians. This principle of indivisibility facilitated the merging of newly conquered and inherited lands, thus laying the foundations for the large territorial states that came to dominate Europe in the eighteenth century. This process of territorial agglomeration was buttressed by another medieval innovation, namely the principle of female inheritance when a royal family died out in the male line. As Samuel P. Finer (1997b: 1269) notes in *The History of Government*, it was only in Europe that states were consolidated through marriage alliances or testamentary succession rather than through war (see also Sharma 2015). Female inheritance contributed to solving the dilemma of succession because it enabled a transfer of realms via marriage in cases where a lineage had no male heir. This, too, stabilized dynastic politics by prolonging time horizons and by allowing a peaceful consolidation of territories, or at least one not based on conquest. But it was solely in hereditary monarchies that this possibility existed—when nobles had the right to choose rulers, they did not elect women (Bartlett 2020: 154).

By changing the rules of succession from elective monarchy (the magnates choosing the king) or agnatic seniority (oldest brother of the monarch taking the throne) to primogeniture, Western European rulers and their elites were thus able to stabilize power relationships, increase political stability, and make their states more durable, thereby prolonging their time horizons. And by abandoning the old practice of partible inheritance they could keep their states intact when passing them on to their eldest sons. The chapters that follow analyse these outcomes, which, we argue, allowed state-builders to invest in the more mundane creation of administrative, fiscal, and military institutions and structures which most prior literature on European state-formation has focused on.

Succession and European state-formation

Empirically, the book sheds new light on European political stability and state-formation from AD 1000 up until the French Revolution. In the tenth and early eleventh century, Western and Central Europe—what is often termed Latin Christendom—was in a sorry state. The Carolingian Renaissance of the eighth and early ninth century was by now a distant memory. West Francia, the future France, had experienced a virtual collapse of public power, which was also felt in other areas of Western and Central Europe, and Viking, Saracen, and Magyar incursions from the west, south, and east, respectively, had laid waste to monasteries, towns, and agricultural areas. The collapse of the urban civilization of antiquity had reached its historical climax, and many of the monarchs of Latin Christendom could hardly be said to rule their realms in any meaningful way. For instance, as mentioned earlier, the Capetian kings who first ascended the throne in 987 were long unable to exercise full authority even in their native Île-de-France region around Paris—and they had virtually no power in the other provinces of the realm of what would become France.

Centralized power was thus at an all-time nadir. Historian Thomas N. Bisson (2009: 34) dubs European authority patterns in this period 'a fabric of lordships' (see also Bisson 1979; Morris 1989). Chris Wickham (2016: 106, 109) refers to this as a 'cellular structure for politics', where local communities and local lordships made up cells of power, 'which became more formalized in the context of royal weakness'. The exercise of public power had effectively become privatized, decentralized, and fragmented, public taxation had virtually disappeared, administrative structures had been replaced by royal and noble households, in many places bishops had stepped in to fill the void where public power had buckled, and European rulers were able to muster armed forces the size and striking power of which were negligible compared to what rulers had done in late antiquity or during the heyday of the Carolingians.[4]

---

[4] Historians used to describe this fragmentation and privatization of power using the concept of feudalism but in recent generations they have largely abandoned this concept, which is why we do

While this collapse of public authority had numerous causes, one of its most important manifestations was to be found in vague rules of succession which generated repeated spikes of political instability and contributed to creating a mosaic or chequerboard of divided possessions. It was against this backdrop that attempts were made to stabilize power by changing the rules of succession, as described earlier. As we show in this book, once implemented, these new solutions of the problem of succession stabilized regime coalitions and ruler tenure, decreased the incidence of civil and international war, and allowed the agglomeration of territories that ultimately resulted in today's European territorial states. This also made family members an asset for the purposes of state-building. We thus show how offspring and siblings stabilized leader tenure and how primogeniture prolonged dynasties.

This process of stabilization of rule via succession arrangements set the Latin west apart from the other civilization areas of Eurasia, with the partial exception of East Asia (see Chapter 9). There was nothing particular about the political fragmentation and succession conflicts that we find in Europe until the adoption of primogeniture. Similar dynamics characterized Muslim polities in the Middle East and the great empire created by Genghis Khan and his descendants in the thirteenth century (Rossabi 2012; Stasavage 2020). Likewise, the Roman, Byzantine, Ottoman, and Russian Empires are merely the most famous examples of polities that, while having a remarkable staying power, were regularly rattled by political conflicts that broke out after the passing of their rulers (Finer 1997a: 623–64; Wickham 2009). For instance, Tim Blanning (2007) emphasizes both how Peter the Great's Russia was destabilized by the problem of succession and how this set it apart from Western Europe:

> Peter's failure to westernize his state was revealed most clearly in his failure to solve what is arguably a monarchy's most fundamental problem: the orderly transfer of power when the current incumbent dies ... In the west, this had been solved by the principle of primogeniture.
>
> (Blanning 2007: 240–1)

It was thus in the Latin west, and to a lesser extent in East Asia, that primogeniture was systematically adopted to combat the centrifugal forces created by partible inheritance or vague rules about succession. As Moore (2000: 66) puts it when describing the eleventh and twelfth centuries' transition to

not use it in this book (see Brown 1974; Ward 1985; Reynolds 1994; Bisson 2009; but see Wickham 2016: 10).

16   THE POLITICS OF SUCCESSION

primogeniture, '[i]t was not the problem which distinguished western Europe, but the solution.'

Outline of the book

In Chapter 2, we use state-of-the-art theory on authoritarian regimes to develop the theoretical idea at the core of the book: the dilemma of succession. As mentioned earlier, there is in practice no optimal solution to the problem of who will succeed the ruler, at least not when power is vested in one person. The absence of a successor causes uncertainty and plotting; the existence of one creates a rival centre of power, with dangerous implications. We show how primogeniture is a reasonable compromise that in 'normal' circumstances allows for an orderly transfer of power while minimizing threats to the incumbent ruler and we describe the corollaries of this for political stability and state-formation.

In Chapter 3, we again turn to theory on authoritarian regimes to conceptualize the character of the medieval monarchies analysed in the empirical chapters. Against this backdrop, we describe the historical data that we use in the book and the way we analyse it. The dataset we have assembled includes more than 700 European rulers in the period 1000–1799, complete with biographical information about their sex, their tenure, their marriages, their paternal aunts and uncles, their siblings, their offspring, and the way they exited office. It also includes information about civil and international wars and parliamentary assemblies. The chapter describes how we have coded this data and provides some simple descriptive illustrations of it.

Chapter 4 uses a historical narrative to shed light on how primogeniture came to be adopted in parts of medieval Europe, emphasizing the Catholic Church's influence on European family structure and heirship practices. This narrative analysis shows that these changes—and therefore the new politics of succession—were enabled by the fragmentation of power and rudimentary royal administrations that characterized the Latin west in the early Middle Ages. It also explains why primogeniture was not adopted in the Byzantine Empire, despite shared Christianity and the advantages that it offered both rulers and elite groups. Finally, we describe how primogeniture spread in our European sample over time.

In Chapters 5–8, we apply our theory about the politics of succession to three core areas of the state-formation experience. In Chapter 5, we study how actual moments of succession have unfolded. Leveraging the natural death of rulers to identify exogenous variation in successions, we find that civil wars were more likely in the wake of natural deaths than in normal years. We also show that the risk of such succession wars was lower in states practicing primogeniture than in states practicing elective monarchy or agnatic seniority. International conflict could of course also be provoked, or at least justified, by succession crisis, as the numerous wars of succession in European history attest to. We find that the natural deaths of rulers were associated with an increased risk of being attacked by rivals, possibly taking advantage of weakness in the regime, or using the succession as a pretext for realizing other political aims.

In Chapter 6, we show how uncertainty about the succession translated into coups and depositions, and how monarchs in states that practiced primogeniture sat more securely on their thrones than monarchs in states practicing elective monarchy or agnatic seniority. This, we argue, is because of the 'shadow of the future' cast by anticipated crises of succession, as well as the incentives of potential successors. When rulers started to enjoy longer tenures, their time horizons also increased, encouraging investment in and development of states.

In Chapter 7, we discuss how the politics of succession affected power-sharing and the development of representative institutions in Europe. A large literature has studied the development of parliaments and generally portrayed these institutions as a concession to subjects demanding representation for taxation and/or as a way to control the same subjects and raise even more revenue. While we do not dispute these accounts, we add that successions, representing moments of weakness in royal authority, also spurred parliamentary activity. Parliamentary meetings were frequently called to legitimize heirs and avoid civil conflict in the wake of successions. They were also convened more often in the wake of problematic successions, such as when the successor was underage and unable to rule on his own. However, we also show that primogeniture mitigated this need to politically stabilize successions.

In Chapter 8, we shift the focus to the monarch's family. To ensure that the state lived on, the monarch had to provide the regime with an heir: primogeniture arrangements are only as credible as the monarch's biological ability to produce heirs. However, in an era when politics was based on personal relationships in general, and blood ties in particular, family also mattered in other ways. Daughters and sisters could be married into important domestic and foreign families to shore up the monarch's alliances, whereas sons and brothers could be used as trusted governors of distant parts of the realm or military commanders. We show that monarchs who had many children and siblings were less likely to be deposed. Female relatives reduced the risk of depositions from both outside and from within the family, whereas male relatives primarily reduced the risk of outside depositions (and of civil wars breaking out). Finally, we show how primogeniture created political stability by prolonging dynasties.

Chapter 9 applies our argument about succession in comparative perspective. We combine a narrative historical analysis of succession arrangements and conflicts in Europe before the introduction of primogeniture and in the other old civilization areas of Eurasia with quantitative data on succession orders and ruler tenure in Imperial China and the Muslim Middle East. Our comparative analysis returns the same findings as in the European analyses—death of rulers repeatedly sparked conflict, but father-to-son successions calmed the stormy waters of succession. The chapter also shows that monarchical systems where hereditary elements were very weak—such as the Byzantine Empire and Mamluk Egypt—were pestered by staggering rates of usurpations and civil wars.

The Conclusions first summarize our findings and then discuss their implications for state-formation and for understanding the workings of modern autocratic regimes. We point out how the perennial problem of succession destabilizes non-democracies such as Russia, China, and Saudi Arabia today. Against this background, we use our findings about the importance of succession for political stability in European history to illuminate how the politics of succession shapes political dynamics in autocracies more generally.

2
The Politics of Succession

Historians have observed how in medieval and early modern monarchies successions were moments of crisis for the leading magnates of the realm (Bisson 2009: 102; Kagay 1981; Weiler 2013; Bartlett 2020). The dead monarch's confidants strove to maintain their status, both against each other and against those members of the elite who had been kept out in the cold and now schemed to get back into favour. The stakes were high. In post-conquest Norman England land tenures reverted to the Crown at the king's death and were handed out again by his successor—often, but not always, to those who held the tenures before (Garnett 2007). Positions as governors of crown fiefs and the rewards that came with them could be lost; as could membership of the king's council (and influence over the government's policies) if the new monarch preferred his own advisors over his predecessor's advisors.

The elite also had to keep a watchful eye on oppressed peasants and townsmen who often sought to exploit the regime's temporary weakness during power transitions to gain greater independence and more rights. Towns were, for example, more likely to introduce self-government in the wake of successions (Doucette 2021). Finally, the elite had to beware of foreign enemies, who were often eager to take advantage of the situation and grab disputed territory or launch outright invasions.

At the same time, successions offered members of the elite an opportunity to improve their standing. In exchange for their consent to the new monarch's accession they could demand a larger portion of the spoils of power, be it lands, rights, or political concessions. Those bypassed by the late monarch could hope for a comeback at court with everything it meant for themselves and their families. Ultimately, one of them might even become the new monarch—or have one of his sons ascend the throne—if he succeeded in outmanoeuvering his rivals.

These dynamics are in no sense unique for the European monarchies which we analyse in this book. The composition of what has been termed the 'winning coalition' (i.e. the cadres who receive the spoils of power) is often rattled when modern dictators die (Tullock 1987: 156; Brownlee 2007; Bueno de Mesquita et al. 2005: 16–18; Svolik 2012; Meng 2020). Power transfers in contemporary autocracies can even have consequences for the career opportunities of lower-level officials (Svolik 2012: 198).

Considering the risks and opportunities that autocratic successions offer, it does not come as a surprise that they often incite power struggles between members of the elite. This is especially true if the autocrat does not leave an heir and the elites must agree on a successor among themselves, or if the new autocrat is not strong enough to shoulder the mantle of his predecessor. The struggles that such power vacuums create sometimes bring with them government collapse or even civil war (Tullock 1987: 156). There is just too much at stake for the elite not to bother, in medieval monarchies just as in today's authoritarian states. However, successions were a more pressing or at least more frequent problem for autocratic regimes historically, as mortality levels were much higher than today, even for monarchs in the prime of their life.

The succession also posed problems for monarchs. Succession struggles could be anticipated, especially if the monarch had not appointed an heir and was old or ailing. In such situations the elite had an incentive to plan for the coming succession struggle and sometimes also to grab power from the incumbent monarch preemptively to gain an advantage over rival contenders for the throne.

In the *The History of Government*, Samuel P. Finer (1997a), when comparing the Byzantine Empire with the Chinese Empire and the Caliphate, takes as a given that hereditary monarchy stabilizes the succession and political life (see Chapter 9). But what is it about primogeniture hereditary monarchy in particular that mitigates the timeless problem of succession? To answer this question, we must first examine the dynamics of autocratic successions in more detail.

The difficulties of succession

The issue of succession lies at the heart of politics. In its most general sense, the succession order designates the way in which political leaders are selected, and thus to a large extent defines the nature of the political system. Where leaders are elected by the people, we have democracy. Where they are selected by a party committee, we have a single-party regime. Where they inherit their position, we often talk of monarchy (Geddes, Wright, and Franz 2014). Where there are no legitimate procedures at all, there is anarchy, at least when the incumbent leader steps down or dies.

But the importance of the succession is not limited to the actual process of selecting a new leader. Since the legitimacy of a ruler is often derived from the way he or she acquired office, a contested succession can come back and haunt the new ruler during his reign. When the principle of succession is based on the consent of some group, that consent can be retracted. And when the elite anticipates a contested succession in the future, the plans they make in advance of it will have repercussions in the present. In an anthropological overview of the practices of succession in a wide range of cultures, Robbins Burling (1974: 2) writes that '[t]hroughout recorded history the failure to achieve smooth transitions of power has repeatedly brought havoc to government, and the need to transfer power has been an important force in fostering the rise of new political patterns' (also see Goody 1966).

At the heart of the problem of succession lies two intertwined challenges, which we refer to as the coordination problem and the crown prince problem. They describe the challenges faced by a ruler who has not designated a successor and the challenges faced by a ruler who has designated one, respectively. Later, we examine how these two problems play out in autocracies.

The coordination problem and the shadow of the future

Life under autocracy is often uncertain and insecure, and even though they may enjoy material wealth, not even members of the elite can sit back and relax. At all times, they must make sure to be in the ruler's good graces, proving their worth, while not appearing too ambitious. As the medieval observer Petrus Alfonsi put it, '[a] king is like a fire—if you are too close, you burn; if you are too far away, you freeze' (quoted in Bartlett 2000: 28). The ruler must balance his supporters against each other, keeping them in suspense about their standing, at times raising someone up, at other times bringing them down, to ensure that no one becomes too confident or too powerful.

Consequently, the members of the elite are in constant competition with each other, prone not to trust their peers, caught in a 'grim, dog-eat-dog world' (Geddes, Wright, and Frantz 2018: 66). In the absence of strong institutions, members of a ruling coalition simply cannot credibly promise to abstain from eliminating or sidestepping each other at some point in the future (Acemoglu, Egorov, and Sonin 2008). This, mind you, is when there is a ruler who can keep competitors in check and provide a focal point around which the elite can focus their attention and scheming. For the ruler at least has an incentive not to alienate the elite entirely; they might then unite and overthrow him. If the ruler leaves office unexpectedly, the most powerful regime insiders will find themselves pitted against each other in a game where the stakes are often life or death.

For elite groups, a vacant throne means opportunity to grab more rents, or even seize power, as someone is bound to become the new ruler. But failed attempts at taking power can prove to be disastrous and the outcomes are uncertain. First, as autocracies are characterized by secrecy, it is hard for contenders to accurately gauge the strength of their rivals (Shih 2010). Second, commitment problems hamper the ability of a challenger to put together a new coalition. Anyone wishing to take power is likely to promise spoils to those who are well placed to support him in the endeavour. But there is no way to credibly commit to upholding those promises, once in power (Bueno de Mesquita et al. 2005: 60). As soon as the new ruler assumes office, his interests start to diverge from those who helped him get there (Geddes, Wright, and Frantz 2018: 93). In the weak institutional environment of an authoritarian regime, there is little that can bind him to his promises, especially if the institutional configuration is in flux because of the transition.

Commitment problems are also common during the reign of a ruler, as pointed out earlier. No one in the elite can be sure to remain part of the winning coalition. But the status quo does provide some comfort and information; members of the elite are likely to trust the ruler who has rewarded them previously over a new challenger, with no proven track record. In Bueno de Mesquita et al.'s (2005) selectorate theory, this is signified by the concept of affinity: an unspecified level of mutual preference between the ruler and his supporters that is revealed only by experience. Given that power corrupts, members of the elite cannot be sure how a challenger will behave in office; if they can work with the current ruler, there are good reasons to prefer the devil they know, even if the challenger's 'bid' might be more attractive in material terms.

The demise of the ruler also risks upsetting the balance of power between the winning coalition's members. This is dangerous as it can result in sub-coalitions that are powerful enough to get rid of the other members of the coalition. Acemoglu, Egorov, and Sonin (2008) have shown that a winning coalition is self-enforcing if and only if it does not possess any sub-coalition that is in itself self-enforcing and sufficiently powerful to get rid of the other members of the coalition. The ruler's demise means that the most powerful member of the coalition is out of the equation. In this situation, there is genuine risk that such a sub-coalition emerges and purges the other members of the coalition.

It is therefore likely that many members of the elite will 'prefer maintaining their status to pursuing a potentially disastrous power grab' (Brownlee 2007: 606). The problem is that it is difficult for them to plan for the demise of the ruling autocrat and coordinate their efforts to uphold the regime if the autocrat does not provide them with a successor. In such circumstances, elite groups will anticipate the chaos that is likely to break out when the autocrat dies and plan for it (Herz 1952). The shadow of the succession looms over what could otherwise be a peaceful and stable reign.

The succession practices—or absence thereof—in the early Ottoman Empire illustrate the fears that a looming succession can raise. As described in detail in Chapter 9, rule passed in the family among the Ottomans, but there was no institutionalized mechanism for choosing between the sons of a previous sultan, other than sheer violence (Imber 2009: 75). As a result, civil war frequently broke out on the death of a sultan. The victor would then execute his siblings, to avoid future challenges to his rule. Needless to say, the expectation that the future sultan would murder his siblings would have been a cause for concern for them, even during the reign of their father. The elite, who had to choose which brother to support, also had to fear ending up on the losing side. It is therefore no surprise that children occasionally waged war against each other before their father was dead.

The shadow of the future looms larger as an anticipated succession draws closer, due to the advanced age or ill health of the ruler. The ability of the ruler to promise future spoils to his supporters—the basis of his rule—diminishes as the risk of his passing away increases (Bueno de Mesquita and Smith 2010) and the prospect of a succession crisis becomes more pressing.

To avoid doubts about the continuity of the regime, rulers have often used propaganda to stress the everlasting nature of the regime, dynasty, or the ruler himself. European monarchs normally concealed information about sicknesses or ill health and frequently took steps to appear younger and sturdier than they really were. Queen Elizabeth I of England, who in contravention of all custom and the protestations from a parliament worried about the succession never married and had children, is a case in point. She went to extreme lengths to keep up a youthful appearance, even into her old age. Paintings of the Queen portray her with a 'mask of youth', showing no sign of aging (Fischlin 1997). In public she wore elaborate dress and heavy makeup so 'that the people might the better perceive her ability of body and good dispositions, which otherwise in respect of her years they might perhaps have doubted;

so jealous was she to have her natural defects discovered for diminishing her reputation,' according to a contemporary observer (cited in Riehl 2010: 58). When continuity cannot be ensured through the preservation of institutions, or a dynasty, the monarch herself must be ageless.

However, even the sturdiest monarch will die, eventually. When the fear of the coming crisis becomes too strong, members of the elite might even be tempted to carry out a preemptive coup. By catching other possible contenders for power unawares, a coup leader can gain an advantage that would not materialize had he waited until the crisis was a fact. Montesquieu (2011[1750]: 61) argues that since possible contenders for the throne in such circumstances know that they are likely to be imprisoned or put to death if they do not manage to grab power for themselves, they have 'a far greater incentive to ambition' than when the line of succession is clear. The absence of a successor is therefore not only highly problematic for the regime as a whole but also for the ruler himself.

Appointing a crown prince has the additional advantage of introducing a 'barrier effect' against potential challengers, as the very existence of a crown prince makes it more difficult for challengers to replace the incumbent (Konrad and Mui 2017). Even if a challenger succeeds in eliminating the incumbent, the crown prince will function as the focal point of the regime. He will also be in an advantageous position relative to challengers, both because he has been allowed to accrue resources due to his status as crown prince and because he inherits the incumbent's resources. Thus, the challenger must also eliminate the crown prince before he can sit safely on the throne. Knowing this, the crown prince will naturally safeguard the incumbent against any threats from potential challengers.

The crown prince problem

However, appointing a crown prince creates problems of its own. Setting aside for the moment the different ways in which succession arrangements can be made credible, the existence of an undisputed heir apparent poses important problems for the ruler, if he becomes too impatient. The appointed successor has strong incentives to stage a coup or assassinate the ruler, as he is designated to assume power when the ruler dies (Tullock 1987: 151–2). Furthermore, the crown prince's status will allow him to accrue power in the regime. Indeed, it is this very power that allows him to function as a barrier against challengers (Konrad and Mui 2017; Meng 2021). In other words, the successor has both the motive and the opportunity to mount a coup, and the ruler therefore risks nurturing a pretender (Brownlee 2007). John Hertz has termed this the 'crown-prince problem' (Hertz 1952: 30). We proceed by discussing three crucial aspects of this problem.

The age aspect

Some crown princes are more dangerous than others, with age being an important factor. A crown prince who is much younger than the ruler can usually afford to wait for the throne, as he can look forward to a relatively long reign after the ruler passes away of natural causes. An older crown prince cannot be as patient, as he himself may well die before inheriting the throne. This is especially true in a world of high mortality. The ruler is therefore well advised to appoint an individual who is much younger than himself, for instance his son, as heir.[1] As Tullock puts it, 'the son is wise to simply wait for his father to die' (Tullock 1987: 163). It is more difficult for brothers, who are usually much closer in age to the ruler, to be as patient (Brownlee 2007). A young crown prince also provides the elite with a longer time horizon. By appointing a young crown prince, the ruler thus not only buys more time in office for himself. He also buys more time in office for his crown prince.

The competence aspect

Competence is another important aspect that decides how dangerous a crown prince is for the ruler, as a competent crown prince is more likely to succeed with a coup if he is so inclined. Hence, it may seem advantageous for the ruler to cut the heads of the tallest ears of wheat, as it is sometimes put, and designate one of the shorter ones as his crown prince, as it would solve both the coordination and the crown prince problem. However, an incompetent crown prince will not function as well as a barrier against challengers, which means that it is not clear that the ruler should prefer an incompetent crown prince (Konrad and Mui 2017). Furthermore, the elite has an obvious interest in the crown prince's competence.

---

[1] The historical examples of fathers and sons quarrelling over power are legion; sons would sometimes rebel, and kings would sometimes disinherit them (Bartlett 2020: 111–12). But, all else being equal, succession conflicts are likely to have been more muted in the case of father-to-son inheritance arrangements.

In bands of animals, such as chimpanzees, leadership contests are determined by physical strength. This 'system' ensures that the band is led by the strongest individual—if a stronger male comes along, the old 'ruler' will soon be deposed. In the same way, small-scale human communities are often led by 'big men' who can promise to protect and provide for their compatriots (Fukuyama 2011: 32). Some larger polities have also had succession arrangements based on physical—or at least military—strength. In the Byzantine Empire, the throne was open to any enterprising military leader who was powerful enough to take it—because a successful power grab was seen as being legitimated by God Almighty (Finer 1997a: 633). As mentioned earlier (and discussed in more detail in Chapter 9), the early Ottoman succession was literally decided on the battlefield between the Sultan's sons (Imber 2009: 75). Such succession-by-the-strongest arrangements may be costly, but at least they ensure that the new ruler is competent at waging war and forging political alliances.

It is obvious that such skills were valuable for rulers historically. At first glance, it may also seem obvious that elites would want a crown prince to be skilled in this way. Just as tribal communities long for leaders who can protect them against external threats, states benefit from having rulers who know how to win wars, make prudent diplomatic choices, and manage the state apparatus effectively. This may be especially true for authoritarian states, in which the ruler often has terrifying powers, and where no one is likely to speak truth to power or to check and balance the ruler's follies. Putting those terrifying powers into the hands of a child or an incompetent, or malevolent, individual can have disastrous consequences.

Foreign enemies constituted a threat to European states throughout the medieval and early modern period (see Chapter 5). These threats always remained a concern for the elite, as they were potentially immensely costly. Although it happened very rarely, they could result in almost complete elite replacement, as in the case of the Norman Conquests of Anglo-Saxon England, Southern Italy, and Sicily, the Ottoman conquest of the Byzantine Empire, and the victory of the imperial, Catholic forces over the Protestant Czech nobility at the Battle of the White Mountain in 1620. Or they could cost the flower of the nobility their lives, as happened at the spectacular French defeats at Crecy (1346) and Agincourt (1415). Hence, it may seem natural that succession orders whose explicit purpose was to produce able and experienced war leaders were common in European history.

One example is testamentary succession, which gives monarchs the right to choose their own successor. However, given how dangerous it could be for particularly weak rulers to designate a competent heir, this principle was no guaranteed way of getting competent rulers. More interesting is elective monarchy, which in theory bestowed the right to select the ruler upon the elite. One of the rationales of elective monarchy was that it allowed the elite to choose the most competent candidate—or at least weed out noticeably incompetent candidates—especially with respect to leading the nation in war (Fritz Kern 1948; Bartlett 2020: 52, 154).

It is not easy to accurately gauge leader quality in advance, especially in autocracies where competence may be a threat to the autocrat. Reliable measures of quality of political leadership are hard to come by, even in the modern world. Education is sometimes used as a crude indicator of leader quality today. Yet, it is an open question whether educated leaders increase economic growth (Besley, Montalvo, and Reynal-Querol 2011) or not (Carnes and Lupu 2016). Educated leaders are also about as likely as uneducated leaders to initiate military conflicts (Horowitz, Stam, and Ellis 2015: 145). There is no reason to assume that it was easier to predict a potential ruler's competence as we go back in history.

While it may be difficult to know who the best candidate is, elective monarchy can still help weed out candidates who are clearly incompetent. Children cannot rule on their own. Chronic illnesses and severe physical disabilities also often made candidates unfit to rule in an age where mortality was high and where monarchs were supposed to rule their lands and armies in person.

However, history is replete with examples of obvious incompetents who have been elected kings. A famous example is Alexander the Great's older and intellectually disabled half-brother Arrhidaeus, who was elected king of Macedonia under the name Philip III in BC 323 after his younger brother passed away in Babylon (Waterfield 2012). Unfit to rule, for several years Arrhidaeus/Philip functioned as a figurehead for more capable generals, until he was finally executed at the orders of Alexander's mother Olympias. Another example is the Swedish king Magnus Eriksson who was only three years old when he was elected king of Sweden in 1319. Although he eventually became Sweden's longest ruling monarch, he was unable to rule in his own right for his first thirteen years as king (Schück 2003). As we show later in the book, such royal minorities—meaning that the king is underage—have tended to destabilize royal power more generally. How come elites chose such candidates, who were unfit to rule at the time of their election?

A likely answer is that a competent ruler not only constitutes a threat to foreign enemies but also to the elite who has elected him. Competence in leading armies, forging alliances, and building up an effective administration may be used domestically to increase the ruler's power vis-à-vis the elite (Tilly 1992; Downing 1992). Consequently, it is not obvious that the elite would want to elect a competent king. All hinges on whether they fear a strong ruler or foreign enemies the most.

In contrast, restricting the succession to members of a particular family, or to the eldest son of the previous ruler, exposes the state to the fickleness of fate. As pointed out by Mancur Olson (1993), the probability that the son of a king is the most talented person for the job is near zero. In the Introduction, we mentioned that Jean-Jacques Rousseau expressed incredulity at the practice of hereditary succession, writing that 'men have preferred the risk of having children, monstrosities, or imbeciles as rulers to having disputes over the choice of good kings.'

History seemingly bears him out, as there have been plenty of unfit monarchs. But how serious this flaw is hinges on the nature of the 'disputes' that are avoided by the automaticity of inheritance: a devastating war of succession, perhaps? Many democracies have managed to institute peaceful competition for power, but in other regimes it is entirely possible that the costs of succession crises outweigh the adverse consequences of sometimes having children or even 'monstrosities' as rulers (especially in a world of high mortality where the average ruler spell was relatively short). The tenth-century philosopher al-Ghazali for instance argued that 'the tyranny of a sultan for a hundred years causes less damage than one year's tyranny exercised by the subjects against another' (quoted in Acemoglu and Robinson 2019: 379).

Moreover, the implications for the crown prince's competence of restricting the succession to members of a particular family should not be exaggerated. Before the birth of modern bureaucracies and public education systems, when most of the population did not even get basic education and lay administrative skills were limited to a handful men in the household of the monarch and the leading men of the realm, royal children were often relatively well prepared to succeed their father. They were given a rigorous upbringing only available to a select few, as shown by the numerous advice books to rulers written in the period (Orme 1984). As they grew older, they were often given responsibilities in government, for example, command over a province or an army (see Chapter 8). Being associated in power 'helped the younger men get considerable experience of ruling' (Jordan 2001: 55). If they were not totally inept, they would therefore have an edge over most of their competitors; a competition that was in any case limited to a small elite, also based on hereditary status (see later and Chapter 3). This relative advantage is likely to have declined over time, as education became more widespread, and administrations grew in size.

But for a long time, it assured that royal children were relatively well prepared for the task of ruling.

In summary, the problem of competence is not easily solved, or even addressed. Furthermore, competence is not the only factor that decides a crown prince's ability to rule effectively. Without the resources to rule he can be as competent as he wants; he will not succeed anyway.

The resource aspect

In contemporary autocracies power resources often come with government positions. Defence ministers and generals can call on support from the armed forces. Interior ministers and directors of security agencies are backed up by various police and paramilitary forces and have access to important intelligence. Ministers of finance and heads of central banks have the financial resources to beef them up in power struggles. To build up a power base and function effectively crown princes must therefore usually be groomed into such positions (Meng 2021).

In the medieval era conditions were very different. There were no standing armies in Western Europe until the fifteenth century, when France established the modestly sized Compagnies d'ordonnance, and even French kings had to rely on mercenaries and nobles and their followers until the seventeenth century (van Nimwegen 2010). It took a long time for other countries to follow suit. England did not form a standing army until the end of seventeenth century. Organized security agencies and police forces were even later inventions. Treasuries and tax incomes did exist and generated important resources. But tax rates were extremely low, both in a comparative and a contemporary perspective. In AD 1300 the kings of France and England were only able to extract about 1 per cent of GDP in revenues whereas the Song emperors of China were able to extract 10 times as much 200 years earlier (Stasavage 2020: 10–13). Most of the wealth in society was simply beyond the reach of the monarchs. One reason was the lack of professional bureaucracies. Day to day affairs in medieval 'states' were run by a handful of retainers and advisors in the monarch's household (Ertman 1997; Stasavage 2020). Councils and councillors often met infrequently. This means that there were hardly any governmental positions in the modern sense that could function as a power base for crown princes. It is a striking fact that almost no monarch in the period we study rose from the ranks of the bureaucracy or the military. Monarchs from peasant and burgher backgrounds are practically unheard of. The overwhelming majority were recruited from royal and noble families.

The reason is that political power in medieval Europe was primarily based on landed wealth owned by the monarch and noble families (see Chapter 3 and Chapter 4).[2] Crown lands did exist. But control was typically limited to the royal family and the leading nobles. Once apportioned crown lands were often run as private estates. Without such landed wealth it was virtually impossible to mobilize sufficient retainers to be a power player in the regime. Consequently, the pool of potential crown princes was in practice limited to the royal family and the leading noble families. No one else had the power resources to participate in the game of thrones.

If a crown prince did not have enough landed wealth to shoulder the king's mantle he was in trouble, as the crown lands were often insufficient to underwrite a stable rule. On the other hand, if he had much larger estates than the king, he threatened not only the monarch (a too-powerful crown prince was dangerous) but also the equilibrium between the monarch and the rest of the winning coalition. In a worst-case scenario, he could aspire to form a new sub-coalition that was self-enforcing in itself and sufficiently powerful to get rid of the other members of the coalition (cf. Acemoglu, Egorov, and Sonin 2008). To uphold the status quo, it was therefore important that the landed wealth of the crown prince and the king were roughly equal. One way to assure this outcome was if the crown prince inherited not only the royal office and the lands that came with it but also the king's private property. As explained later, this fact had important repercussions for how stable succession orders were.

To sum up, it was important that a crown prince had the resources needed to rule, which in the period we study mainly consisted of landed wealth. But he should preferably not have more landed wealth than necessary, as a too powerful crown prince threatened both the monarch and the balance of power in the regime. Having the right amount of landed wealth likely mattered more than being competent, as it was next to impossible to compete in the game of thrones without such wealth. As we shall argue later, from the vantage point of political stability it therefore makes sense to prioritize finding a crown prince with the right resources rather than finding the most competent one.

Succession orders in medieval Europe

We proceed by specifying the succession orders that operated in the medieval monarchies we analyse in this book and by relating these to the

---

[2] The Church was, of course, also a large landowner and did influence succession conflicts. However, it did not try to impose candidates from within its own rank on lay thrones.

problems of succession described earlier (for a more comprehensive review of succession orders in monarchies, see Duindam (2016: 127–42)). In the eleventh century, where our analysis begins, the prevailing succession orders in European monarchies could be divided roughly into three categories: election, agnatic seniority, and primogeniture (partible inheritance was also practiced and is discussed in the next section). As we shall see in Chapter 9, each of these succession orders have analogues outside of Europe as well but here we contextualize them based on our sample of European monarchies.

Election or acclamation of monarchs was a common practice in much of medieval Europe at the dawn of the second millennium, for instance in Anglo-Saxon England, France under the Capetians, the Scandinavian countries, and, perhaps most famously, the Holy Roman Empire. It is misleading to think of these monarch-elections as elections in the modern sense of the word, for three reasons. First, it was primarily the privileged (i.e. nobles and prelates) who were allowed to vote; second, the elected normally came from a common pool (the royal family); third, often the procedure is better described as acclamation[3] than election (Douglas 1964). However, the fact that the pool of candidates was limited did not solve the coordination problem. Uncertainty about the succession was a constant factor of concern. And in some polities practicing acclamation, such as the Byzantine Empire, the dynastic principle was very weak, meaning that non-relatives of the prior ruler also stood a chance (Finer 1997a: 633–55). On the positive side, the monarch did not need to fear a crown prince.

In some monarchies with elective elements, succession by appointment—that is, the monarch deciding who would be his successor—became an established custom. In Russia under Peter the Great, this principle even achieved legal status (Whittaker 2001; Lieven 2006). However, succession by appointment does not solve the coordination problem unless the appointment process is strictly regulated. First, monarchs often avoided appointing a successor. Peter the Great himself, who failed to do so, is a case in point (Whittaker 2001). Second, if the appointment process was not strictly regulated, so that

---

[3] Strong monarchs were often able to render the elective element moot by forcing the nobility to elect their sons as heirs during their own lifetime. Such ceremonies frequently included anticipatory crowning of the heir to rule as co-king until the death of the father, as in Capetian France during the eleventh and twelfth centuries and in the Holy Roman Empire in the same period (Lewis 1981; Bartlett 2020: 93–5). In such circumstances the coordination problem was temporarily solved. However, even when such practice became established custom, elective ceremonies were kept and took on the role of acclamation (Bendix 1980). In addition, far from all monarchs were able to have their sons elected heirs during their rule. Elections could also regain importance after weaker monarchs, as happened in the Holy Roman Empire after 1250 (Le Patourel 1971; Bartlett 2020: 95).

it was obvious for the elite who the appointed crown prince was, it could create confusion and competing claims. William the Conqueror's justification for the Norman Conquest of Britain in 1066 was, for example, that he had been designated heir by the previous king, Edward the Confessor. This was disputed by Harold Godwinson, who instead claimed that the dying king had promised the crown to him on his deathbed. Even though the issue was settled by raw power, in the Battle of Hastings, more ambiguity meant more leeway for potential challengers to legitimize their claim (Oleson 1957). Public appointment ceremonies and testamentary appointment would alleviate doubts about who had been appointed crown prince and help solve the coordination problem (Wang 2018). But such arrangements could also aggravate the crown prince problem, if they did not guarantee the crown prince that he would remain the heir even if the incumbent had a change of heart. The fear of being replaced was a powerful motivation to take preemptive action.

Elective monarchy also enabled great shifts in landed wealth between incumbents and their crown princes. There was no guarantee that a newly elected king had the same resources to draw on as his predecessor. When Queen Margrethe of Denmark and Norway was elected Swedish regent in 1363, she could draw on vast estates in her two other kingdoms, as well as their treasuries. In contrast, her deposed predecessor Albrecht of Mecklenburg only had his father's resources in the duchy of Mecklenburg. The shift in royal power in Sweden was profound and the Swedish nobility saw its prerogatives diminish (Schück 2003).

The coordination problem is seemingly automatically solved by the other succession order that dominated in Europe at the start of the second millennium: agnatic seniority.[4] Under this rule, which was practiced primarily in Slavic countries, such as Piast Poland and Rurikid Kiev, the eldest living brother of the current ruler inherited the throne (Dvornik 1962; Fine 1986). It was then supposed to pass to his younger brothers until the last living brother, who at his death was to hand it over to the oldest brothers' eldest living son (to pass it on to his brothers, cousins, and their offspring). Consequently, the system in ordinary circumstances produced a large pool of potential successors who were only slightly younger than the current ruler.

---

[4] There is reason to assume that the systems of 'agnatic seniority' that later historians have interpreted to have existed in Eastern Europe in reality were often mixed with succession based on competence and appointment. Likewise, many elective monarchies—for instance in Scandinavia early in the period we analyse—in practice often produced agnatic seniority successions, as adult younger brothers were preferred over their nephews, especially if the latter were underage.

It is quite likely that the crown prince in such a system may die before the ruler. Even if he lives to succeed, he will in normal circumstances provide the regime with a relatively short time horizon. Therefore, members of the regime may be better off grooming the next in line for the succession. However, even that person—perhaps the third-youngest brother—could be too old to be a safe wager. There is thus a huge risk that elites will bet on the wrong heir and end up with a successor whom they have not had the chance to groom properly. Agnatic seniority may therefore have been a less optimal solution to the coordination problem than it appears at first sight.

The large pool of relatively old successors also aggravated the crown prince problem, as the next in line for the throne could usually not afford to wait for the incumbent monarch to die of old age if he wanted to enjoy the benefits of ruling (Brownlee 2007: 605). This fact may also have made the monarch keen on discouraging his elites from grooming his brothers, as he knew that their incentives to remain loyal to him were low.

Seniority-based systems also meant that the monarch often did not leave his private wealth to his successor, as this would mean that he disinherited his own children. Although the crown prince tended to have his own private landed wealth, he usually ended up poorer than the monarch (monarchs tend to have more opportunities to amass private wealth). There was thus a risk of a gradual erosion of monarchs' private resources in states with seniority-based succession arrangements.

At the same time, the system guaranteed that there were normally successors of an adequate age who were ready to lead the people in war if the incumbent monarch died; at least if they were not too old and sick, which was always a risk when the succession was based on seniority. This capacity to produce capable successors seems to be one of the reasons the system was adopted in the first place (Fletcher 1979; Engel 2001; Merrills 2010). The successors also worked as barriers against challengers from outside the royal dynasty who were tempted to grab the throne (see Chapter 8).

As discussed in more detail in Chapter 4, the third succession order that dominated medieval Europe was primogeniture.[5] The most common version of primogeniture practiced in medieval Europe was *agnatic primogeniture*, according to which the eldest living son and his male offspring inherited.

---

[5] The rivalling principle of proximity of blood yields the same result as primogeniture if the monarch's eldest son is alive, which is why we have not chosen to treat it separately. The two principles could yield different results in more complicated situations, but from the point of view of our theoretical argument the differences between the principles are unlikely to matter for autocratic stability and ruler survival.

Females were excluded entirely from inheritance.[6] Some states practiced the principle of *male preference primogeniture*, which allowed daughters and their offspring to inherit if the monarch had no living male offspring.

Both rules assured that there was only one legitimate crown prince who could function as a focal point for the ruling regime as long as the monarch produced eligible male children. The crown prince also functioned as a natural barrier against challengers (Konrad and Mui 2017; Bartlett 2020: 62). The pool of heirs was not limited to the crown prince, but encompassed all living male relatives (and female relatives where they could inherit). Its fully developed forms even allow for inheritance via deceased predecessors. With the introduction of primogeniture, the regime thus went from being a 'one bullet regime', or two if an appointed crown prince existed, to a 'many bullets regime'. As in states practicing agnatic seniority, outsiders had to eliminate the whole royal family before they could feel safe on the throne.

For natural reasons, crown princes were also considerably younger than their fathers and could afford to wait to inherit the throne. In addition, monarchs tended to be young when ascending the throne and thus provided the elite with a relatively long time horizon. Finally, it was difficult for the king to shift successor because he by definition only had one eldest son (Tullock 1987: 164). The crown prince could therefore be relatively certain of his place in the succession.

Another advantage of primogeniture was that the crown prince usually inherited the bulk of his father's private power resources and thus did not upset the balance of power between members of the winning coalition. In theory, he just replaced his father in this coalition, in contrast to the upheavals associated with elective monarchy and, to a lesser extent, agnatic seniority discussed earlier.

The main drawbacks of primogeniture were that the system sometimes produced successors who were underage, inexperienced, or otherwise unsuitable for the job. However, as pointed out earlier it is not certain that better monarchs were chosen in elective monarchies and monarchies where the succession was based on appointment. Royal children may not have been such bad candidates all things considered, as they both had the necessary power resources to

---

[6] Most famously, this principle was expressed in the so-called Salic law, practiced in France. The law was created by King Clovis, who first united the Franks in the seventh century but was for a long time forgotten. At the beginning of the fifteenth century, French scholars brought it back into practice and thereafter engaged in revisionism to create the impression that the law had always been used (Taylor 2001).

shoulder the monarch's mantle and were better prepared for the task of ruling than most contemporaries.

This leads us to two conclusions. First, monarchs' risk of being deposed from within the regime is likely to have been lower under primogeniture than under competing succession orders, as primogeniture in contrast to the other succession orders addressed both the coordination problem and the crown prince problem (Tullock 1987: 18). The fact that the principle reduced successions' effect on the balance of power between members of the winning coalition more than other succession arrangements and provided better barriers against challengers than succession arrangements based on election and appointment only reinforces this conclusion.

Second, the risk of succession wars is also likely to have been lower under primogeniture than under other succession arrangements. Because the principle solved the coordination problem and was better at keeping the balance of power between members of the winning coalition intact during successions (i.e. provided the crown prince with the right resources), this is also true for successions that were not spurred by depositions. Indeed, it is this effect that (to a large extent) explains why the principle reduced the risk of depositions.

But why the eldest son? Some cultures, such as the Mongols (see Chapter 9) and peasantries in parts of England (known as Borough-English), have instead favoured the youngest son in the inheritance: i.e. practiced ultimogeniture. Ultimogeniture on average produces younger crown princes than primogeniture and may at first sight seem to be a better solution to the crown prince problem. However, ultimogeniture introduces several other problems, especially in a high mortality setting such as medieval Europe. The first problem is that the identity of the youngest son is much more volatile than that of the eldest son: every time a new son is born to the monarch the old crown prince loses his status and the elite must shift its allegiances to, and begin grooming, the new crown prince. There is thus less stability in elite–crown prince relations than under primogeniture.[7] This problem was aggravated in the medieval era due to high infant mortally rates (between a third and a half of all children never reached adulthood). An older son, who had survived the first critical years, had much higher chances of surviving into adulthood than a newborn (see Chapter 8).

---

[7] Indeed, in medieval Europe the birth of younger brothers who received lands previously allotted to older brothers often caused unrest and sometimes rebellion, as in the case of the older sons of Henry I of England rebelling against their father in 1173–1174 because he bequeathed lands to their younger brother John Lackland (Bartlett 2020: 196–8). This has been referred to as the problem of the 'late lamb' (Bartlett 2020: 195).

Second, if the monarch dies before the new crown prince reaches adulthood and can have children of his own, we end up with a situation where the new monarch's crown princes are his older brothers. Older brothers who have previously held crown prince status and owned the elite's allegiances, who have had more time than the new monarch to accrue power and experience, and who might not be underage themselves. So, if ultimogeniture solves the crown prince problem better in the father's generation—itself a thorny issue—it easily introduces a much worse crown prince problem in the next generation.

Third, even if the older brothers remain loyal it is obvious that ultimogeniture produces underage kings who are unable to rule on their own for the first years of their tenure more frequently than primogeniture does. Finally, it is a fact that parents can invest more of their time in their first-born, giving them an advantage in life whereas they must divide their time between children if they have more than one (Blake 1981). Research shows that being an older sibling increases the chance of having a political career even in the modern era (Oskarsson et al. 2021). The eldest son may thus have had a slight competence or leadership advantage over his younger brothers.

Overall, these factors strongly suggest that ultimogeniture does not produce the same stability in relations between the monarch, the elite, and the crown prince as primogeniture does, which is probably why the latter principle was almost always preferred in royal succession in hereditary monarchies.

Partible inheritance

So far, we have ignored the fourth succession arrangement that was common in medieval Europe, especially early in the period we study, namely partible inheritance. The practice of partitioning a monarch's realm(s) between sons (and sometimes also other male relatives) goes back at least to the Merovingians (van Dam 2008) and it continued under the Carolingians (Nelson 2008a; 2008b; Wickham 2009). It still survived in parts of the Holy Roman Empire in the seventeenth century (Fichtner 1989; see Chapter 4).

Partible inheritance brings a strong hereditary element to the succession, as the principle treats the monarch's lands as his private property, to be shared between his heirs. However, partible inheritance was practiced in monarchies which also had strong elective elements, such as the Frankish realm (Nelson 2008a; 2008b). There were also often limits to when and how the principle was practiced. In the Iberian Peninsula in the eleventh to fourteenth centuries, partible inheritance was seemingly practiced only when a monarch had conquered, or inherited, new lands that he could leave to younger sons (see Chapter 4). In the high and late Middle Ages, there are very few examples of monarchs partitioning their lands without such acquisitions outside the Holy Roman Empire (and even within the Empire core lands were often kept intact when there were many sons, but no acquisitions).

Partitions thus usually followed the borders of pre-existing polities in the period we study; a practice that was made easier by the fact that almost all monarchies in medieval and early modern Europe were conglomerate (also known as composite) states, in which the constituent parts had their own political institutions and laws and elites and were kept together by bonds of loyalty to the monarch and his family (Elliot 1992; Gustafsson 1998; Nexon 2009). This has implications for understanding how the principle affected political stability.

Many historians have blamed partible inheritance for political instability and the fragmentation of political power (Fichtner 1989; Scheidel 2019: 153–4). Although it is obvious that the principle did cause a fragmentation of political power—the partitioning of a monarch's lands by definition fragments power—we do not believe that it necessarily caused political instability beyond this in the period we study. When applied to already existing polities in a predictable way (for instance, the eldest son inheriting the patrimony and younger sons inheriting acquisitions or their mother's dowry in order of their seniority) partible inheritance solves the coordination and crown prince problem in much the same way as primogeniture does: it provides the elites in the monarch's realms with heirs and these heirs, being the sons of the monarch, can afford to wait to inherit their thrones. The sons also function as barriers against challengers, both in the realm they expect to inherit and in the realms their brothers expect to inherit (as they will inherit these if their brothers pass away).

The main difference to primogeniture is that heirs do not inherit the power resources their father controls in other realms, which potentially could tilt the balance of power within the winning coalition in the realm they inherit. However, this difference should not be exaggerated, as monarchs in a world of composite states often had a difficult time using their resources as monarch of one realm to influence politics in their other realms. A case in point is Eric of Pomerania, King of Denmark, Norway, and Sweden, who was deposed as Swedish king at least in parts because the Swedish nobility refused to serve him in his campaigns against the insubordinate Duchy of Schleswig, which was a part of Denmark (Lönnroth 1934: 67–8). Other famous examples include Habsburg Emperor Charles V's and his son King Philip II's difficulties in mobilizing their composite territories for campaigns in Germany and the Low Countries (Møller 2014).

It should also be pointed out that in cases where the monarch only leaves one live legitimate heir/son, partible inheritance and primogeniture yield identical results. This often happened after the Catholic Church transformed strategies of heirship in late antiquity and the early medieval period, strictly limiting the number of legitimate children born to monarchs (see Chapter 4). Indeed, excluding bastard siblings who could not inherit, half of the monarchs in our data did not have a living brother when they ascended the throne. Hence, partible inheritance often defaulted to de facto primogeniture after the transformation of heirship practices.

Admittedly, partible inheritance may have caused more instability if practiced in a disorderly manner, when several sons outlived their father and when there were blurred lines of legitimacy for heirs. A cause of discord and confusion was that it was sometimes unclear who would inherit what. This was especially the case when there were many potential heirs, with different mothers who had different status, as under the Merovingians who practiced polygamy and concubinage (van Dam 2008; Wickham 2009). It was also the case when new polities were created out of old polities without consideration of pre-existing borders and institutions, as had happened under the Merovingians (van Dam 2008; Scheidel 2019: 153–4), and as sometimes happened under the Carolingians (Nelson 2008a; 2008b) and in the Holy Roman Empire (see Chapter 4). As Bartlett (2020: 201) puts it when describing the frequent divisions of the Merovingian realm between brothers, 'there was no fixed system.' In such situations there was both a risk of coordination problems (who would inherit what) and a risk of upsetting the winning coalition (splitting it into several smaller winning coalitions). For example, the succession wars that broke out in anticipation of and following Louis the Pious' death in 840 were triggered by disagreements between his sons over how to split up the empire after their father; a problem that was made worse by the fact that Louis on several occasions redivided the empire between them (and their sons) before he died (Nelson 2008b).

It was this uncertainty, a common feature of partible inheritance in the early Middle Ages, that created the centripetal dynamic and political instability that we described in the introductory chapter. But where there was a clear expectation about who would inherit what and where pre-existing borders were respected, partible inheritance may not have been much worse than primogeniture, especially in a world of nuclear families and few legitimate sons. Yes, the principle hindered the consolidation of larger composite monarchies and increased the number of smaller polities that could eventually wage war against each other; but the polities it produced were probably no more prone to coups and civil wars than states practicing primogeniture.

Succession and state-formation

We have argued, first, that hereditary monarchy stabilizes the succession and therefore limits conflict in autocracies, second, that primogeniture is the best way of realizing the stabilizing windfalls of hereditary succession. We can conceive of this as the consequences of primogeniture for political stability. Observable implications include longer ruler tenures and less frequent depositions and civil wars. But what were the longer-term consequences for state-formation?

If we look at the two maps in Figure 2.1, we can see that over the course of 600 years states practicing primogeniture came to dominate Europe. Issues of succession affected the territory of states, in several ways. First, in the anarchic international system of medieval and early modern Europe, states that practiced primogeniture would, due to their internal stability and associated incentives to engage in state-building, over time swallow many of the states that did not, meaning that states with ineffective models of succession were selected out. The most famous example is probably the elective kingdom of Poland whose weak eighteenth-century rulers neglected to invest in state-building and therefore lost out to stronger neighbouring states (Tilly 1992;

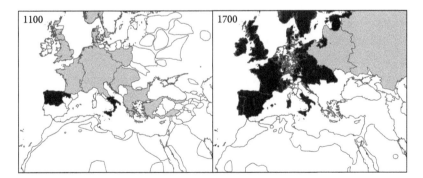

Fig. 2.1 States with primogeniture and orderly partible inheritance (black) and other principles of succession (grey) in 1100 (left) and 1700 (right). White indicates missing data

Ertman 1997). As Palmer (1970: 21) once provocatively put it, '[l]iberal writers everywhere subsequently condemned the Partitions of Poland as a crime; but was it murder, or suicide?'

This is where we find the most important difference between primogeniture and partible inheritance. Even if partible inheritance when practiced in an orderly manner stabilized the succession, the principle—by its very nature—meant that states over time were divided and hence grew smaller and weaker (Fichtner 1989). In contrast, primogeniture monarchies remained intact after a succession, as impartibility is a defining feature of primogeniture (Broms and Kokkonen 2019). Hence, in the long run primogeniture monarchies had a huge survival advantage over states practicing partible inheritance.

Our focus in this book is limited in the sense that it does not deal with other forms of political organization than monarchies. As pointed out by Charles Tilly (1992), the political geography of medieval Europe was a rich tapestry of different types of states: kingdoms, yes, but also city-states, empires, principalities, republics, religious orders, etc. Over time, they converged on one dominant form of organization, what Tilly terms the national state, but through different paths: via concentration of coercion, concentration of capital, or a combination of the two.

Our story is primarily about what Tilly terms 'capitalized coercion', of how stability in ruler–elite relations enables monarchs to build stronger states while also drawing on the resources of towns. The issue of succession was of course also present in non-monarchical states, they just had other ways to deal with it. However, as Tilly points out, the capitalized coercion strategy of primogeniture monarchies such as England and France over time had a competitive edge. In a quantitative sense, all the major states of present-day Europe are the descendants of the monarchical states we analyse in this book, with the exception of Switzerland and the partial exception of the Netherlands. And among monarchies, those with primogeniture succession crowded out those with other succession orders.

Another aspect in which successions and succession arrangements affected control over states and territory is purely dynastical. Primogeniture often failed spectacularly in one way: monogamous ruling families regularly died out in the male line. In states with monarch elections this situation would simply be solved by elevating someone else to the throne, either another member of the broader royal or princely family or a foreign candidate who could appeal to the electors. However, in primogeniture monarchies—and especially those practicing male preference primogeniture—a common solution was dynastic unions with other primogeniture monarchies who had not run dry in the direct male line (see Bartlett 2020: 425). This is where female inheritance comes to the fore. In primogeniture states lacking a live male heir, the vacant throne could often be filled via marriage in the female line. This tendency was further strengthened by the fact that the Church's encouragement of exogamy, which we describe in Chapter 4, created a pattern where monarchs often sought marriage partners for themselves or their sons and daughters from abroad (Bartlett 1993: 230; 2020: 15–26). All primogeniture monarchies that lost their 'independence' in the period we analyse passed to other realms via marriage; primogeniture allowed a peaceful transfer of realms via dynastic unions.

Primogeniture was not a panacea for all ills of a state, or a guarantee of good outcomes in general. What it did do was to increase political stability, making rulers sit more safely on their thrones, allowing for more predictability and longer time horizons for them and for the elite. Such stability could encourage investment in state capacity and economic infrastructure. But it could also, in the long run, lead to stagnation. We started the introductory chapter with the example of Louis XIV and seventeenth-century France, a stable state with a powerful monarch. Yet, it was not here modern economic growth started; this happened across the Channel, in England, where the monarch was weaker and constrained by parliament. A similar perspective can be applied to an even broader comparison, between Europe and China. Walter Scheidel (2019) argues that the root cause of the extraordinary political and economic development of Europe was not stability, but fragmentation and competition (see also Hall 1985: 139; Jones 2008[1981]: 239–45; Landes 1998: 37–8; McNeill 1982: 68–9, 112–16). After the fall of the Roman and Carolingian empires, no other polity ever laid claim to the same territory in Europe. In contrast, China was normally dominated by huge empires, stifling competition and innovation.

However, we need to distinguish between stability at different levels. Interstate competition has generally been assumed to foster innovation (Tilly 1992) and internal stability, in contrast to a united empire which might lead to complacency, as Scheidel argues. But a lack of internal stability in a smaller state, exposed to international pressure, is unlikely to lead to development. It is more likely that the combined weight of the two will cause the state to buckle, as Poland did. In contrast to international war, which can have positive consequences for state building, civil war is entirely destructive. Daron Acemoglu and James Robinson (2019) in a similar vein argue that liberty—and with it innovation and development—can only flourish when there is a balance of power between state and civil society (see also Boix 2015; Stasavage 2020). Development takes place not when both are stuck at a low level, but when an increase in the capabilities of the one is matched by the other. As we will see in the empirical chapters, problems of succession rile the state, thereby impairing development.

Conclusion

To ensure the continuity of the regime as a whole, and the well-being of the individual members of the elite, smooth transitions of power are necessary. But this is difficult to achieve when we balance the problem of coordination and the crown prince problem (with its three aspects of age, competence, and resources). From the ruler's perspective, a good principle of succession solves the coordination problem without exacerbating the crown prince problem. From the elite's perspective, a good principle of succession mitigates conflict, but does not cement the superiority of the ruler. The ways in which these contrasting aims have been balanced in different systems have had profound implications for the development of individual fortunes as well as entire states.

Successions thus provide critical junctures where the winning coalition can be—and often is—upended. Personal loyalty to a ruler is not easily transferred to his successor, which creates problems for both the new ruler and for the members of the elite who risk being sidelined or even proscribed for being too closely associated with the old leadership. Successions have often triggered civil wars and on occasion acted as catalysts for interstate wars. Moreover, fears of succession struggles have sometimes led members of the elite to depose monarchs. And when conflicts were resolved peacefully, elites still had to be won over to secure the new ruler's hold on the throne, in some cases leading to economic or political concessions.

We have argued that primogeniture solved the problems of succession better than most alternative succession arrangements that were available in medieval monarchies (with partible inheritance as a partial exception): election, agnatic seniority, and appointment—not to mention free-for-all contests. More generally, this book argues that the introduction of primogeniture, coupled with female inheritance, lies at the heart of the impressive European state-formation experience in the period after AD 1000 (see Tilly 1992; Downing 1992; Ertman 1997). In later chapters, these ideas are further specified theoretically and applied using new data on monarchies in medieval and early modern Europe.

However, while primogeniture may seem like a natural succession order for those well-acquainted with the latest 1000 years of European history, it was originally a revolutionary idea, which for the same reason has been very uncommon historically. At the start of the second millennium, where our empirical analysis begins, only a few Christian kingdoms in Latin Europe adhered to the principle (and here it was often coupled with partible inheritance when monarchs acquired new lands). Over time the principle gradually spread, and this, we argue, was to have important consequences for European political stability and state-formation. In Chapter 4, we use narrative historical sources and a comparison with Orthodox Christianity to trace how primogeniture, coupled with female inheritance, arose in the Latin west. The chapter shows both why this succession order is a historical anomaly and it argues that, at least in long-term historical perspective, it was exogenous to European societies. But first, we need to say a little more about the concepts we use and the data we have coded.

3
Conceptual Framework and Data

To apply the theoretical ideas developed in Chapter 2, we need valid and reliable data on monarchs and succession arrangements. However, to understand these data, it is necessary to briefly outline the core features of the medieval monarchies we study in this book. In this chapter, we first use the existing literature on modern-day authoritarian regimes to describe the central actors in our story: the ruler, the elite, and the people, both in general terms and in the context of medieval and early modern European monarchies. We then describe the setting in which they interact—the stage, if you will. In the second part of the chapter, we introduce our dataset on medieval monarchs and present some simple descriptive developments that put flesh on the bones of our conceptual framework.

Central concepts

The ruler

The protagonist of this book is the ruler. In an influential model of authoritarian politics, 'selectorate theory' as developed by Bueno de Mesquita et al. (2005), the ruler is defined as 'one or more central individuals with the authority to raise revenue and allocate resources' (Bueno de Mesquita et al. 2005: 38), a definition that also includes elected leaders and even collective bodies. We are only interested in authoritarian or autocratic leaders in monarchies. In the historical universe we study, their title would normally be king or queen but sometimes also emperor, tsar, prince, or archduke. The defining characteristic is not this title but instead the position at the top of the political pyramid.

The word 'autocratic' does not mean that these rulers necessarily held absolute power, as the word literally implies. Some monarchs in our study were constrained by institutions such as charters, law systems, courts of laws, or parliaments; others had more freedom of action in theory but were in practice hemmed in by the existence of other powerful individuals or by limited state capacity. We thus do not define rulers according to their de facto power—some were rather weak—but based on the notion that there was one individual who held the highest executive authority and who was not accountable to a parliament in the way modern constitutional monarchs and executive powers in democracies are.

It is common to define dictatorship (and by extension dictators) using a negative: the absence of free and competitive elections and/or the absence of selection of the chief executive (Svolik 2012: 22; Geddes, Wright, and Frantz 2018: 1). By that standard, all the polities in the empirical universe we analyse—medieval and early modern Europe—obviously qualified as dictatorships (by virtue of not being democracies). The only possible exception are republics, and even these would not pass the bar of political inclusion based on modern definitions of democracy (e.g. Dahl 1971). These electoral autocracies, for want of a better word, are not included in this study as they were not monarchies.

However, the mere presence of elections does not exclude the possibility that a state is a monarchy. In elective monarchies the ruler is chosen, normally by the magnates, but then bears the title of emperor, king, tsar, archduke or prince, serves for life, and holds power. In contrast to Gerring et al. (2021), we do not consider hereditary succession a defining characteristic of monarchy;[1] it is our main independent variable.

The elite

No one can rule alone. Even rulers who wielded immense power did so by virtue of command: armies must be directed, taxes raised, rebellions forestalled, and orders carried out. The group in charge of this, helping the ruler to govern the country, is called *the elite*. To win power, an authoritarian leader needs the support of a large enough subset of this elite: what in the literature is interchangeably referred to as the winning coalition, the dominant coalition,

---

[1] Besides election, there are also other non-hereditary monarchical succession orders, including appointment by the old monarch. Defining monarchy in terms of hereditary succession conflates a general regime type with a particular trait shared by many empirical instances of this type—or, to put it differently, it confuses defining and accompanying attributes of monarchy (Sartori 1984). It also has very strange results, as illustrated by the fact that it would mean that early Capetian France or eighteenth-century Poland-Lithuania (both with king-elections) were not monarchies. Coding elective monarchies as instances of monarchy only when they were de facto hereditary creates other paradoxical situations. For instance, both the Holy Roman Empire and the Byzantine Empire was de facto hereditary in some periods but not in others (Bartlett 2020: 95).

or the ruling coalition (Bueno de Mesquita et al. 2005; North, Wallis, and Weingast 2009; Acemoglu, Egorov, and Sonin 2008).

That rulers need the help of elite groups is true for all societies except possibly small bands, where one individual can dominate the others personally or the entire group can police the behaviour of each individual (Boix 2015: Chapters 1-2). But it holds a fortiori for medieval and early modern Europe, where power was fragmented and where elites were all that mattered in political terms (Koeningsberger 1971: 3-4; Zagorin 1982: 61-5; Bisson 2009; Wickham 2009; Oakley 2010). A genuine challenge to princely power could only emerge from these quarters. Just as today, but in an even more accentuated form, autocrats were normally removed by regime insiders, if at all (Svolik 2012: 4; Sharma 2017). Elite groups—primarily lay magnates, such as dukes, counts, and barons, and high clergy, such as bishops—therefore serve as the main antagonists of this book.

The people

The third main actor in modern scholarship on authoritarian regimes is the people. Milan Svolik dubs the attempt to avoid popular rebellions *the problem of authoritarian control*, and argues that it reflects the 'original sin' of dictatorship, the absence of popular consent (Svolik 2012: 20). A recent overview of autocratic regimes found that popular uprisings were the third most common way in which autocratic regimes came to an end: 17 per cent ended this way. If we also count elections (26 per cent), 43 per cent of autocratic regimes fell because of popular pressure (Geddes, Wright, and Frantz 2018: 179). The problem of authoritarian control is the most conspicuous feature of autocracies as its solution is mainly to be found in large-scale repression of the masses.

However, before the French Revolution the people represented much less of a threat to the ruler and the regime. Peasant revolts were legion, and the wars of religion of the sixteenth century had important popular dimensions (Zagorin 1982; Cohn 2006). Yet very few—if any—monarchs were deposed purely by popular uprisings (Kokkonen and Sundell 2014). The great mass of the population were peasants who simply did not have the resources to organize a rebellion that genuinely threatened the ruler; tellingly, the vast majority of medieval and early modern European *Jacqueries* were local, with the resident landowners or local clergy bearing the brunt of the violence. As our focus is on ruler survival and general political stability, the people do not feature prominently in our book.

Institutions

An influential account of authoritarian regimes takes as a point of departure that they are characterized by two basic features: first, there is no independent authority that can enforce agreements between the ruler and other members of the elite or uphold the rules of the game; second, violence is the ultimate arbiter of conflict (Svolik 2012: 2). Whereas democratic politics is orderly, authoritarian politics is unruly. The basis for authority is simply the distribution of means of violence (Bueno de Mesquita et al. 2005; North, Wallis, and Weingast 2009; Boix 2015). Whoever is at the head of the coalition that has the highest capacity for violence rules, and the options available to the ruler are primarily determined by his relations to the members of that coalition. Under such circumstances, institutions would seem to be of no consequence. This augurs ill for the main argument of this book, that the rules regulating the succession are important. If all rules can be broken, and no agreements are credible, why should succession arrangements, or any other institutions or traditions matter?

Here, we can start with the simple observation that there is a plethora of institutions in authoritarian states. Today, virtually all states have some form of legislature and hold some form of elections, though their actual importance varies considerably. A large literature discusses the different incentives authoritarian rulers have for setting up institutions that constrain them, such as legislatures. The main argument is that institutions can co-opt opposition groups and alleviate commitment and monitoring problems between the ruler and other members of the regime, which makes the ruler's commitments more credible and thereby facilitates his staying in power (Boix and Svolik 2013; Gandhi and Przeworski 2006, 2007; Wright 2008; Magaloni 2008; Svolik 2012; Schedler 2013).

Such institutions might even change the underlying distribution of power. If members of the elite are given better access to state resources through appointment to key positions in the executive, the legislature, or the party apparatus, it will strengthen their ability to credibly threaten the ruler (Meng 2019, 2020). Institutions that regulate the access to these resources, for instance, rules concerning appointment, recruitment or budget allocation, can thus acquire importance by virtue of changing de facto power relations.

But even when this is not the case, institutions need not merely be the handmaidens of the underlying balance of power, epiphenomenal structures carrying no weight of their own. Staging a coup or rebellion is an extremely risky undertaking that faces gargantuan collective action problems. A member of the elite who rebels on his own will be stopped and punished, harshly. In order to remove the ruler, the rebellious party must be unified and coordinated. In the secretive environment of an authoritarian regime, riven by suspicions, such coordination is inherently difficult. Here, institutions often matter by providing signals and focal points that help members of the elite plan and coordinate their behaviour.

Formal institutions give rise to expectations about other actors' behaviour, over time altering informal norms and even beliefs (North, Wallis, and Weingast 2009: 15; Acemoglu and Robinson 2019). Deviation from established norms requires more justification and attracts more attention. By creating a default expectation about the behaviour of others, miscalculations and misunderstandings that could give rise to conflicts are prevented. In this way, institutions can help control or at least mitigate the use of violence.

In the historical context under study in this book there were sometimes written rules or charters that regulated the relationship between the monarch and the barons of the realm, such as the English *Magna Carta*, first granted by King John Lackland on Runnymede in 1215. In itself, Magna Carta proved to be non-binding, as King John, supported by his liege-lord Pope Innocent III, quickly annulled it. Nonetheless, the Great Charter established a precedent and idea that had important repercussions later, as successive English monarchs reissued the charter, beginning with John's son Henry III in 1216 and 1217 (Maddicott 2010; see Chapter 7).

We find similar charters all over the Latin west in the medieval period (Bloch 1971[1939]: 451–2). However, more important were established traditions or precedents, often in the form of group-specific privileges or liberties, which helped regulate behaviour and expectations. These were hugely influential in a society that cherished tradition—authority was normally justified by being old—and where rulers could not easily make and unmake laws. The principles of succession that we focus attention on in this book were in practice often governed by a mix of informal norms, established tradition, and legal documents (see Bartlett 2020: 99–104).

Family and dynasty

Due to the weakness of institutions in authoritarian regimes, personal relations are key. The weaker the legal and institutional framework, the more the state resembles Max Weber's description of the *patrimonial state*, defined as a state where the relationship between the ruler and his subjects is the same as the one that has—in most historical societies—existed between a father and his children (Weber 2019; Siedentop 2014). The father enjoys virtually unrestricted authority over his children, circumscribed only by tradition, and the children are expected to obey and be loyal to the father.

In many modern authoritarian regimes, especially of the personalist kind, family or kinship ties remain important. Many dictators have tried, with varying degrees of success, to pass on power to their children and where possible they have relied on relatives as trusted advisors and agents (Brownlee 2007).

While promotion of relatives to political positions today risks breaking norms of impartiality and elicits allegations of nepotism, the patrimonial character of rule was *comme il faut* as well as deeply institutionalized in the high politics of medieval and early modern Europe. This was a world of dynastic politics, where family ties had a legitimate and much broader political significance than they do in today's autocracies (Sharma 2017; Bartlett 2020). Territory, and even royal offices, were often seen as the property of their holders, and could be passed on to family as any other inheritance.

The societies we analyse in this book were therefore ones where individuals catered not solely to themselves but to the interest of their house or lineage. To understand this social context, we have to recall that most monarchs saw themselves as part of a larger chain, with a key aim of perpetuating their lineage's hold on the throne (Greengrass 2014: 16, 276–7; Bartlett 2020: 360). In other words, monarchs sought not only to stay in power but to hand over this power (as well as other spoils of power) to their own offspring or family members. This strong sense of dynasty is illustrated by the high frequency of child kings (Bartlett 2020: 115; see also Chapter 7).

The state

The classic Weberian definition of a state is the 'community that (successfully) claims the monopoly of the legitimate use of physical force within a given territory' (Weber 1948: 78). This definition does not hold up for the polities we focus on in this book, at least not for most of the period we analyse. Monarchs, the heads of the states in question, were—especially as we delve far back in time—relatively weak.

The ninth and tenth centuries had seen a virtual collapse of public power across large swathes of Western and Central Europe (Bisson 2009; Wickham 2009, 2016; Oakley 2010). In areas such as West Francia and Catalonia, public taxation had all but disappeared, no medieval Western or Central European monarch had anything resembling a centralized administrative apparatus—not to speak of a local administrative apparatus—at his or her disposal, and nobles and bishops had stepped in to fill the void left by the absence of public authority. Power was therefore carried via interpersonal ties between rulers and elites in the localities (Strayer 1987 [1965]; Poggi 1978; Finer 1997a; Bisson 2009; Oakley 2010; Sharma 2017). As a consequence, there were often overlapping claims to authority in each territory (Bartlett 2020: 421–7). Some territories were held as crown lands, under direct control of the king. Others were held by the monarch, but in a personal capacity. Still others were under the control of another lord, such as a duke or a baron, who in turn owed formal allegiance to the monarch.

The relationship between the monarch and his supposedly subordinate lords was in practice often strained. For instance, the eleventh-century Capetian kings of France were weaker in terms of military power than their most important vassals, the dukes of Normandy and the counts of Flanders, and in later centuries they were often weaker than the English kings who were also their vassals (Bartlett 2000: 17; Jordan 2001: 52–62; Wickham 2016: 102). If we relate this to Svolik's (2012) work, the point is that medieval monarchs' power vis-à-vis that of the elite was low to medium (see also Oakley 2012: 149–51). No medieval monarch could rule without the support of at least a significant proportion of the lay magnates and high clergy. It follows that power relationships at the apex of society were based on negotiated relationships between elite groups and monarchs, as elites would bargain with their kings over their loyalty.

Dukes, counts, and barons who ruled rich lands could carve out substantial power and sometimes challenge the monarch. One of the foremost examples were the dukes of Burgundy, who over the fourteenth and fifteenth centuries gradually acquired more and more territory in both the Kingdom of France and the Holy Roman Empire. During the Hundred Years' War, Duke Philip the Good even allied with the English against the French king Charles VII, only ending the conflict with a treaty that guaranteed the duke virtual independence within his French territories (Putnam 1908). Philip's son Charles the Bold was even more ambitious, seeking to turn Burgundy into a kingdom (Vaughan 1973: 55). Burgundy's ascendancy was however cut short by the death of Charles the Bold in 1477. Lacking male heirs, the disparate Burgundian holdings disintegrated (illustrating one of the main points of this book).

Moreover, the territorial boundaries of states were in the earlier part of the period much looser than those of modern-day states. Kingdoms were in places separated by 'marches', borderlands whose marcher lords had authority not enjoyed by their counterparts in the central parts of the kingdom (Lieberman 2010). Examples include the Welsh Marches in Britain and the Austrian March in the Carolingian Empire, which later developed into Austria. More generally, medieval Europe made up a form of patchwork of political authority structures—so-called composite or conglomerate states (Elliot 1992; Gustafsson 1998; Nexon 2009)—where even kings could be vassals of other monarchs for certain territories and were many nobles owed allegiance to several monarchs for different territories (Bartlett 2020: 421–4).

Weber's definition of the state thus does not apply to the more vaguely delineated and loosely held kingdoms of medieval Europe. Nevertheless, there is still a clear continuity between, for example, the Kingdom of the Franks ruled by Hugh Capet in the late ninth century and the France in which his descendant Louis XVI was guillotined eight centuries later. The geographical space of the kingdom varied, as well as the power of the monarch versus nobility, but the monarchs were all part of the same tradition, deriving their authority from the same fount.

As our focus in this book is on the institutions and practices of royal succession, we are primarily interested in the workings of the central authority and the relation of the monarch towards the elite, which remains comparable throughout the period, even though the territorial nature of the state itself changes.

Introducing our dataset

To apply the theoretical arguments presented in Chapter 2, and to capture the most important of the above-mentioned conceptual distinctions empirically, we have coded a dataset that registers 741 monarchs and succession arrangements in 27 European medieval and early modern monarchies between AD 1000 and 1800. In Chapters 5–9, we enlist these data to test the theoretical arguments developed in Chapter 2, or more precisely to analyse how successions and succession arrangements affected depositions, civil and interstate war, parliamentary activity, and dynasty. We here proceed by introducing this dataset and discussing some of the crucial challenges we faced coding it.

States/polities

This book is about European state-formation and political stability. As we are interested in autocracies and want to keep potential confounders constant, we only include Christian monarchies in our dataset. This means that we exclude Muslim monarchies, such as the *taifas* in *al-Andalus*,[2] Christian republics, such as Venice and the Dutch Republic, and Christian religious polities, such as the Papal States and the State of the Teutonic Order.

The choice of which among the very many Christian monarchies to include has been guided by two factors: (1) data availability and (2) the importance of the polities in European history. Our ambition has been to include as many of the monarchies that have played important roles in European history as possible. However, sometimes—especially early in the period—information on monarchs, succession arrangements, and outcome variables are too scarce, or of too low quality, to warrant inclusion. This is particularly the case for some states in Eastern Europe and the Balkans. Likewise, we only include monarchs on whom we have reliable information, which means that there are gaps for some polities in the period we study. For example, Sweden only figures from AD 1130 in our data, even though a Swedish monarchy, or at least Swedish monarchs, probably already existed at the turn of the millennium. But we only have fragmentary evidence of the tenures and political fates of Swedish monarchs before 1130 so we are unable to code these earlier monarchs.

For pragmatic reasons we have also had to prioritize more important monarchies (where 'importance' is measured primarily in terms of polity and population size). It would simply have been too time consuming to code all smaller principalities, especially those in the Holy Roman Empire and the Italian Peninsula.

The Empire alone encompassed several hundred polities and from among these we have chosen to include (i) the Empire itself until it stopped functioning as a de facto state in the mid-fourteenth century (see later) and (ii) the most important of its constituent units, namely the secular prince electors, the archdukes of Austria, and the kings of Bohemia.

One might worry that the choice to primarily include more important monarchies introduces a form of survivorship bias to our study. However, as Scott F. Abramson (2017) has shown, small polities continued to thrive in Europe well into the age of the territorial state and they were actually more likely to survive than large states. Some of the states we include in our study also lost their independence, or disintegrated, in the period we study. It was not until the nineteenth century, well after our study ends, that large states came to dominate Europe. Hence, it is not obvious that there is any survival bias in

---

[2] However, in Chapter 9 we enlist data on ruler tenure in these Iberian Muslim polities for purposes of comparison.

the data. However, there is still clearly an overrepresentation of larger monarchies (except for the models comparing Christian Europe with Muslim states in Chapter 9). This should be kept in mind when interpreting the results.

Another difficult issue is how to conceive of 'sovereignty' in an era of composite monarchies and personal unions (Philpott 2001; Nexon 2009). Given our focus on the succession we have chosen to treat states as sovereign as long as they retained their own political institutions, such as councils and parliaments, and had their own succession arrangements. This means, for example, that we treat polities that were ruled by the Habsburgs, such as Bohemia, Austria, and Hungary, as separate states until they adopted a unified succession when they agreed to the Pragmatic Sanction in the eighteenth century. We treat polities that were parts of other personal unions, such as the Kalmar Union, in the same way (i.e. Denmark, Sweden, and Norway are coded as separate states when they were part of the Union). We also stop counting the Holy Roman Empire as a functioning state after the Golden Bull of 1356 was issued (we count Bohemia as a sovereign state from 1212, when the Golden Bull of Sicily was issued). Although the Empire continued to exist on paper, and also for some practical purposes, long after 1356, the fact of the matter is that its constituent units grew more independent over time until they for all practical purposes acted as sovereign states. Setting the threshold later, as in 1648 when the Thirty Years War ended, does not substantially change our results.

The resulting dataset consists of 27 states, described in Table 3.1 (Chapter 7 on power-sharing institutions builds on the subset of these states that at some point in time had parliaments or representative institutions, which is 26 out of 27, the exception being the Byzantine Empire).

These polities cover most of the European landmass as shown in Figure 3.1. This is especially true early in the period where we treat the Holy Roman Empire as a sovereign state (i.e. until 1356). Later on, there are quite some white spaces in what is today Germany, Switzerland, and northern Italy, reflecting that we have been unable to code all the small states that emerged from the (de facto) imperial collapse. Similarly, Greece and its surrounding areas become white after the Ottoman conquest of the Byzantine Empire.

Monarchs

For these 27 monarchies, we have collected detailed information on more than 700 monarchs, their families, and their political fates. If there is one piece of information medieval states cared to record for the afterworld it was information

Table 3.1 States in the sample

State	First year in sample	Last year in sample
Aragon	1035	1479
Austria	1359	1792
Bavaria	1651	1799
Brandenburg/Prussia	1356	1799
Byzantine Empire	1025	1453
Bohemia	1230	1740
Castile	1035	1516
Denmark	1014	1799
England	1066	1799
France	1031	1793
Hungary	1001	1740
Holy Roman Empire	1002	1378
Leon	1028	1230
Lithuania	1382	1569
Naples	1071	1504
Navarre	1004	1610
Norway	1000	1559
Palatinate	1356	1799
Poland	1025	1795
Portugal	1095	1788
Russia	1359	1799
Savoy	1383	1799
Saxony	1356	1799
Scotland	1034	1707
Sicily	1282	1409
Spain	1516	1788
Sweden	1130	1792

about their monarchs and their lineages (see also Blaydes and Chaney 2013). In a few states early in the period birth dates and information on families can sometimes build on sketchy, or conflicting, evidence. But for most of the sample the information is very reliable, and it is probably *the* historical indicator of importance we can code most accurately when delving back into medieval Europe.

The key feature of this data is information about successions, which usually builds on the same historical sources. Even if we do not know much else, we almost always know when a monarch ascended and descended the throne. We also often have good information on *how* monarchs ascended and descended the throne. In a few cases there is ambiguity surrounding the death of monarchs. For instance, was English King John Lackland killed by dysentery caused

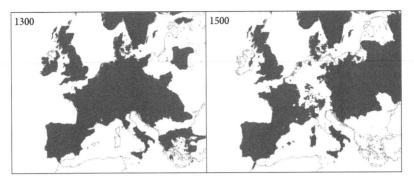

Fig. 3.1 Area covered by states in the sample in 1300 and 1500

by gluttony, as his chronicler Ralph of Coggeshall wrote, or was he poisoned by a monk of Swineshead Abbey, as claimed in the Brut Chronicle? Claims of poisoning made 800 years ago are hard to ascertain, but in most cases historians agree on the interpretation of the available evidence. In King John's case the majority opinion is that the idea of his being poisoned was invented long after his death in order to blemish his reputation—the Brut Chronicle was written 50 years after the events took place.

In general, the data on how monarchs left office are therefore both reliable and detailed enough to allow for separating successions caused by the natural deaths of monarchs and successions brought about by depositions, murders, and deaths in battle (Kokkonen and Sundell 2020). We use this data to construct a series of succession variables, described in more detail in the empirical chapters.

Succession arrangements

Succession arrangements were often not written down until rather late in the period we study, though there were exceptions (Bartlett 2020: 99–104). Genuine succession laws codifying primogeniture, such as the Norwegian Law of Succession of 1260 (Helle 1981, 1995; Orning 2008) and the *Siete Partidas* that was compiled during the reign of Alfonso X of Castile (MacDonald 1965: 653), first start to appear in numbers during the thirteenth century. When such laws are available, we use them to code succession arrangements until they were formally repudiated. Our primary focus is thus on *de jure* succession arrangements.

Before the appearance of written laws, succession was normally guided by customs that must be inferred from the historical sources, which means that interpretations to a large extent rely on actual succession patterns (Bartlett 2020: 99). However, there are often clues to succession arrangements in the ceremonies associated with royal successions. One of the most important of these clues is the fact that many monarchs early in the period took the precaution to have their eldest sons elected (or acknowledged) as co-kings during their reigns to assure their later succession (Bartlett 2020: 93–5). It would have been unnecessary to take such precautions if they were sure of their sons' succession by hereditary right. Nobles sometimes also protested against these 'premature' elections with the motivation that they were attempts to circumvent the elective character of the monarchy (Bartlett 2020: 72). Thus, co-regencies between fathers and sons strongly suggest that the succession had an elective character. This explains why we code France as an elective monarchy until Philip II Augustus (r. 1180–1223) abolished the habit of co-rule between fathers and sons, even though the Capetians had by then succeeded in turning over the throne to their eldest sons (i.e. had practiced de facto primogeniture) for more than 200 years (Lewis 1981: 28; Bartlett 2020: 93).

However, we have rerun all our models with an alternative coding that counts longer periods of de facto primogeniture in (what we interpret as *de jure*) elective monarchies as primogeniture. This alternative coding of primogeniture produces similar—indeed, even stronger—results (in addition to the Capetians' rule in eleventh and twelfth centuries France there were such periods in Poland under the Jagiellonian dynasty, in Habsburg Bohemia, and Hungary before the states adopted primogeniture in the seventeenth century, as well as several other places).

A more important problem is that succession practices early in the period often mixed elements of several different succession orders. Hereditary succession arrangements could, for example, contain elements of acclamation. Such elements were sometimes kept as ceremonies long after they had lost all political meaning and it is not always easy to know when they became purely symbolic. In short, we seldom find instances of pure primogeniture, pure elective monarchy, or pure agnatic seniority early in the period—only a dominant tendency towards one of these succession orders.[3] As a result the interpretation of succession arrangements can sometimes be difficult as we venture far back in time. We have tried to follow the established view among historians in such circumstances (Lustick 1996; Møller and Skaaning 2021).

---

[3] It also took a long time for hereditary succession laws to become specified enough to deal with many complex situations that conflicting succession claims created. For example, one motivation for the Hundred Years War was a dispute over whether men could inherit the French throne via their maternal line (the English claim) or not (the French claim). We return to this issue in Chapter 7.

Another problem is that conflicts occasionally broke out over the choice of succession principles. For instance, in fifteenth-century Russia (the Grand Principality of Moscow) different branches of the Rurikid dynasty clashed over whether agnatic seniority or primogeniture should guide the succession (Martin 2019). Although such conflicts are relatively well documented as we come closer to our own time, for early parts of the period we analyse they must often be inferred from poorly described events.

When conflicts are well documented, and in cases where new succession arrangements were adopted, we have chosen to only code changes in succession arrangements that were followed by a succession which obeyed the designated procedure and where the successor was not deposed shortly afterwards (cf. Cheibub et al. 2010). This 'turnover test' ensures that changes in succession arrangements that resulted in at least one succession, according to the designated principle adopted, are counted as being implemented. A change in succession arrangements that fulfils this criterion is counted as implemented from the beginning of the reign of the monarch who adopted it.

We use the resulting *de jure*-based coding to construct a dummy variable that differentiates between primogeniture and partible inheritance on the one hand and elective monarchy and agnatic seniority on the other. As argued in Chapter 2, primogeniture and partible inheritance (if the latter is practiced in an orderly manner, as it came to be in the period we analyse) are likely to have similar effects on political stability. Elective monarchy and agnatic seniority should both be worse for political stability; which of these two principles is worst hinges on the relative importance of the coordination problem and the crown prince problem.

The consequent dummy variable—distinguishing primogeniture and partible inheritance from other succession orders—functions as the main specification of succession arrangements in most of our models. However, we have rerun all our models with more fine-grained variables that separate all four succession arrangements mentioned earlier. These models show that primogeniture and partible inheritance have very similar effects on political stability. Notice here that more than 80 per cent of the monarch-years in this merged category are due to primogeniture—partible inheritance was much less frequent. Add to this that many monarchs in the states that practiced partible inheritance lacked brothers when they ascended the throne (and thus defaulted to de facto primogeniture) and that many of the states only partitioned the inheritance if there were substantial acquisitions to divide (see Chapter 4) and the real number of primogeniture years increases to more than 90 per cent of the monarch-years in the merged category. For this reason, when using this specification in our empirical analyses, we will simply refer to primogeniture (and as already mentioned, all reported results are similar if we only use undisputable primogeniture monarch-years).

Agnatic seniority and elective monarchy also have quite similar effects (with the former principle being somewhat more destabilizing than the latter). However, we separate the four succession arrangements when this is warranted (i.e. when they could be expected to have and/or do in fact have different effects). A more detailed description of the development of succession arrangements in Europe, which provides the basis of our coding, is provided in Chapter 4.

Conclusion

In this chapter, we have described the key conceptual characteristics of authoritarian systems in general and medieval monarchies in particular. The central dynamic in authoritarian states is the tension between the ruler and the elite. Rulers and elites need to cooperate to uphold the regime in the face of foreign threats and internal opposition, but they also constantly compete for distribution of power and spoils. This is done in an environment where there is no independent authority that can adjudicate conflicts or underwrite agreements, which means that commitments are only credible when backed by force. Politics play out under the threat of violence.

All but the weakest of modern autocracies are more institutionalized than pre-modern states, and reverence for dynasty and lineages has in many cases been replaced by party loyalty. But in key respects modern autocracies resemble medieval and early modern monarchies. Authoritarian politics is still defined by repression of the masses. Members of the elite also constantly jockey for a place in the winning coalition at the same time as they collectively try to bargain with the ruler over the distribution of spoils within the regime. These general political dynamics are timeless, but the problems were compounded in the medieval and early modern era, where rulers were weaker, dynasty more important, and ownership of territory tied to the fates of individuals.

In this setting, violent scrambles for power often broke out when succession became a political or legal issue, for instance due to the death of a monarch and vague succession rules (Acharya and Lee 2019; Sharma 2017: 194–5). These power scrambles, triggered by succession, can be likened to 'lawsuits in which violence was considered to be a legitimate mechanism of conflict resolution' (Sharma 2017: 194). To understand the consequences of succession, and how principles of succession moderated the associated risk, Chapters 5–9 apply the theoretical arguments from Chapter 2, using our new dataset. But first we devote a chapter to shedding light on the historical origins of primogeniture.

4
The Origins and Spread of Primogeniture

If primogeniture is an asset in state-formation processes, and if it is in the interest of both rulers and elite groups, why was it not adopted by state-builders everywhere? The idea that the eldest son takes the entire inheritance, or at least the bulk of it, has played such an important role in European history that many today conceive it as the normal—perhaps default—heirship practice. As mentioned in Chapter 1, sixteenth-century philosopher Jean Bodin even saw it as a law of nature, which had been observed among all peoples.

Yet Bodin could hardly have been more wrong. When it first arose in Europe, the idea of disinheriting all family members save one was revolutionary. In the eleventh century, Western Europeans invented something quite new: a 'harsher but more efficient principle to govern the inheritance of landed property' (Moore 2000: 2). While we find a looser form of primogeniture practiced in some areas of East Asia, including China, it was novel to medieval Europeans, and in historical perspective it was also very rare (see Chapter 9).

In this chapter, we show how the road leading to the adoption of primogeniture was paved with a thorough transformation of family structures and heirship practices in the Latin west, which sundered broader kinship ties and brought about the monogamous marriage and the nuclear family. The main aim of the chapter is to understand this fundamental transformation which provided new ways of dealing with the problem of succession in the period after AD 1000. We shall argue that the main transformative force was the Catholic Church, which promoted the nuclear family at the expense of the wider kin and the inheritance rights of the eldest son within that elementary family.

The chapter first describes how the Christian Church transformed strategies of heirship in late antiquity. Next, we argue that this transformation gradually brought about primogeniture in Western and Central Europe, a development that was further facilitated by an ambitious attempt by the Catholic Church to assert itself in the eleventh century. We then describe how and when primogeniture was adopted, or not adopted, among the countries in our sample. Finally, we use a comparison with the Orthodox Church to understand why

The Politics of Succession. Andrej Kokkonen, Jørgen Møller, and Anders Sundell, Oxford University Press.
© Andrej Kokkonen, Jørgen Møller, and Anders Sundell (2022). DOI: 10.1093/oso/9780192897510.003.0004

the Church's ability to transform strategies of heirship was much more effective in Western and Central Europe than in Eastern Europe and in the Balkans. This comparison reveals that the development of new heirship practices, and ultimately the introduction of primogeniture, was related to state weakness in the Latin west.

The heirship practices forbidden by the Church in late antiquity

Historically, most societies have been characterized by a high incidence of 'in-marriage', meaning marriage within a broader line of kinship or agnatic lineages (Goody 1983; 2000; Hall 1985; Fukuyama 2011; Schultz et al. 2019). This was still the case in the late Roman Empire where we find a strong patrilineal agnatic family structure. The father was the undisputed master of the household and could even kill his slaves or children (Siedentop 2014). Roman men were monogamous on paper but had much sexual leeway outside the marriage—especially with their social inferiors—and could also divorce their wives. Marriage to cousins was allowed, in some forms (Henrich 2020: 163).

Germanic, Celtic, and Slavic tribes beyond the Roman borders seem to have been organized in clans or agnatic families. One aspect of these broad kinship structures was that women who inherited property when their husbands died were under social pressure to return it to the family, often symbolized by the widow remarrying a younger brother of the deceased husband, a practice that was also widespread in the Mediterranean world.

According to British anthropologist Jack Goody (1983), 'in-marriage' was gradually replaced by 'out-marriage'—that is, marriage outside agnatic lineages, though normally within the same social class—in Europe after the late fourth century. Goody argues that the early Christian Church was the main driver of this change (see also Goody 2000: 27–44). The Church forbade a series of traditional strategies of heirship, including divorce and subsequent remarriage, consanguineous marriages within certain degrees (for instance between cousins), marriage between younger brothers and deceased older brothers' wives (known as the levirate), adoption, and concubinage. Children born out of wedlock were seen as illegitimates who could not inherit property or the family name. Finally, testaments and wills were encouraged by the Church, and widows could retain property and even bequeath it outside the family (Henrich 2020: 166).

Goody points out that all the forbidden practices were normal in Western Europe in antiquity, and that they continued to be common for centuries after the early spread of Christianity. It was only in the fourth century that this began to change as the Church hierarchy actively intervened in heirship policies. The first prohibition seems to have been introduced at the Council of Neocaesaria in 314, where the levirate was banned (Goody 2000: 27–8); other milestones include the council of Epaon in Burgundy in 517 and Emperor Leo III's Ecloga of 741 (Bartlett 2020: 44). The Church attempted to bolster the new prohibitions with reference to Scripture. However, the ban on divorce was the only new principle that could clearly be justified in this way, more specifically based on Matthew 19:3–9, 'What therefore God has joined together let not man put asunder.' All other forbidden practices had precedent—and were often portrayed as legitimate—in the Old Testament, and occasionally in the New Testament as well. On this basis, Goody (1983: 42) raises the following question:

> Why should the Christian Church institute a whole set of new patterns of behaviour in the sphere of kinship and marriage, when these ran contrary to the custom of the inhabitants they had come to convert, contrary to the Roman heritage upon which they drew, and contrary to the teachings of their sacred texts?

Goody's answer is straightforward. Rather than look at the religious implications of these policies, we should understand them in the context of their effects on the social system. The Church had an economic interest in changing strategies of heirship because this allowed 'shifts from private ownership to the hands of the Church' (1983: 46). By severing kinship ties, the clergy stood to gain from testamentary gifts from widows who could refuse family pressure to remarry and no longer had to give up their property to relatives within a broader agnatic structure.[1] In other words, the Church attempted to prevent return of property to the family via cousin marriages, remarriage, and the levirate, and to make it more difficult to secure an heir by forbidding adoption and

---

[1] Of course, to the extent that passages from the Bible could be invoked to defend the new heirship policies, they were. Besides Matthew 19:3–9, a good example is the Book of Numbers (27:8), where God vindicates the principle of female inheritance—for rulers—by advising Moses as follows: 'When a man dies without a son, his inheritance shall pass to his daughter' (Bartlett 2020: 151). More generally, in the New Testament Jesus tells his followers to abandon their families. Goody might be said to have underestimated the normative power of Biblical passages such as these.

by making children born out of wedlock illegitimate. As a result, lineages died out more frequently. Simply put by Joseph Henrich (2020: 167), these reforms ensured that the Church 'got rich on death, inheritance, and the afterlife'.

The new prohibitions completely transformed notions of legitimacy with respect to unions between men and women and their offspring. What we have here is thus a revolutionary development, allowed by the Christianization of Europe and spearheaded by the Church, which stood to benefit from it. Cousin marriage, levirate, and legal adoption had all been standard ways of extending the family and thereby keeping property intact. All these practices, sinews of the old social order, now gradually disappeared from European culture. But as we show in the following sections, the process was not straightforward.

The gradual spread of the new heirship practices

While some of the forbidden practices were effectively suppressed very early on in the Latin west—adoption is probably the best example[2]—other prohibitions were de facto flouted by the high and mighty for a long time. In the early Middle Ages, marriages within the forbidden degrees were frequent, kings and nobles often repudiated childless wives (or wives who displeased them) in order to remarry, concubinages were common, and the offspring of such liaisons were often able to inherit properties and even titles (see Duby 1984).

The Merovingian kings of Francia were thus effectively polygamous, something that virtually no cleric of the period dared question (Goody 2000: 52; Wickham 2009: 188).[3] Likewise, the founder of the Carolingian dynasty that in the early eighth century replaced the Merovingians, Charles Martel, was born by one of his father Pepin's mistresses but nonetheless managed to rally enough support to take the inheritance from Pepin's legitimate but underage son Theudoald. In fact, there were institutions of semi-legitimacy well into the eleventh century, which served to perpetuate lineages, in clear contravention of the Church prohibitions. For instance, despite his nickname, William the Bastard (later known as the Conqueror) was not entirely illegitimate. His

---

[2] While adoption remained in use in the Byzantine Empire and was sometimes practiced among the Merovingians, it is hardly ever documented in the medieval west. Strikingly, adoption was only reintroduced in France in 1892 and in the United Kingdom in 1926 (Goody 1983: 73).

[3] They probably had good reason to be cautious. When the Irish monk and monastic founder Columbanus in 610 refused to bless the illegitimate sons of King Theuderic II, he was exiled from Francia and had to relocate to Northern Italy (Brown 1997: 156).

mother was married *more danico* (in the Danish way) to count Robert of Normandy, meaning that William could inherit if no sons were born in genuine wedlock (Duby 1984: 42–3).

However, as the clergy gradually became more self-assertive in policing the prohibitions, the rules became more consequential. During the Carolingian renaissance of the eighth and ninth century, intellectuals—which in effect meant clergy in this period—steadily achieved more normative power, including the power to criticize the elite for their ways with respect to, among other things, marriage (Brown 1997: 269; Wickham 2009: 411; Siedentop 2014: 152–71). Wickham (2009: 555) identifies this as a major cultural shift based on a moralizing political practice of clergy policing the behaviour of kings and nobles.

The Carolingians even tried to force their nobles to accept monogamous marriages and they made divorce more difficult (Moore 2000: 89; Goody 2000: 52; Bartlett 2020: 155). While they were not always successful in this, marriage laws were clearly tightening in this period (Goody 2000: 28, 51–2; Wickham 2009: 420–1). Consanguineous marriages were forbidden to the seventh degree of kinship at a Carolingian church council in 747. In the ninth century Pope Nicholas I (r. 858–867) managed to make Lothar II of Francia remarry his renounced wife Theutberga with reference to the prohibition against divorce (Wickham 2009: 420–1; Oakley 2010: 213–14). Christian societies in Europe thus seem to have gradually internalized many of the new norms about heirship and family.

Here, the strength of the ecclesiastical infrastructure obviously mattered. The Church had a more developed organization in areas with a longer Christian tradition as there were more monasteries, older and more established bishoprics, a stronger ecclesiastical presence at the parish level, and a stronger presence of clergy in royal administrations, all of which made it easier to gain broader acceptance of the norms for marriage and heirship.

We can use data on the spread of bishoprics to proxy which areas were most affected by these teachings. The map in Figure 4.1 shows how long each region in Europe had been exposed to the Western or Catholic Church in the year 1500, using data from Schulz et al. (2019). Darker shades mean longer exposure. The epicentre was in the Carolingian empire, reflecting the alliance between the Frankish kings and the Church (Henrich 2020: 186). We can also see the effects of Islamic rule in Southern Spain, which meant that although the area Christianized early, it had fewer centuries under direct (Western) Christian influence.

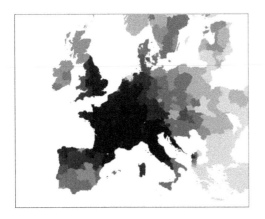

Fig. 4.1 History of exposure to the Western church, in 1500. Darker shades indicate longer exposure (no data for Serbia, Macedonia, Bosnia and Herzegovina, and Russia)

Areas that had been Christian for a long time were more ready to accept new (or more strictly enforced) Church regulations than areas that had only recently been Christianized.[4] For instance, the first generations of Christian kings in Scandinavia—who were Christianized long after the Franks—would often have heirs born out of wedlock (Bartlett 2020: 4–5).[5] A striking example is Danish king Svend Estridsen (r. 1047–1076), five of whose bastard sons were successively elevated to the throne.

The tenth- and eleventh-century Church reform movement

In the late ninth century, the papacy entered a centuries-long period of crisis, both in esteem and power (Ullmann (1970[1955]); Southern 1970; Berman 1983; Morris 1989), which meant that most popes of the tenth and early eleventh centuries could not enforce the marriage and heirship prohibitions in the way Pope Nicholas I had attempted in the ninth century.

However, we find other progressive forces within the Latin Church in this period. The most important example is the Cluniac reforms of the tenth and early eleventh centuries (Howe 2016; Southern 1956: 163; Moore 2000; Melville 2016). The Cluniac reform movement was a bottom-up social

---

[4] Schultz et al. (2019) show that even today there is a very strong positive relationship between centuries under the medieval Catholic Church and cousin marriage rates; the longer the Catholic legacy, the lower the propensity for cousins to marry.

[5] During the high and late Middle Ages, there are a number of examples of bastard sons who were able to claim the throne—and sometimes start their own dynasties—in the old Christian core areas. A prominent example is the House of Trastámara, which ruled Castile from 1389, and which was founded by Henry II, an illegitimate son of Alfonso XI of Castile (Bartlett 2020: 169–80). But as opposed to the situation under the Merovingians or in early Christian Scandinavia, these bastard sons had to fight an uphill struggle for the throne, they could not inherit it merely by being sons of the former ruler.

coalition between clergy and popular masses. It emerged in West Francia in the late tenth century in response to the collapse of royal power in this area and the secularization of church tithes and property this had created in the 150 years after the death of Charlemagne (Moore 2000: 10, 28; Siedentop 2014: 186-7; see also Møller and Doucette 2022: Chapters 1 and 3). The main aim of the Cluniac reform programme was to free ecclesiastical institutions—particularly monasteries—from secular influence to be able to follow Scripture and church tradition in an uncorrupted way (Fried 2015: 134–5). More specifically, the Cluniac movement spread new ideals about clerical chastity and the prohibition against simony (the selling of church offices) and lay investiture (Moore 2000). As we show later, this had important repercussions for lay heirship practices.

The Cluniac reforms were succeeded by—and helped foster—the eleventh- and twelfth-century Gregorian or papal reforms (Moore 2000; Howe 2016: 9). These papal reforms began around 1050, as a string of assertive reform popes were elevated to the see of St. Peter. Inspired by the Cluniac reforms, the reform popes first lashed out against simony and tried to enforce clerical celibacy. But they soon turned on lay rulers. Pope Gregory VII (r. 1073–1085), after whom the movement takes its name, attempted to assert papal supremacy over lay rulers and questioned their right to invest clerics (most prominently bishops) with church offices. These principles had originally been formulated by the fifth-century popes Leo I (r. 440–461) and Gelasius I (r. 492–496) but had never been effective (Ullmann 1970[1955]: 197–204; Tierney 1988: 25; Berman 1983: 93; Oakley 2010: 208).

The great conflict over lay investiture between 1075 and 1122 has attracted most attention in the literature (see Ullmann 1970[1955]; Southern 1970; Berman 1983; Morris 1989; Jordan 2001; Oakley 2012). But another part of this development was a much stricter enforcement of the prohibitions against marriage within the family, divorce, remarriage, concubinage, and a disavowal of the tacit acceptance of children born out of wedlock inheriting property and the family name. The reform popes were thus much more vigorous in sanctioning the prohibitions than their predecessors had been (Goody 1983: 134–5, 142). One important aspect was that it became less common to accept offspring from liaisons as legitimate (Duby 1984). Another was that it became increasingly difficult to obtain permission for divorce and remarriage (Bartlett 2020: 9).

A good example of this shift is the protracted struggle between King Philip I of France and one of the reform popes, the former Cluniac monk Urban II (r. 1088–1099). The struggle revolved around Philip's second marriage to

Bertrade de Montfort in 1092, after Philip had repudiated his first wife, Berthe. According to Canon law, the new union was unlawful because it fell within the prohibited degrees of kinship and because Bertrade was already married to Fulk IV, Count of Anjou. Philip nonetheless refused to separate from Bertrade, and he was therefore excommunicated by the papal legate Hugh of Die in 1094. The sentence was subsequently confirmed by Urban II at the Council of Clermont in November 1095. The ban was lifted and reinstated several times, until the king finally repudiated Bertrade in 1104 (Duby 1984: 16–17).

In subsequent centuries, popes would regularly force monarchs to annul consanguineous marriages or marriages with divorcees or to take back wives they had repudiated unlawfully (see e.g. O'Callaghan 1975: 242–5; Procter 1980: 49). Famous examples include Innocent III's interdict on France in 1200 to force King Philip Augustus to take back his repudiated wife, Ingeborg of Denmark, and the two occasions in the mid-thirteenth century when the papacy placed Portugal under interdict due to King Alfonso III's marriage within the prohibited degrees (Jordan 2001: 205, 245).

We can use our dataset to illustrate the increasingly strict norms of marriage after AD 1000. Figure 4.2 plots the percentage of marriages entered into

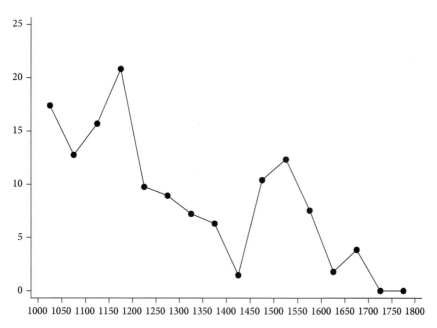

Fig. 4.2 Percentage of marriages that ended in divorce, grouped according to the half-century of the monarch's accession

by monarchs in our sample which ended in divorce, grouped according to the half-century in which the monarch in question took the throne. Although there are some bumps in the data, the trend is clearly decreasing, with fewer and fewer divorces. The trend would probably have been even starker had we had similar data for the period before AD 1000.

The advent of primogeniture in the Latin west

To better grasp the gradual development of primogeniture, a closer look at family patterns and inheritance among the elite in the early Middle Ages is helpful. Under the Merovingians, the Frankish realm was virtually always divided between brothers: in the period between 511 and 679, we only find 22 years of Frankish unity (Wickham 2009: 114). This changed after the ascendancy of the Carolingians. Between 751, when Pepin III officially became king of the Franks, and the death of Louis the Pious in 840, the Frankish realm was unified for all but four years (768–771). One reason was that the Carolingians sired fewer heirs because they had fewer legitimate wives. While the Carolingian kings would often have multiple offspring from liaisons, these illegitimate children would normally not be able to inherit—unlike the situation under the polygamous Merovingians and early Christian Scandinavian kings (Wickham 2016: 64).

For instance, despite all his power and prestige, Charlemagne took the trouble of having his marriage with the Langobard princess Desiderata annulled in 771 before remarrying, and henceforth he only remarried once the present queen had died (altogether he was married four times). One of the consequences of this practice of monogamy was that many Carolingian kings and later emperors, by biological chance, only left one legitimate male heir who could inherit the realm intact.[6] While Charlemagne had at least twenty children by nine or ten different women, he was thus only survived by one legitimate son in the form of Louis the Pious. The resulting pattern of accidental primogeniture explains why the Frankish realm remained intact for most of the time from Charles Martel to Louis the Pious (Riché 1993). This occurred in a situation where partible inheritance between sons was still the norm, so if the Carolingian kings had been survived by several legitimate sons, the realm would have been divided, as it was between the sons of Louis the Pious in the ninth century.[7]

---

[6] This was ultimately the reason the Carolingian family died out in the male line.
[7] In the aptly titled document *Divisio Regnorum* dating to 806, Charlemagne had in fact specified the future division of the realm among his then three living legitimate sons. However, two of these

It seems probable that this 'Carolingian wonder', and other similar examples of de facto primogeniture brought about by the Church's regulations on marriage and heirship, demonstrated the advantages of succession based on primogeniture and eventually inspired monarchs in polities where the influence of the Catholic Church was strong to let the eldest son inherit the bulk of their possessions even when they had many surviving children. Moreover, this demonstration effect was probably amplified by the fact that the clergy insisted that the Carolingians abandon the practice of partible inheritance in one crucial respect: the imperial crown. The Christian idea of empire was indivisible (just as there was only one God, there could only be one emperor), and the imperial title was never split between several heirs (Wilson 2016: 40–1).

Over time, the logic of primogeniture therefore made headway in the Latin west. A tendency towards primogeniture first became noticeable in the ninth century (Moore 2000: 70) and it then became more prominent in the tenth century.

Figure 4.3 shows the average level of primogeniture (and orderly partible inheritance that usually resulted in de facto primogeniture) in different areas of Europe between 1000 and 1800, based on our data. Each spot on the map has been shaded according to the number of years it has been part of a state that practiced primogeniture, with darker colours representing more primogeniture. As in the earlier map (Figure 4.1) the shading highlights the western parts of Europe in general and the Frankish realm in particular, with higher levels of primogeniture in France, England, Scotland, the Iberian Peninsula, and Southern Italy. The correlation with exposure to Western Christianity in Figure 4.1 is not perfect. For instance, only the northern parts of the Iberian Peninsula were consistently under Christian influence, but the entire area is dark in this map. To some extent this is an artefact of the way the map is made—we do not have data on the Muslim kingdoms that ruled the southern part of the Iberian Peninsula in the early part of the period, and the average level of primogeniture is therefore based only on the years under which it was under Christian rule, as part of Castile, Aragon, Portugal, and later Spain. The same is true for parts of the Holy Roman Empire—after the Golden Bull of 1356, the empire as a whole is not included, only the secular electors are, meaning that we do not have data on the small states in the area. And the coding of Ireland is entirely based on the part of the island under English rule.

---

sons predeceased Charlemagne, meaning that the youngest, Louis, was the only one still alive when the emperor died in 814 (West 2019: 7).

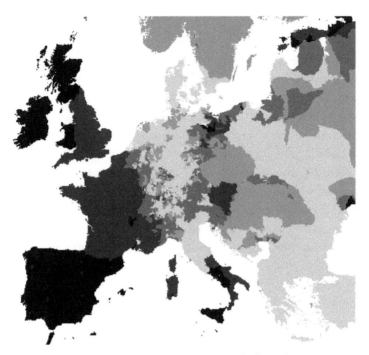

Fig. 4.3 Average primogeniture in our sample (based on those years where we have data for the region). Darker shades indicate more primogeniture

While family structures in a region can leave a deep mark on social life and psychology (Henrich 2020), royal succession is not a perfect reflection of social practices in the area under rule. After the *Reconquista*, Christian state structures were layered on top of areas that had been under Muslim rule for centuries, meaning that there was not necessarily a strong link between the values and traditions of the populace and the institutions governing the state. Similarly, southern Italy was in the early parts of the millennium conquered and ruled by an elite of Norman origin. But these conquests also spread the Frankish inheritance strategies, especially on the elite level. As Bartlett (1993) describes, both the Iberian Peninsula and Southern Italy were in this sense colonized by the Frankish core areas, where the new heirship policies and then primogeniture had advanced most.

Overall, we thus find a clear correlation between an area's exposure to the Western Church and eventual adoption of primogeniture in the royal succession, which becomes even stronger if we factor in the elite-level cultural spread of social practices via colonization.[8]

The role of state weakness

What enabled the clergy of the Latin west to impose the prohibitions on even kings and emperors? As the narrative earlier shows, the backdrop of the Western change in heirship practices was one of feeble public power (see Stasavage 2020: Chapter 5). After the fall of the Western Roman Empire in the fifth century, the first generations of Germanic successor states preserved an ex-Roman tradition of public authority, which now came to revolve around an assembly model of politics where the freeborn would gather at frequent assemblies (Wickham 2009: 101–5; 2016: 33–4). Moreover, they controlled the churches within their realms (Oakley 2010).

These societies thus still had meaningful government and power was in the hands of the Merovingian kings in France, Visigoth kings in Spain, and Langobardic kings and dukes in Italy rather than local lords. But public authority was much weaker than it had been in the Roman Empire. For instance, the Roman land tax seems to have disappeared after AD 550, which made it impossible to pay a standing army and an administration that went beyond the royal household (Wickham 2005; 2009).

It was this state weakness that empowered the Catholic Church and enabled it to gradually force its norms of inheritance on lay rulers and nobles. The Catholic Church was the one major Roman institution that survived the collapse of the Western Roman Empire (Wickham 2009: 59, 74), and it became a form of surrogate state apparatus in a situation where lay rulers had little in terms of a genuine administration. In comparative perspective, this state weakness—and the powerful position it gave to the Church—is the main difference between the Byzantine Empire, which we introduce for purposes of comparison later, and the Latin west (Kaldellis 2015).

It is therefore not a coincidence that the final breakthrough for the Church policies on family structures and heirship strategies took place after the large-scale breakdown of public order that began in West Francia in the ninth century (Wickham 2009: 444; Bisson 2009). This breakdown did not affect all of Western and Central Europe to the same extent. While the old heartlands

---

[8] In a supplementary analysis, we have divided Europe into grid cells and regressed the average level of primogeniture on exposure to the Western Church (using the same data presented in the two maps). This analysis shows that the relationship is strong and statistically significant.

of the Carolingian realm in West Francia were hit the hardest, East Francia—what was to become the Holy Roman Empire—emerged as the strongest of the Frankish successor states (Southern 1956: 19–20; Wickham 2009: 430, 523). That said, public power was everywhere more feeble, more localized, and more decentralized in AD 1000 than it had been in AD 900 or in the glory days of Charlemagne (Wickham 2009: 444). More specifically, power increasingly became associated with local lordship and the royal writ ceased to apply outside a few core areas, at least in West Francia and Catalonia (Bisson 1986; 2009; Moore 2000).

The final assertion of the new heirship practices by the Roman reform popes thus occurred in a context where state power had collapsed. The ninth- and tenth-century breakdown of public authority enabled first the bottom-up Cluniac reform movement and then its top-down successor, the Gregorian reform movement, to finally wrest power over marriage and heirship practices from lay rulers and lay nobles. Moreover, the reform programme opened new career possibilities for disinherited younger ("second") sons of nobles and monarchs. Clerical celibacy was a way of freeing the Church from outside interests, including the interests of kinship and lineages. Until around 1100, it was normal for Western clergy to marry and produce heirs who would often inherit their benefices. The reform popes' stricter enforcement of clerical celibacy—or at least the fact that any offspring of clerics was now considered illegitimate—ensured that each new generation of younger noble sons could enter the Church and gain powerful positions and valuable benefices (Bartlett 1993; Sharma 2015; Gorski and Sharma 2017).

This, in turn, facilitated the final transition to primogeniture. Moore goes so far as to argue that clerical chastity and primogeniture were a form of quid pro quo, which 'guaranteed that the land which was handed over to them [the Church] would not at any time in the future become the basis for the foundation of a new secular dynasty' (Moore 2000: 88, see also 155). Primogeniture therefore first became a common succession practice in the very area where public power had buckled most and where the tenth- and eleventh-century Church reform programme had been most vibrant: West Francia and the Christian statelets in Northern Spain (Moore 2000). But even outside of this area, the Church actively spread the new succession rules. For instance, Pope Gregory VII directly tried to promote strong hereditary monarchy—'preferably from father to son' (Cowdrey 2000: 351)—in the Scandinavian countries and in England, to stabilize power in these newly Christianized areas and to solidify church–state relations (Bartlett 1993: 248; Cowdrey 1998: Chapter 6; Cowdrey 2000: 322, 347–51). The only exception was the Holy

Roman Empire where popes—from Gregory VII henceforth—insisted that the crown was elective (Southern 1970: 145; Cowdrey 1998: 620–8).

Moreover, the restrictive marriage and family practices not only constrained monarchs—our focus—but also their rivals, influential aristocratic families. By hindering the formation of tight-knit aristocratic clans, the hand of kings were strengthened. There was thus a mutually beneficial alliance between the Church and the Frankish kings (Wickham 2009). The Church gained immense power as regulators of social life and economic wealth from inheritance, and the kings gained legitimacy, weakened the nobility, and could draw support from a more professional bureaucracy (Henrich 2020: 186–7). We proceed by describing the adoption (or non-adoption) of primogeniture in the royal succession in the countries in our sample in more detail.

Succession practices around Europe

France, England, and Scotland

The most famous example of the transition to primogeniture is that of the Capetians kings, who replaced the Carolingians on the throne of West Francia in 987 when Hugh Capet was elected king. At the time, Francia or France was an elective monarchy. However, the Capetians had already established a custom of transmitting the principal honour of the family and their vast patrimonial lands undivided to the eldest son, whereas younger sons were married off to heiresses, given positions within the Church (including lucrative benefices), or compensated with lesser territorial acquisitions (Lewis 1981: 7–16; Moore 2000: 70). The Capetians were thus part of the early tendency towards primogeniture in West Francia, described earlier.

After being elevated from ducal to royal family, the Capetians adopted much the same approach towards the crown, which was 'quickly assimilated to the family and its lands as a patrimonial honor' (Lewis 1981: 28). Securing the succession of the eldest son to the throne required special tactics and procedures. Most Capetians kings had their eldest son elected co-king during their lifetime to assure their claim on the throne vis-à-vis younger sons and outsiders (Bartlett 2020: 93). The Capetians' attempt to make their eldest sons their successors were so successful—in large part due to biological fortune as monarchs repeatedly produced healthy sons—that the royal elections gradually lost their meaning, until they were finally abolished under Philip II Augustus (r. 1180–1223). The triumph of primogeniture was clear for everyone to see when the beginning of Philip III's reign was officially dated to 1270, even though he was only crowned in 1271 because he had been away on crusade when his father, Louis IX (whom he accompanied), died at Tunis in 1270 (Jordan 2001: 241).

Although the Capetians were early adopters of the principle of primogeniture for their patrimonial lands, similar customs were adopted in the tenth and eleventh centuries by most of the French higher nobility (Lewis 1981: 30; Bartlett 1993: 49–50). The Capetians' succession policies were, thus, barely indistinguishable from those of other noble families in West Francia, a fact that may have made it easier for the latter to accept the transformation of the French crown from an elective into a hereditary monarchy.

The Norman conquest of England in 1066 brought French succession practices to the British Isles, but the adoption of the new rules was slow. Before the conquest, succession in Anglo-Saxon England had been guided by a mix of appointment by the incumbent king and election by the elite assembly *Witenagemot*. In the centuries leading up to the conquest, most kings were descendants of king Alfred the Great, and candidates from this Wessex dynasty frequently stressed their ancestry as an argument for their election. However, lack of ancestry does not seem to have precluded an outsider's accession (Marafioti 2014: 19). As earlier described, both Harold Godwinson and William the Conqueror thus based their royal claims on appointment by the previous king.

Succession in Normandy was by contrast guided by primogeniture, and William's eldest son, Robert Curthose, succeeded him in the Duchy of Normandy. The Kingdom of England was given to his second eldest son, William Rufus (Douglas 1964; Holt 1997: 149–51). William the Conqueror's division of his lands was not unique for the time. Medieval monarchs who came in possession of several polities frequently divided them among their sons, with the inheritance (i.e. the polity that the monarch had himself inherited) going to the eldest and acquisitions (i.e. polities that the monarch had acquired in one way or another in his own lifetime) going to the younger ones (e.g. Holt 1997: 313); we will see the pattern repeated in the Iberian Peninsula.

William's appointment of his second oldest son to the throne of England—and the fact that he himself had claimed the throne based on appointment—created confusion about the Norman-English succession. The situation was not helped by the fact that neither Rufus nor his immediate successors Henry I and Stephen of Blois managed to put a son on the throne. Not until Richard I (Lionheart) succeeded his father, Henry II, in 1189 do we see a transfer of the English throne from father to eldest surviving son (Bartlett 2000: 4). That transfer only came about because Richard revolted against his father in fear of being disinherited (Painter 2001[1933]: 62; Turner and Heiser 2013:

70). Richard, who died childless, bequeathed England to his brother John (Lackland), even though his deceased older brother Geoffrey's son Arthur of Brittany—who was entitled to inherit according to strict primogeniture—was still alive (Holt 1997: 307–26; Barlow 1999: 305).[9] The principle of succession by appointment thus lingered for a long time in England.

However, hereditary monarchy did take root in the centuries after the Norman Conquest, and primogeniture was conclusively established during the thirteenth century (Barlow 1999: 42). When John's son Henry III died in 1272 the principle had gained such strength that his son, the future Edward I, who was on crusade in the Holy Land, did not even bother to go straight home when he heard about his father's death, but instead travelled around Europe for almost two years before returning to receive the crown (Prestwich 1997). As in France under Philip III, Edward I's reign was officially dated not from this crowning but from the death of his father (Jordan 2001: 241; Bartlett 2020: 107–8). Edward's absence thus did not create any interregnum, illustrating one of the advantages of primogeniture that we return to in later chapters.

A parallel, but earlier, development took place in Scotland, where primogeniture had become the established tradition for the royal succession by the early twelfth century, also due to Norman influence (Stephenson 1927; Penman 2007).

The Iberian Peninsula

The second millennium began tumultuously for the Christian principalities in the north of the Iberian Peninsula, and the development of primogeniture was not as straightforward as in France, even though it was in many ways more precocious. In the early eleventh century, the King of Pamplona (later Navarre) Sancho 'the Great' managed to unite almost all Christian realms on the peninsula under his rule. However, he did not leave his inheritance intact, but divided the realms among his sons: Navarre was given to the eldest legitimate son; the County of Castile and the County of Aragon were bequeathed to his two younger sons. All sons were granted the title of king, transforming Castile and Aragon into kingdoms (O'Callaghan 1975: 194).

---

[9] Primogeniture includes the principle of succession by representation, which means that the eldest son's male heirs inherit before his younger brothers inherit. However, at this time the alternative principle of proximity of blood, which gave cadets (i.e. the eldest son's brothers) a better claim, was also in vogue. Some of John's supporters also defended his claim by appealing to proximity of blood (Holt 1997: 307–26; Barlow 1999: 305). John would later defeat and probably also murder Arthur of Brittany who did not relinquish his claim on the English throne.

Traditions in Navarre, Leon, and Castile normally prescribed undivided inheritance of the patrimony to the eldest son (O'Callaghan 1975: 198; MacDonald 1965: 650). However, matters were complicated by the fact that Iberian kings sometimes acquired new polities with long traditions of independence, which they did not recognize as part of their 'inheritance'. On a few occasions monarchs also created entirely new 'offshoot' kingdoms from conquered Muslim territory and handed them to younger sons, despite primogeniture being 'firmly established' as the main principle of inheritance (Ruiz 2004: 104). The common denominator seems to be that acquired territories were not seen as part of the patrimony and therefore not governed by existing practices of succession.

It was not until the thirteenth century the principle of undivided inheritance by primogeniture was codified for Castile and Leon in the *Siete Partidas* and became 'both practice and rule thereafter' (MacDonald 1965: 653). After its creation in 1150, the Crown of Aragon, encompassing the Kingdom of Aragon, the County of Barcelona and later the Kingdom of Valencia, was never divided in the way Castile and Leon were, and the Aragonese succession was guided by primogeniture (Ruiz 2004: 104). However, offshoot or 'cadet' kingdoms—usually explicitly subordinated to the Crown of Aragon— were sometimes created for younger sons from new acquisitions outside the Iberian Peninsula, such as the Kingdom of Majorca and the Kingdom of Sicily.

The Italian Peninsula

In the high and late Middle Ages, there were very few monarchies in the Italian Peninsula, most of which was formally ruled by the German Emperors but de facto by city-states and princes. The major exception is southern Italy, which was conquered by Norman mercenaries in the eleventh and early twelfth centuries, creating the Kingdom of Sicily, which in the thirteenth century was subdivided into the Kingdom of Sicily and the Kingdom of Naples. Succession in these Norman kingdoms of the South seems to have been based on heirship practices in the Normans' ancestral lands, i.e., primogeniture (Bartlett 1993). Later dynastic changes did not alter the succession, as the Capetian House of Anjou and the House of Aragon already practiced primogeniture when they conquered the kingdoms. Primogeniture was also adopted by the few other monarchies that we find in Italy after AD 1000. When Savoy emerged as an independent state from ruins of the failing Holy Roman Empire in the fourteenth century, it had thus already practiced primogeniture for a long time (Previté-Orton 1912; Cox 1974).

The Holy Roman Empire

The Empire itself was an elective monarchy throughout its existence (Kern 1948; Gillingham 1991; Kannowski 2007; Weiler 2007; Whaley 2012). Initially the emperor was elected by ad hoc gatherings of nobles and prelates, but in the thirteenth century the imperial elections were confined to seven prince-electors (three bishops-princes and four secular princes). With some minor additions of secular prince-electors in the seventeenth and eighteenth century this small body of prince-electors continued to elect the emperor until the empire was dissolved in 1806. Before the fifteenth century the throne alternated between different dynasties, but from 1438 to 1740 a Habsburg was always elected.

The noble families of the Empire stuck to their old Germanic tradition of partible inheritance for centuries (Arnold 2009; Whaley 2012; Greengrass 2014: 55; Lyon 2017). However, in 1356 the Imperial Diet issued the Golden Bull (of 1356), which fixed the constitution of the Empire for the rest of its existence. The document stipulated that the lay Electorates (the Kingdom of Bohemia, the County Palatine of the Rhine, the Duchy of Saxony, and the Margraviate of Brandenburg) henceforth were to be handed down undivided via primogeniture (Whaley 2012: 426). The Habsburgs gave similar instructions—in the document *Privilegium Maius*—for their own territories, which were elevated to an Archduchy (Berenger 1994). However, the prince-electors and the Habsburg archdukes often bequeathed parts of their domains to younger sons, even though the Electoral title and the core lands associated with it in 1356 were given to the eldest son (Whaley 2012: 486). The Electors of Brandenburg forbade such partible inheritance in the *Dispositio Aqillea* in 1473 and the Electors of Saxony practiced a form of primogeniture from 1547 when the Electorate was taken over by the Albertine line, which had adopted primogeniture in 1499 (Whaley 2012: 487). However, the Electors of the Palatinate and the Habsburg archdukes continued to practice partible inheritance down to the seventeenth century (developments in Bohemia are described later) (Fichtner 1989).

Scandinavia

The northern parts of Europe were Christianized late. It was not until the second half of the tenth century that King Harald Bluetooth 'made the Danes

Christian'. At the turn of the century Norway was converted under Olof I Tryggvason, whereas Sweden did not become Christian until the eleventh century. As a result, Scandinavia lagged behind with respect to the Christian family practices described earlier. Kings frequently took concubines and had illegitimate children, some of which eventually took the throne (Bartlett 2020: 180). It also took a long time until primogeniture was adopted in Scandinavia.

Early in the period, monarchs in all three countries were elected at provincial assemblies, so-called *things*, where the election was usually limited to members of certain prominent dynasties (Helle 2003; Lindkvist 2003; Skovgaard-Petersen 2003). Later, when the royal administration had become more centralized, the right to elect the monarch was both in practice and *de jure* transferred to the councils of the realms (Schück 2003).[10] The elective principle had strong support among the nobility, especially in Denmark and Sweden, and the requirement that the elected king had to be of royal blood was gradually abandoned (Schück 1984).

Norway was the first country to abandon elective monarchy and introduce primogeniture. This happened under Haakon IV in the middle of the thirteenth century, in the wake of a more than 100-years-long struggle over the succession commonly known as the 'civil war era' (Helle 1981; 1995; Orning 2008).[11] However, elective monarchy was reintroduced in Norway 150 years later, after the ruling Bjälbo dynasty died out in the male line at the turn of the fourteenth century and Denmark, Sweden, and Norway were united in a personal union—today known as the Kalmar Union—under the last Norwegian king's mother, Queen Margarethe, and her sister's grandson Eric of Pomerania (Schück 2003). Norway then remained an elective monarchy until the country lost its independence to Denmark in the sixteenth century.

Sweden held on to its elective monarchy until it seceded from the Kalmar Union under Gustav Vasa. Primogeniture was adopted at a parliamentary meeting in 1544 (Schück 1984). Denmark remained an elective monarchy even longer. Only in 1660, under Frederik III, was primogeniture formally introduced—more than 600 years after the kingdom had been founded (Kurrild-Klitgaard 2000).

---

[10] In Norway this process took place after the reintroduction of elective monarchy during the Kalmar Union.
[11] In 1163 one of the civil war factions adopted a succession law that included a half-baked attempt to introduce primogeniture, but which allowed for elections if the eldest son was deemed unfit to rule ('evil or mad'). However, the faction's king, Magnus V, was contested and later killed in the battle of Fimreite, without being able to pass on the throne according to the succession law (Helle 1973; 1981).

East-Central Europe

At the start of the period we analyse, succession practices in East-Central Europe were seemingly unregulated. The succession was often confined to a certain dynasty (the Arpads in Hungary, the Premyszslids in Bohemia, and the Piasts in Poland), but it took time to establish clear rules of succession within the dynasty. However, there seems to have been a tendency towards agnatic seniority over time (Dvornik 1962). Boleslaw III Drymouth of Poland for example established this principle in his testament in the early twelfth century (Davies 2005: 60). The principle of agnatic seniority was probably also influential in the selection of early Arpad kings and Premyszslid dukes (Sedlar 1994: 31). In addition, there may have been an elective element to early succession in these three states (Agnew 2004; Davies 2005). In Bohemia, which was formally a part of the Holy Roman Empire, dukes sometimes also had to be approved by the emperor.

Eventually, primogeniture was adopted in all three polities, but only for brief periods. In the Golden Bull of 1212, Bohemia was granted the status of kingdom by the German emperor (Agnew 2004). A few years later the Bohemian king Ottokar I established primogeniture for his son (Grant 2015: 8). But when the Premyslid dynasty died out in the male line in 1305, the throne was filled by means of an election, which weakened the hereditary aspect of the crown. Subsequent 'elections through capitulation', where monarchs had to agree to constraints on their power, further strengthened the nobility at the expense of the monarchy in Bohemia (Betts 1955; Agnew 2004). With the Golden Bull of 1356 Bohemian kings were once again granted the right of succession by primogeniture, but in the long term the Bohemian nobility refused to give up their electoral rights.

Hungary also enjoyed a period of primogeniture in the thirteenth century after the Pope intervened to secure the right of the eldest son of the king to succeed, at the expense of the king's brothers (Kristó and Makk 1996: 227, 231, 247). However, when the Arpad dynasty died out in the male line in 1301 the Hungarian nobility started to interfere more actively in the succession, a process that escalated when the Angevin king Louis I failed to produce a male heir and the elective element came to dominate Hungarian succession.

Poland also seems to have practiced primogeniture for a short period after Wladyslaw I Lokietek reunited the country under his rule and Poland was raised to a hereditary kingdom by the Pope in 1320 (Davies 2005). However, when the Piast dynasty died out in the male line towards the end of the fourteenth century, the nobility took advantage of the situation and claimed the right to elect new monarchs. The election of Grand Duke Jogaila of Lithuania as King Wladyslaw II Jagiellon of Poland in 1386 marked the beginning of the new monarchy (Stone 2001; Davies 2005). Jogaila had himself been granted hereditary rights to the Grand Duchy of Lithuania by the Pope when he converted to Christianity (to take the Polish throne via marriage). However, this right was contested by the Lithuanian nobility, who throughout Lithuanian history claimed the right to elect their ruler (Stone 2001). Poland remained an elective monarchy until its dismemberment in the eighteenth century (Davies 2005).

Bohemia and Hungary were eventually incorporated in the Habsburg possessions. Although the countries formally remained elective monarchies, the nobilities generally accepted the dynastic transfer of power within the Habsburg family. But the electoral principle made itself felt occasionally, most spectacularly when the Bohemian estates in 1619 deposed their Catholic king Ferdinand II, and instead elected the Protestant Frederick of the Palatinate, sparking the Thirty Year's War. After the Habsburg emperor Ferdinand II regained power in Bohemia, he promulgated a new constitution in 1627 that abolished the elective monarchy and introduced primogeniture (Agnew 2004). A similar process occurred in Hungary where Leopold I and the Hungarian Diet introduced primogeniture in 1687 after a victory over the Ottomans (Kann 1974: 55–7).

Russia and the Byzantine Empire

As we describe in more detail later, the Byzantine Empire never formally adopted hereditary succession, with the succession remaining vaguely elective (based on acclamation) down to the final conquest of Constantinople by the Ottomans in 1453.

Succession in Muscovite Russia was initially guided by a tradition of agnatic seniority going back to the Rota system that was instituted by Yaroslav the Wise in Kievan Rus in the early eleventh century (Stokes 1970; Kollman 1990; Martin 1995: 27–9). Although the rotation of princes between different principalities was gradually abandoned, collateral succession continued to be practiced until the fifteenth century. It was not until Vasily II won the Muscovite civil war—fought over which succession principle should prevail—against his uncle Yury of Zvenigorod and his sons that primogeniture became the established principle of succession (Martin 1995: 239–44). Primogeniture continued to guide the succession until the Rurikid dynasty died out in the male line with Feodor I in 1596.

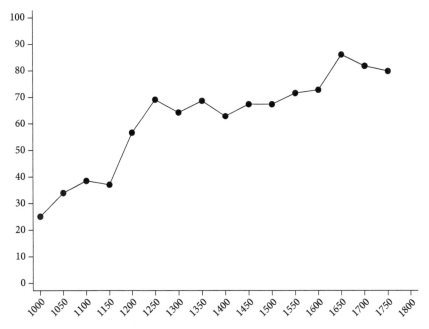

Fig. 4.4 The percentage of states in the sample each half-century that practiced primogeniture (and orderly partible inheritance that usually yielded de facto primogeniture)

After a long period of civil war and unrest, Michael Romanov was elected Tsar in 1613. The succession was then guided by primogeniture until 1722 when Peter I, the Great, who hated his eldest son, introduced the *New Law of Succession*, which allowed the Tsar to choose his own successor, be it a relative or not (Whittaker 2001; Lieven 2006). When a tsar died without appointing an heir, which Peter himself failed to do, negotiations among the elite decided the succession—a practice that was referred to as 'elections' in accession documents (Whittaker 2001). Peter the Great's succession law continued in use until his great-grandson, Paul I, abolished it and reintroduced primogeniture in 1797.

An overview

Figure 4.4 shows the proliferation of primogeniture over time, displayed as the proportion of all country-years in our sample for each half-century that practiced primogeniture. As we described earlier, the spread of primogeniture was gradual, and dynastic fortunes and accidents in various places either sped up or blocked the process. Nonetheless, across the Latin west the norm was increasingly that the eldest son inherited the patrimonial lands and the family title intact, first in the areas with a longer history of Western Christianity, then spreading outwards to the more recently Christianized periphery.

The Catholic Church in comparative perspective

The advent of primogeniture in the high Middle Ages can be seen as the crowning achievement of the strategies of heirship that the Church had first introduced in late antiquity. Had the Church not broken the agnatic family and clan structures, the introduction of a strategy of heirship where one son merely by virtue of being the eldest takes the entire inheritance, dispossessing all siblings, uncles, nephews etc., would probably have been inconceivable. Moreover, primogeniture only became a practical possibility due to strict rules about legitimacy, reducing the number of potential claimants.

The Orthodox Church

But if the prohibitions of certain marriage and heirship practices by the Christian Church created primogeniture in the Latin west, one would expect similar developments in Orthodox Christendom, centred on the ecumenical Patriarchy in Constantinople. This did not happen, at least not to the same extent. One reason was that the prohibitions were not sanctioned to the same extent in the east, especially not within the families of emperors and kings. In a statistical investigation of the Catholic Church's effects on kinship ties and individualistic values, Schultz et al. (2019: 2) simply write that while the Orthodox or Eastern Church 'did adopt some of the same prohibitions as the Western Church, it never endorsed the Western Church's broad taboos on cousin marriage, was slow to adopt many policies, and was unenthusiastic about enforcement.'

However, the story is more complicated than this. The point of departure in the Latin west and the Orthodox east was similar. The late fourth-century Church principles about marriage and heirship characterized both areas (Goody 1983; 2000). Moreover, we find numerous examples of how patriarchs in Constantinople criticized and sometimes even excommunicated Byzantine emperors who transgressed the marriage practices sanctioned by the Church. For instance, in the tenth century, patriarchs twice banned emperors from church services in the great church of Hagia Sophia to force them to dismiss their concubines (Wickham 2009: 303).[12]

Similarly, Leo VI, the Wise (r. 886–912), struggling to provide a male heir, came into conflict with the Church hierarchy in Constantinople when he married his mistress Zoe Karvounopsina to legitimate their son (the future Constantine VII) (Bartlett 2020: 70–1). This was Leo's third marriage and while the Orthodox Church allowed one divorce and one remarriage, it frowned upon multiple remarriages (Gregory 2005: 227). The Eastern Church's ban on remarriage after the death of the second wife was thus stricter than what we find in the West in the same period—recall Charlemagne's four lawful marriages described earlier. It is telling that Leo VI solved his problem by appealing to the Pope in Rome, who was happy to offer him a dispensation.

The main difference between west and east lies not so much in doctrine as in implementation, that is, in the normative power of the Church to voice and enforce the bans. As Wickham (2009) points out, the east never in the same way as the west developed the moralizing politics where clergy were expected to police the behaviour of their rulers. Even more important was the absence of a clergy independent of lay power. The reason for this was that the state structures of the old Roman Empire never broke down in the same way as in the west. Byzantine rulers inherited a well-functioning fiscal system and a long tradition of legitimate imperial rule and were thus not in the same way in need of administrative help or legitimization from the clergy (Acemoglu and Robinson 2019: 187; Stasavage 2020). There was no alliance between equals, as in the Latin west.

This does not mean that lay–religious conflicts did not exist in Orthodox Christendom (Oakley 2010: 99). The most famous example is the eighth- and ninth-century iconoclast struggle where the strong Isaurian emperors tried to forbid religious icons (Brown 1997: 235–53). The emperors lost this struggle and the Byzantine Church remained fundamentally conciliarist, based on the collective authority of particularly bishops to set doctrine at the great ecumenical councils. Even 'an emperor as powerful as Justinian could not legislate religious belief to his subjects' (Gregory 2005: 135).

However, the Eastern Church never experienced anything like the Western eleventh-century 'crisis of church and state' (Bisson 2009: 8), and the emperor retained a solid hold on the Church throughout the 1000 years the Eastern Empire lasted, with emperors appointing and deposing patriarchs (2010: 103;

---

[12] For other examples, see Gregory (2005: 170, 200, 213).

Gregory 2005: 227–8). As a result, the church had no institutional basis for policing marriage practices at the royal court, as in the west.

Other Orthodox political systems inherited this theocratic model where the secular ruler also controlled the Church. One important manifestation was the creation of what were de facto national churches (say, of Bulgaria, Serbia, and later of Russia) where the local grand princes or tsars would hold sway over the Church within their territory, just as Byzantine emperors did in Constantinople. This meant that there was never an independent international organization called the Orthodox Church. Orthodox Churches, while nominally acknowledging the primacy of the ecumenical patriarch in Constantinople, were de facto independent from early on. This can be contrasted to the much more united and centralized Catholic Church in the Latin west (MacCulloch 2009: 551).

Orthodox Christianity was thus much less of an integrated whole than the Latin or Roman Church. And after the two great disasters of 1204 where Latin crusaders conquered Constantinople and created a Latin empire ruling Constantinople until 1261 and 1453 when Constantinople fell to the Ottomans, Orthodox theological innovation and inter-church relations were stifled. The Patriarch in Constantinople ceased being an active force in transforming society in the sense that the Roman popes did in the high Middle Ages (MacCulloch 2009: 499).

These differences between the Orthodox east and the Latin west probably go a long way in explaining why primogeniture only came to characterize Orthodox Christian areas when it was borrowed from the West (see the description of the Russian case earlier). We do find several spells of de facto hereditary emperorship in Byzantium, but unlike in Latin Christendom, hereditary kingship, including primogeniture, at no time became a formal principle of succession in Constantinople (Kaldellis 2015). In fact, like the Roman Empire, the Byzantine Empire never devised a 'constitutional' mechanism regulating succession (Gregory 2005: 5, 22). The emperor took the throne based on a vague notion of acclamation that has been described as akin to a form of heavenly mandate where whoever was strong enough to take the purple was, *ipso facto*, the one favoured by God Almighty (Finer 1997a: Chapter 1).[13] In Chapter 9, we show how this inevitably led to political instability, and the Byzantine Empire thus represents an important counter-factual to the kingdoms of Western and Central Europe.

---

[13] As described earlier, even in the West the Church insisted that the imperial throne should be elective, not inherited. The survival of empire in Constantinople might therefore have been another reason that primogeniture was resisted.

Protestant churches

The Reformation broke the Catholic Church's ecclesiastical monopoly in Latin Christendom. There are some indications that Protestant churches did not enable primogeniture in the same way as the Catholic Church did. To take an extreme example, a few Protestant sects denounced outright the family and heirship policies introduced by the Catholic Church in the Middle Ages. The first generation of Anabaptists and later the Mormons thus reintroduced polygyny because they found that it was legitimized by passages in the Old Testament (Goody 2000: 112–13). However, this was the exception. At first, most Protestant denominations retained the established prohibitions, including the ban on divorce. Yet, there were other differences, which are relevant for understanding the spread of primogeniture. Like the Orthodox churches, Protestant churches were normally beholden to the state and the Reformation, including the abolition of monasteries and the demotion of the importance of bishops, affected the extent to which the Church was a relevant player in dynastic politics.

To what extent did this affect the adoption of primogeniture? This is difficult to unravel empirically because the first-born-male succession principle had already won the day in some of the polities which became Protestant, for instance England and Scotland. In other Protestant countries, the Reformation and the adoption of primogeniture virtually overlaps, for instance, in Sweden where both date to the mercurial rule of Gustav Vasa. But this was a revolutionary time in Sweden, so the transition to primogeniture may be completely unrelated to Protestantism. In Sweden's neighbour, historical competitor, and most-similar-case, Denmark, it took more than a century after the Reformation for primogeniture to win the day.

The more general problem is that the Reformation arrived late in the day, in areas where primogeniture had already been adopted or was in the process of being adopted, meaning that it is difficult to tease out its effects. However, there is one important exception, namely the Holy Roman Empire where primogeniture had generally not been adopted before AD 1500, and where some polities became Protestant while others remained Catholic. In a seminal analysis, Fichtner (1989) argues that the Reformation retarded the adoption of primogeniture in this region. Fichtner shows how from 1526 to 1650, most German Protestant princes retained partible inheritance, while in the same period primogeniture won the day among German Catholic princes. This is surprising, Fichtner points out, as Protestantism has often been associated with state-building, and as partible inheritance repeatedly created territorial disintegration.

Fichtner makes the point that religious considerations tended to delegitimize primogeniture both among Catholics and Protestants because it meant dispossessing most of one's children. However, 'Catholics had a better way to enjoy the advantages of primogeniture, yet live with their consciences over the treatment of younger sons. They could still arrange appropriate living for their offspring in the church' (52–3). Among Protestants, on the contrary, the Reformation to a large extent put a stop to the widespread practice of placing younger sons of rulers or nobles in the Church. Add to this that in Catholic areas ecclesiastical careers did not mean abandoning the ability to interfere in secular dynastic affairs, but instead meant political influence.

According to Fichtner, this eased the adoption of primogeniture in the Catholic areas of the Holy Roman Empire but slowed it down in the Protestant areas. It took a shock of the system—the havoc wreaked by the Thirty Years' War (1618–1648)—to make Protestant princes adopt primogeniture to ensure their dynastic survival. After 1700, partible inheritance was thus broadly abandoned in the German area, even among Protestants. However, the differences in timing are pronounced and Fichtner's analysis illustrates some of the important ways in which the Catholic Church facilitated the adoption of primogeniture, long after the invention of the principle in the high Middle Ages.

Conclusion

This chapter has traced the historical origins of European primogeniture. We have argued that this new succession arrangement—crystallizing in the tenth and eleventh centuries—was a consequence of Church prohibitions of hitherto common practices such as divorce, marriage with relatives, concubinage, and adoption. These bans had been devised in late antiquity, but they were consolidated by the Carolingians in the ninth century and then further sanctioned by the eleventh-century reform popes. Primogeniture was thus ultimately a byproduct of the Church's attempts to, first, sever kinship ties in late antiquity to be able to receive bequests via wills and testaments and, second, to free itself from lay control in the eleventh and twelfth centuries.

The non-emergence of primogeniture in the Byzantine Empire shows how and why the Catholic Church was able to change heirship policies in the Latin west. In the Byzantine Empire, we find similar Church prohibitions, but we do not find an independent church that could systematically police rulers' immoral behaviour. This indicates that the eleventh-century reform papacy must be factored in to fully understand the Western transition to *de jure* primogeniture, even if spells of de facto primogeniture occurred earlier due to the increasing monogamy of kings and emperors, itself a product of the Church prohibitions. For this reason, Max Weber claimed that "dominance of monogamy as the sole legitimate form of marriage has been one of the most important reasons for continuity of monarchic power" (Weber 1968:1138).

Similarly, there is some evidence that the Protestant Reformation slowed the adoption of primogeniture because it closed the door to the lucrative and powerful Church careers that younger sons of nobles and monarchs had previously enjoyed and continued to enjoy in much of Catholic Europe. A comparison with the Orthodox and Protestant churches therefore underlines the crucial role of the Catholic Church. In Chapter 9, we further broaden the view via comparisons with other areas of Eurasia. While a form of primogeniture is to be found in parts of East Asia, and arguably created political stability and strengthened state power in e.g. China, it remains the exception in historical perspective, probably because it so clearly clashes—head on—with the broader kin interests that have provided the sinews of social order in most places.

The comparison with the Byzantine Empire more specifically shows that the change of heirship practices that culminated in primogeniture was conditional on state weakness. Had the Latin west been governed by a polity—or even multiple polities—as strong as the Byzantine Empire, the Catholic Church would have been unable to enforce its norms among the high and mighty to the same extent. This is reflected in the final timing of primogeniture after the ninth- and tenth-century breakdown of public power in West Francia. The social constellation of factors that allowed the advent of primogeniture was thus a very particular one.

Nevertheless, the introduction of primogeniture was not an inevitable consequence of the Church's heirship policies. Reproductive chance such as the 'Capetian miracle' where a long succession of kings managed to produce sons who survived facilitated the introduction of primogeniture in some places, whereas the genetic lottery did not favour it in other places, for instance the Holy Roman Empire where kings died without leaving male children in 911, 918, 1002, 1024, and 1125 (Bartlett 2020: 72). But once adopted, primogeniture would further change the social context that had allowed this succession order to emerge, with important political consequences.

5
Civil War and International War

> If we compare the wars of succession, foreign and civil, which have laid waste to Europe between the Norman Conquest and the French Revolution, it will be found that they exceed all other wars put together in number, and still more in duration
>
> (Brougham 1845: 11).

Although the British statesman Henry Brougham may have exaggerated, Europe has certainly seen its fair share of long and bloody succession wars: the Norman Conquest of England, the English Wars of the Roses, the Hundred Years' War between France and England, and the Wars of the Spanish, Polish, and Austrian Successions, to mention only a few.

Many of these wars were extremely costly for the belligerent parties. The Norman Conquest resulted in almost complete elite replacement in England (Bartlett 2000; Garnett 2007) whereas the Wars of the Roses depleted the resources of the warring houses of Lancaster and York to the extent that a third house—the upstart Tudors, of Welsh origin—was able to usurp the throne. The Wars of the Roses also caused 24 other English noble houses to die out in the male line between 1450 and 1474 (McFarlane 1981). Other succession wars, such as the Anarchy in England (King 1994)—'the nineteen long winters' after the death of King Henry II in 1135—and the Civil War Era in Norway from 1135 to 1240 (Helle 2003) laid waste to both countries and drove the opposing sides to the brink of exhaustion. Monarchs and elites thus had strong incentives to fear successions and the disputes they caused.

In this chapter, we analyse how successions affected the risk of civil and interstate war and ask how different principles of succession mediated this risk. We start the chapter by recapitulating why successions often cause war. We then discuss the nature of succession wars and provide descriptive statistics on wars in European history between AD 1000 and 1800. Lastly, we test our argument, presented in Chapter 2, that the gradual adoption of primogeniture mitigated the coordination problem, thus reducing the risk of succession wars, and we discuss the broader implications of our findings.

Why successions cause civil war

In the absence of an appointed successor, an autocrat's death usually leaves the regime in a power vacuum. This offers both opportunity and risk for elite groups. A claimant might become the new leader and his supporters might improve their standing within the regime. But power struggles in autocracies are risky. Losers may forfeit their livelihoods and possibly even their lives (cf. Egorov and Sonin 2015) and backers of claimants cannot be sure they will be rewarded even if their preferred candidate wins, as would-be kings cannot credibly commit to rewarding those who supported them, once in power (Bueno de Mesquita et al. 2005).

Although elite groups may in theory reestablish order by peacefully finding a new leader among themselves, the nature of power relations in autocracies makes it difficult for them to do so. One problem is that the demise of the ruler risks upsetting the delicate balance of power between the winning coalition's members, so that sub-coalitions that are powerful enough to get rid of the other members of the coalition emerge (Acemoglu, Egorov, and Sonin 2008).

Another problem is that authoritarian power relations are characterized by secrecy to prevent members of the regime and outside actors from co-ordinating coups and rebellions (Shih 2010). Sharing military and security information without the autocrat's permission tends to be strictly forbidden. Ideally, key supporters should also remain in doubt whether other members of the regime will remain loyal to them in conflicts and dangerous situations, as bonds of trust can be used to plot against the autocrat. Members of the regime furthermore have an incentive to hide their true capabilities in order not to appear as a threat to the autocrat (cf. Egorov and Sonin 2011). Most powerful actors will therefore have vague and partial information about the distribution of power within the regime, including their own relative strength vis-à-vis other regime insiders, before the succession takes place.

The demise of the leader can also alter facts on the ground in ways that make the distribution of power even less transparent than in ordinary circumstances. For example, it may be difficult to know who has the loyalty of military regiments that were formerly under the personal control of the leader.

Adding to the confusion, the incentives to misrepresent strength change in the wake of a succession. Members of the regime who aspire to become the new leader now have an incentive to appear stronger than they are to persuade possible contenders for the throne to back down and to convince those who are unsure about whom to support to bandwagon behind them (Brownlee 2007; Tullock 1987). All contenders of course know that rivals have an incentive to overstate their strength to gain a more favourable deal in future bargains. In such circumstances, regime members may easily end up disagreeing about their relative strength. Research has demonstrated that similar disagreements between international actors are among the most important causes of interstate wars (Fearon 1995). We argue that they may also lead to civil war in autocracies.

Even if elite groups eventually manage to agree on a successor, other actors can take advantage of the period of uncertainty. Later, we return to the case of foreign states and how successions can cause international conflict. However, important groups within the country might also be incentivized to act when there is a succession, even if they are not interested in taking the throne for themselves. Separatist groups, for instance, might make a push while the elite is occupied with their internal dealings.

The existence of a crown prince changes these dynamics. The natural assumption is that the crown prince will inherit his predecessor's power and position (including his private property if primogeniture is practiced), so that relations between the autocrat and the rest of the regime will remain essentially unaltered after the succession. Members of the regime can expect to stay on and do not have to choose between different claimants, with a risk of ending up on the losing side. In short, regime members only need to accept the crown prince's ascension to power to assure regime continuity and to avoid civil war.

However, as noted in Chapter 2, primogeniture is better than other succession arrangements at providing suitable crown princes. The principle automatically provides the regime with a successor in advance of the succession, as long as the ruler manages to produce an eligible heir or has other male relatives (Acharya and Lee 2019; Wang 2018). This son is likely to outlive his father, thus ensuring the regime a long time horizon. Primogeniture also prevents the leader from tampering with the succession, as the line of succession is public knowledge and as heirs cannot be disinherited in normal circumstances. Combined, these facts make the succession procedure virtually automatic.

Of course, monarchs sometimes produce heirs who are incapable of ruling. The eldest son could be too young, sickly, or too mad to rule at all. In such circumstances, the regime needs to replace him or take over his functions until he becomes capable of ruling effectively on his own and a new coordination problem is created. On the other hand, primogeniture guarantees that the new king has the same private landed wealth as his predecessor, as the eldest son usually inherits his father's private property, as well as the property of the crown. This guarantees that he can shoulder his father's mantle (with respect to resources) and that his accession does not alter the balance of power between the monarchy and the rest of the regime. Royal children were also often relatively well prepared for the task of ruling, as they were educated to become leaders from a very young age. Overall, primogeniture therefore handles the coordination problem relatively well, especially compared to the other succession orders practiced in Europe after AD 1000.[1]

Agnatic seniority (brother-inheritance) also normally provides the regime with an heir that the leader cannot replace in advance of the succession. However, the fact that the heir is usually only a few years younger than the leader, and therefore not certain to outlive him, makes it inherently difficult to know if it is worth betting on him, or better to groom the next in line for the succession. Even that person—perhaps the third-oldest brother—can be too old to be a safe bet. There is a huge risk that the regime will bet on the wrong heir and end up with a successor whom they have hardly had the chance to groom. The principle also means that the new king is likely to have fewer power resources at his disposal than the old king, as he will not inherit his predecessor's private property if the latter has children. Combined, these factors point to the conclusion that it should be more difficult to solve the coordination problem in states practicing agnatic seniority than in states practicing primogeniture.

Even worse is the scorecard of elective succession arrangements, as elections usually take place after the death of the monarch. Therefore, the regime will be left without a focal point when the incumbent leader dies. And even if the elite can agree on a successor, it is not certain he will have the private power resources necessary to shoulder his predecessor's mantle.

Hypotheses

Two hypotheses about our sample of medieval and early modern monarchies follow from this discussion: (1) successions increase the risk of civil

---

[1] As argued in Chapter 2, the same applies to partible inheritance when practiced in a stable manner, as it came to be in Europe in the period we analyse. It is for this reason that we have merged the two categories in our empirical analysis in this chapter. As mentioned in Chapter 3, because the merged category of primogeniture and partible inheritance in reality consists of more than 90 per cent primogeniture monarch-years, we simply refer to primogeniture when interpreting the results (all reported results are robust to using a specification that only counts undisputable primogeniture monarch-years).

war, and (2) primogeniture mitigates the effect of succession on civil war, as the principle in ordinary circumstances solves the coordination problem better than other succession arrangements.[2] Given the nature of the coordination problem, we also expect succession wars to break out shortly after the old leader's demise. Once a new monarch sits safely on the throne, the coordination problem is solved.

Why successions cause international conflict

The risk of civil war is only half the story about the turmoil caused by successions, however. There are also reasons to expect successions to increase the risk of interstate war (Bartlett 2020: 72). The confusion that follows if a regime is left without a successor, or is split between different claimants, may tempt foreign leaders to take advantage of the situation in several different ways.

The most obvious example is when a foreign ruler had a claim (invented or real) to an empty throne. This happened when Edward the Confessor died in 1066 and both William the Conqueror and the Norwegian King Harald Hardrada laid claim to the English throne and invaded (Oleson 1957). Foreign rulers could also throw their weight behind one particular candidate for the throne to secure a more beneficial policy towards their own country or to hinder an enemy state from placing their man on the throne, thereby tilting the geopolitical balance of power in its favour. Both the Spanish War of Succession (1701–1714) and the Polish War of Succession (1733–1735) developed into broader European conflagrations, in which different groups of states backed different claimants. The former war was caused by the extinction of the line of Spanish Habsburg monarchs following the death of Charles II in 1700 (Lynn 1999: 91–108). The resulting conflict pitted the Bourbon candidate Philip (the later King Philip V of Spain), backed by France, against the Austrian Habsburg candidate Charles, backed by France's traditional enemies, the Holy Roman Empire, Great Britain, and the Netherlands.

In the Polish case, the spark was not the lack of an heir—Augustus II had left an adult son (also named Augustus and supported by Russia)—but rather the opportunity elective monarchy allowed other candidates (Sutton 1980). A

---

[2] In the empirical analyses in this chapter, we only distinguish between primogeniture (and partible inheritance) on one hand and (all) other succession orders on the other hand, as the proportion of country-years characterized by agnatic seniority is too small for us to tease out the consequences of elective and agnatic succession arrangements, respectively.

rival claimant thus appeared in the form of the French-backed Stanislaus, who had held the Polish throne previously.

In both conflicts, the country in which the succession took place became a theatre of war between great powers, vying for influence. Foreign states of course often try to influence the selection of leaders of neighbouring states, through diplomacy or other forms of support, but the death of a monarch creates an urgency that might lead to military action. This was especially the case in European history where monarchs often ruled several polities at the same time, and the balance of power could be upset overnight by inheritance, or a royal election. For example, the War of the Spanish Succession was triggered as much by fears of a unified French and Spanish monarchy as by real concerns over who was the legitimate heir to the Spanish throne (Lynn 1999: 91–108; Schmidt Voges and Solana Crespo 2017: 2).

Even when foreign powers showed no genuine interest in who inherited the throne, they sometimes pressed their own interests while the new monarch was preoccupied with internal politics. Upon the death of Holy Roman Emperor Charles VI in 1740 (the same Charles who had been a contender for the Spanish throne during the War of the Spanish Succession), his daughter Maria Theresa inherited the Habsburg possessions. That she was able to do so despite being a woman was the result of a protracted diplomatic effort by her father, culminating in acceptance of the 'Pragmatic Sanction', which allowed female inheritance in most of his realms. However, when Charles died, Maria Theresa's rights to inherit were disputed by the King of Prussia, Frederick the Great, who invaded and took control over the rich region of Silesia (Anderson 1995).

Frederick used the succession as the *casus belli* for invading but seemed to have harboured few illusions about the strength of his arguments. His legal claim to Silesia was 'a face-saving afterthought' and it was not even brought up in the confidential discussions between Frederick and his ministers (Anderson 1995: 69). Still, the succession gave Frederick a crucial opportunity to cover his expansionist ambitions with a veneer of legality, which in medieval and early modern Europe often proved to be important when rulers sought alliances. Striking quick—the war started less than two months after the death of Charles VI—Prussia was able to seize Silesia easily, though Frederick would have to fight several tough wars to keep it.

A second reason succession can trigger international war is that a new leader and his predecessor may not have the same resolve to fight wars. Scott Wolford

(2007) argues that this gives antagonistic states an incentive to challenge a new leader to test his resolve (or hers, as in the case of Maria Theresa), and the new leader an incentive not to back down in order to establish a reputation as a strongman, which will benefit him in future bargaining situations. If the new leader has private information about his true resolve, this dynamic makes succession 'a kind of informational trap' (Wolford 2007: 773) that risks triggering war. Simply put, both parties have yet to get to know each other and cannot be sure how the other will react in a tense situation. Research also shows that leaders are more prone to engage in war early in their careers (Chiozza and Goemans 2003; 2004; 2011; Gaubatz 1991; Gelpi and Grieco 2001).

Primogeniture (or any other succession arrangement for that matter) cannot do much about the second problem as a successor always differs from his predecessor in some respects and might be tempted to make a mark early. The sixteenth-century philosopher Jean Bodin noted that, '[i]t is a matter of common experience that when a new prince succeeds, all sorts of new plans, new laws, new officials, new friends, new enemies, new customs, new social habits spring up. Most princes are pleased to introduce novelties of all sorts, just to get themselves talked about' (Bodin 1967: 196).

Primogeniture can alleviate the first problem, at least in theory, as the principle in normal circumstances prevents conflicting claims to the throne by only acknowledging one claimant. It also increases the cost of invasions, as it allows the regime to rally relatively fast around the true claimant. In contrast, elective monarchy allows for many claimants and leaves the state leaderless until the elections are over (which often took considerable time in an era where, as French historian Fernand Braudel once put it, distance was 'public enemy number one').

However, primogeniture can also foment trouble, as it does not allow actors to pay due respect to the international balance of power. An important reason the War of the Spanish Succession broke out was that the French crown prince had a right to inherit the Spanish throne according to primogeniture (Kamen 2001: 6). In a Europe where dynasties were closely related, primogeniture caused similar crises with regular intervals because numerous actors, from popes to other lay rulers, had 'an interest in ensuring that the accidents of birth, marriage and death did not produce dangerous mega-states' (Bartlett 2020: 427). Royal elections, in contrast, allow the electors to consider the international situation and avoid tilting the balance of power in ways that provoke foreign invasions. It is difficult to say, a priori, which effect will dominate.

Hypothesis

Given that no succession order alleviates the problem that a leader and his successor may differ in resolve or the problem that other rulers might seek to press their interests when a king dies, we do not expect primogeniture (or any other succession order) to mitigate the effect of successions on foreign invasions. We therefore only propose one hypothesis about external war in our sample of monarchies, namely that successions—in general—increase the risk of such conflicts.

War in medieval and early modern Europe

In European history, war and the threat of war have been constants until the political and economic integration of Western Europe in the second half of the twentieth century. Wars were a natural and frequent element in international politics and millions died in the bloodiest conflicts, such as the Thirty Years' War from 1618 to 1648 (Wilson 2009: 786-94).

Figure 5.1 plots the percentage of countries in our sample that were involved in at least one war in each year, averaged by decade. Across all countries and years, the mean value is 40 per cent; at any point in time, almost every other country was involved in at least one international conflict. The high (or low) point was reached during the Thirty Year's War, followed by the period around the turn of the eighteenth century that saw the outbreak of the War of the Spanish Succession.

Unsurprisingly, the data show that the most warlike states were the major players of the era: Spain, Austria, Russia, France, and England, in that order. The least afflicted countries in our sample were small states such as Navarre, Brandenburg (until it developed into militaristic Prussia), Sicily, Norway, and the Palatinate.

Not all wars were as devastating as the Thirty Years' War, of course. Before the military revolution of the sixteenth and seventeenth centuries (Parker 1996[1988]; Downing 1992), conflicts involved far fewer men-at-arms. However, the civil population could still suffer immensely. Some historians have construed William the Conqueror's Harrying of the North in the winter of 1069-1070 as an act of genocide (Kapelle 1979: 3). According to the Doomsday Book, written in 1086, only 25 per cent of the population had survived and 60 per cent of all holdings in the North remained wasteland 16 years after the Harrying (Palmer 1998).

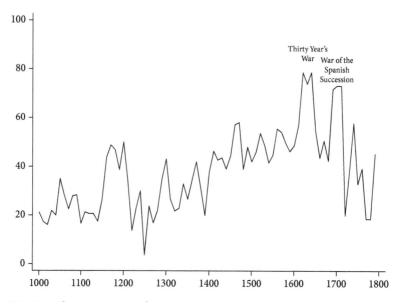

Fig. 5.1 The percentage of countries in at least one international war, averaged by decade

These two conflicts also illustrate the wide range—in type and scale of conflicts—that took place in the period we study. From peasant rebellions to civil wars between contenders for the throne; from minor skirmishes between professional mercenaries to the destruction of entire cities (such as the razing of Milan in 1162 or the Sack of Magdeburg in 1631). In this book, we distinguish between 'civil' and 'international' war. In modern social science literature, civil war is normally defined as 'internal war'. An influential article thus defines civil war as 'fighting between agents of (or claimants to) a state and organized, nonstate groups who sought either to take control of a government, to take power in a region, or to use violence to change government policies' (Fearon and Laitin 2003: 76).

In a period where states were much more loosely organized and where rulers did not have a monopoly of violence within the borders, such distinctions were less clear-cut. Personal unions, in which a monarch ruled different states simultaneously, illustrate the problem. We have adopted the approach used in modern literature and define civil wars as armed conflict between groups living permanently within a polity's borders. However, this means that the same war can be interpreted differently based on the vantage point. For instance, during the dying days of the Kalmar Union (1397–1523), which united Denmark, Norway, and Sweden in a personal union, Swedish peasants and some

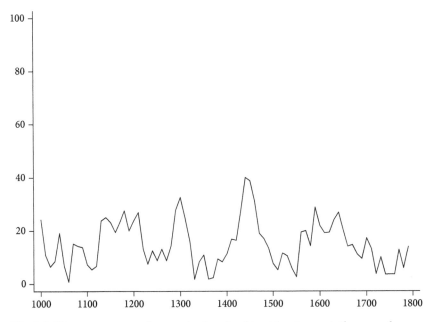

Fig. 5.2 The percentage of countries involved in at least one civil war each year, averaged by decade

Swedish nobles rebelled against King Christian II, who sent Danish troops to suppress the rebellion (Schück 2003). For Sweden, we count the conflict as a civil war, as part of the population was in rebellion against the king of Sweden (Christian II), who still had loyal supporters in the country. However, for Denmark, we count it as an interstate war, as Christian was sending Danish troops 'abroad'. There was no civil strife in Denmark.

Figure 5.2 plots the percentage of countries in our sample that were involved in at least one civil war each year, averaged by decade. We see that the incidence of civil war was substantially lower than that of international war, with on average 15 per cent of countries being embroiled in one each year. The rate is also fairly constant over time, with less evidence of clear secular trends.

Not all the international and civil wars included in Figure 5.1 and 5.2 were caused by successions. We therefore proceed to discuss how to distinguish succession wars from other wars.

Wars of succession

'Succession wars' originate in disputed successions, i.e. successions in which more than one contender present conflicting claims to the throne. Although this definition seems straightforward, it is also vague, especially when it comes to the timing between the disputed succession and the initiation of war. Can a 'succession war' break out years, or even decades, after a disputed succession? Or must it break out during, or immediately after, the succession to count as a 'succession war'? We argue that there are strong methodological and theoretical reasons for preferring an operational definition that restricts succession wars to wars that break out close in time to successions.

One reason is that medieval and early modern European monarchs sometimes used disputed successions as pretexts for wars that were fought for other reasons. One indication is that many 'succession wars' 'originated' in disputed successions that took place long before the wars broke out. The Hundred Years' War, for example, did not break out until 1337, nine years after the French king Charles IV died without male issue and a French assembly invoked Salic Law to pass over his nephew, Edward III of England, in the succession in favour of Charles's patrilineal cousin Philip, Count of Valois. Although Edward declared the disputed succession as his *casus belli*, the true cause of the war seems to have been Philip's confiscation of Edward's French lands in the years before the outbreak of the war (Sumption 1999; Prestwich 2003). Edward had acknowledged Philip's right to the French throne by paying homage to him for his French possessions in 1329 but faced with the confiscation of his lands, he reactivated his claim to the French throne and declared war. Edward would thus probably have declared war even if the disputed succession of 1228 had never taken place and only used it to strengthen his bargaining position vis-à-vis Philip.

It should be easier to rule out such alternative explanations the closer in time the succession is to the outbreak of war. Claims invoked years after the fact can be taken less seriously than claims made, and acted upon, during the succession. There is also another important reason for focusing on wars that broke out during, or immediately after, successions: our theoretical argument for why successions increase the risk of war focuses on the short-term effects of successions. The coordination problem, for example, says that successions increase the risk of war because a leader's demise creates a period of uncertainty that lasts until one of the contenders to the throne has been accepted by the elite as the new ruler. When Edward II declared war on Philip VI, that period of uncertainty was long gone. It was probably over when the assembled French nobility and prelates declared Philip king in 1328, two months after his predecessor Charles IV's death, and it definitely ended when Edward paid homage to Philip in 1329, meaning that the elite could be certain that Philip's claim to the throne had won the day.

Table 5.1 The percentage of country-years in which a war broke out

	Civil war start (%)	International war start (%)
No succession	2.3	6.7
Succession—natural death	9.1	12.2
Succession—deposed (excluding depositions by foreign powers)	14.5	11.6

For these reasons, we focus on wars that broke out in years when successions occurred. Table 5.1 shows the percentage of years in which wars broke out based on whether there was a succession or not, and whether it was caused by a natural death of a monarch or a deposition.

If we compare succession years to years without successions, we see that successions were indeed tumultuous events: the risk of an international war breaking out was almost doubled and the risk of a civil war breaking out was four to six times higher. However, there are a number of reasons why successions may be endogenous to war. The objective of many civil wars was to replace the monarch. Leaders who lose international wars frequently resign or are deposed (Croco 2011; Chiozza and Goemans 2004; 2011) and, especially in the earlier parts of the era we study, monarchs risked dying in battle or of diseases while campaigning.

A closer look does indeed reveal that civil wars are strongly associated with depositions. In 14.5 per cent of the years a monarch was deposed, a civil war broke out in the same country, which is more than six times higher than the norm. A likely interpretation is that the wars led to the depositions, even if the opposite could also happen. For international wars, depositions are not as strongly associated with the initiation of wars, but the risk is still almost double that of normal years.

If we instead focus on deaths by natural causes and accidents, we should be able to get closer to the causal effect of successions on war (cf. Jones and Olken 2005; 2009). We argue that natural deaths are exogenous to wars. As we show later, wars can cause abdications, battle deaths, and depositions but they are unlikely to increase the risk of natural deaths significantly. If there is an increased risk of war breaking out in such years compared to normal years, there is strong reason to assume that successions *caused* wars.[3]

---

[3] Years that both saw natural deaths and depositions (or battle deaths) are counted as years with depositions.

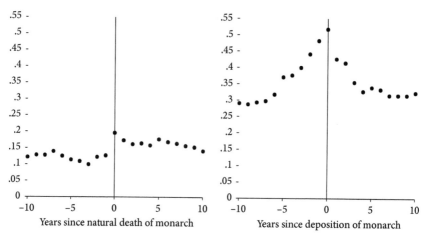

Fig. 5.3 Proportion of countries involved in at least one civil war the years before and after a natural death of a monarch (left graph) and before and after a deposition (right graph)

Table 5.1 shows evidence of such an effect. The risk of a civil war breaking out is four times higher in years in which a monarch died from 'natural'—meaning unpolitical—causes than in other years. If the assumption holds that war is unlikely to have caused these natural deaths, the data suggest that successions were dangerous moments in which elite coordination could fail and spiral out of control.

Another way to show this is to compare the periods just before and after a succession, divided according to whether the succession was caused by natural death or deposition. Figure 5.3 shows the percentage of country-years in which the country was involved in at least one civil war, for each year relative to the succession.

The graphs depict two different dynamics: natural deaths occur at the start of a period of conflict, and depositions at the peak. Countries were involved in civil war in about 13 per cent of the years before the natural death of a monarch but this figure jumps to 20 per cent in succession years. In contrast, years leading up to depositions were much more frequently characterized by civil war; the figure then drops after the deposition. As we are interested in the effect of successions on conflict, we focus on natural deaths in the analyses that follow.

Successions, primogeniture, and civil war

Successions were thus seemingly linked to the outbreak of war, especially civil war. But did primogeniture mitigate the risk, as we have argued? Table 5.2 compares the observed risk of civil war in a country-year, depending on whether a monarch died a natural death that year and whether the country practiced primogeniture or had other succession arrangements. The table shows that the risk of civil war onset was higher in years where a monarch died naturally but that this pattern is accentuated in elective monarchies and monarchies practicing agnatic succession. In this part of the sample, civil wars broke out in 2.8 per cent of the normal country-years and in 16.8 per cent of the country-years when a monarch died a natural death. Succession years are thus associated with a sixfold increase in the risk of civil war. In states practicing primogeniture, civil war broke out in 2.3 per cent of normal years and in 5.1 per cent of the years when a monarch died a natural death. In other words, succession years only doubled the risk of civil war when primogeniture was practiced. These descriptive statistics strongly suggest that primogeniture mitigated the risk of succession wars and hence that succession orders mediate the relationship between succession and domestic conflicts.

However, the observed differences may be due to other factors associated with states practicing primogeniture. There is also the possibility that years in which natural deaths occurred systematically differed from other years. It is therefore necessary to control for plausible confounding factors in a regression framework.

As is standard in the literature on civil war onset, we control for peace spells between civil wars with variables that measure years and years squared since last civil war (e.g. Collier and Hoeffler 2004). Following the literature on the importance of parliaments for leader–elite negotiations (e.g. Blaydes and Chaney 2013; Boucoyannis 2015; Downing 1992; Møller 2017; Stasavage 2010; 2016), we also include a variable that controls for the presence of

Table 5.2 Frequency of civil war onset in a country-year (per cent)

	No natural death	Natural death
Primogeniture	2.3	5.1
Other succession orders	2.8	16.8

parliaments. This variable, which is based on data on the history of European parliaments from van Zanden, Buringh, and Bosker (2012), measures for each state and century whether the state had a parliament. If the state had a parliament it is assigned a value of 1; if it did not it is assigned a value of 0 for the century in question.

As larger countries are more exposed to local revolts, we control for the log of the geographical area, measured in 100-year intervals using data from Euratlas.net. Using the same data, we include a variable for mountainous terrain, the presence of which could make it easier for rebel groups to evade capture (Blattman and Miguel 2010; Collier and Hoeffler 2004). This variable is constructed as the percentage of the country located at an altitude of at least 500 meters. Finally, we control for the monarch's tenure, age, and age squared.

The framework we use is based on the country-year structure of the data, where the outcome of interest is whether a civil war broke out in any given year. We use linear probability models, estimated with OLS regression, with standard errors clustered at the country level. All models also include country and century fixed effects. The coefficients from our models are shown in Figure 5.4.

The figure shows that natural deaths increased the risk of civil war (by on average 7 percentage points) when other factors are taken into account. This general effect hides considerable heterogeneity: a natural death only increased

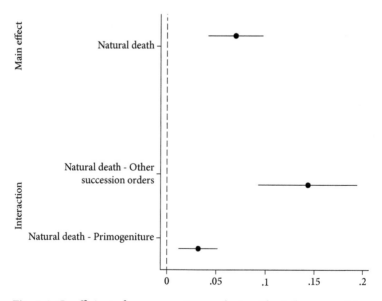

Fig. 5.4 Coefficients from regression analysis with civil war onset in a year as the dependent variable

the risk of civil war by 3.2 percentage points in states that practiced primogeniture, compared to 14.3 percentage points in states with other succession arrangements. To put these increases into perspective, the risk of civil war breaking out was below 3 per cent in both types of states in non-succession years.

It is obvious that primogeniture mitigated the effect of successions on civil war, as successions increased the risk of civil war much more in states with other succession arrangements. Of the 441 country-years in the sample in which a monarch died a natural death, civil war broke out in 40. Had all natural deaths occurred in primogeniture states, the expected number would be 25, compared to 73 had they all happened in elective monarchies and states practicing agnatic seniority.

Successions and international war

So far, we have shown that successions increased the risk of civil war and that primogeniture mitigated this effect. We now turn our attention to how successions and succession orders affected international wars. Table 5.3 compares the observed risk of international war in any given country-year, depending on whether a monarch died a natural death that year and whether the country practiced primogeniture or had other succession arrangements. The first two columns show that successions increased the overall risk of international war onset regardless of the principle of succession. In states that practiced primogeniture, wars broke out in 6.5 per cent of normal years and in 11.3 per cent of succession years. The corresponding figures for states with other succession arrangements were 7.5 per cent in normal years and 14.1 in successions years. The risk of interstate war was thus somewhat lower in states practicing primogeniture, but successions seem to have increased the risk equally in both types of states.

A somewhat different pattern appears in the columns that separate defensive from offensive wars (i.e. wars in which states were attacked by another

Table 5.3 Frequency of international war onset in a country year (per cent)

	All wars		Defensive wars		Offensive wars	
	No death	Death	No death	Death	No death	Death
Primogeniture	6.5	11.3	3.5	6.2	2.9	5.1
Other	7.5	14.1	4.1	10.1	3.3	4.0

state or were allied with an aggressor versus wars in which they attacked another state or were allied with the defender). Here we see that states were more likely to be attacked in the wake of successions regardless of succession arrangements. However, while states that practiced primogeniture were more likely to attack other states in succession years, the risk of offensive international war increased much less in other states, indicating that their new rulers had their hands full shoring up the situation at home instead of embarking on foreign adventures.

These patterns could of course be affected by other factors. We therefore test the effects of successions and succession arrangements using regression models. The models again build on the country-year structure. The dependent variable is whether an international war broke out in any given year. We use linear probability models, estimated with OLS regression, controlling for geographical factors, as well as century dummy variables. Standard errors are clustered at the country level. The standardized coefficients are shown in Figure 5.5.

The figure largely confirms the impressions from Table 5.3. Natural deaths increased the risk of international war both in states that practiced

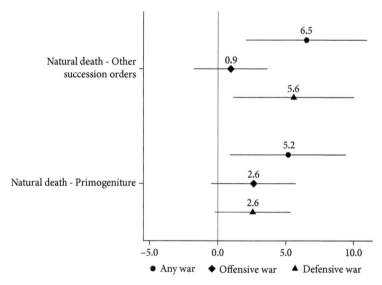

Fig. 5.5 Coefficients from regression analysis with international (defensive and offensive) war onset in a year as the dependent variable

Note: 95 per cent confidence intervals. Unit of analysis is country-year. Models include controls, century fixed effects, and country fixed effects.

Table 5.4 Risk of war breaking out depending on death or not, and the outcome of wars (per cent)

	Any war	Offensive war	Defensive war	Winning war	Losing war
No death	3.3	1.5	1.8	1.5	1.4
Natural death	6.7	2.7	3.9	2.5	3.9

primogeniture (5.2 percentage points) and in states with other succession arrangements (6.5 percentage points). In the latter, the effect seems to have been driven primarily by an increase in defensive wars (i.e. foreign invasions). In the former, the effect seems to have been driven by an increase in both offensive and defensive wars. States with other succession arrangements thus seem to have been somewhat more vulnerable in the wake of successions. However, the differences between the two categories are not statistically significant and the overall increase in the risk of international war in the wake of successions does not seem to depend on succession arrangements.

For a subset of wars in the dataset, we have information on victors and vanquished from one of the five sources we have used to compile our list of wars, namely Phillips and Axelrod (2005). We present this information in Table 5.4.

The pattern in Table 5.4 is similar to the one in Table 5.3: wars, especially defensive ones, were more likely to break out in years with natural monarch deaths. The most interesting observation is that wars which broke out in such years were more likely to end in a loss for the country in which a succession took place. This pattern can, in part, be explained by the fact that a majority of the wars which broke out in such years were defensive wars, and defensive wars were more likely than offensive wars to end in defeat. Regardless, this shows that succession wars were on average more dangerous than other international wars.

Natural monarch deaths were as common in states practicing primogeniture as in states with other succession arrangements, due to the high mortality rates of the era. However, successions caused by unnatural factors, such as depositions and assassinations, of course also increased the risk of international war. As we show in Chapter 6, such successions were less common in states practicing primogeniture. Primogeniture therefore indirectly reduced the risk of devastating succession wars even though there is only weak evidence that the principles mitigated the effect of successions on international war.

Children and succession crises

Primogeniture solves the coordination problem by tying succession to biological processes. However, the principle requires that there are eligible heirs. In the period we analyse, lineages would regularly die out in the male line due to biological chance (see Chapter 8). Given that offspring from liaisons were illegitimate as heirs and adoption was prohibited, biological reproduction was therefore a constant worry for monarchs. Henry VIII of England's attempts to produce a male heir to perpetuate his Tudor line and avoid future civil strife eventually caused England to break with the Catholic Church when the Pope refused to grant the English monarch a divorce.

Avidit Acharya and Alexander Lee (2019) argue that most elective monarchies operated under a norm that gave a monarch's male children precedence in the order of succession and that failure to produce male heirs was therefore a universal source of succession disputes in European history regardless of *de jure* succession order (see also Wang 2018). They substantiate this claim by showing that the absence of male heirs increased the likelihood that European regions were embroiled in civil wars.[4] Oeindrila Dube and S. P. Harish (2020) argue that unmarried female monarchs were more vulnerable to challenges than their male counterparts due to their perceived weakness. These findings raise the question of how the availability of male heirs affected the risk that succession wars broke out.

Table 5.5 presents the observed frequency of war onsets in years with natural monarch deaths, depending on whether the monarch had at least one living son when he died, and whether the state practiced primogeniture or had other succession arrangements.

Table 5.5 Frequency of civil war onset in years with natural monarch deaths (per cent)

	No son	Son
Primogeniture	8.7	3.2
Other	21.3	12.2

---

[4] Acharya and Lee's dependent variable is ongoing civil war and not war onset, which is the focus in this chapter.

The table shows that the risk of civil war was considerably lower following a monarch's death if he was survived by one of his sons. In states practicing primogeniture, the risk of civil war was 3.2 per cent if the monarch had a living son when he died and 8.7 per cent if he did not. The corresponding risk for elective monarchies was 12.2 per cent if the monarch had a living son and 21.3 per cent if he did not. These patterns seemingly confirm that a monarch's ability to produce sons was important for avoiding succession wars regardless of which succession arrangements were practiced. However, to understand these dynamics fully, it is necessary to control for confounding factors.

In Figure 5.6, we present results from models that are similar to those presented in Figure 5.4, but with the addition of the full set of interactions between natural death, practicing primogeniture, and the dummy measuring whether a monarch had at least one living son. The figure presents the estimated conditional coefficients and confidence intervals for natural death at the four combinations of practicing primogeniture and having at least one son.

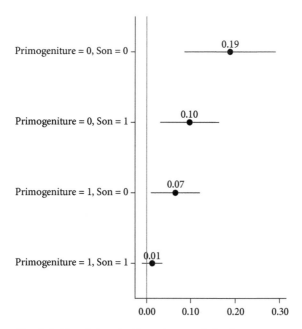

Fig. 5.6 Conditional effect of natural death on probability of civil war onset, at different levels of primogeniture and at least one living son

Note: 95 per cent confidence intervals. Unit of analysis is country-year.

The figure shows that the natural death of a monarch increased the risk of civil war by 19 percentage points if the monarch did not have a son and primogeniture was not practiced. If the monarch had a son, this risk dropped to 10 percentage points and it dropped to 7 percentage points if primogeniture was practiced. If the monarch had a son *and* primogeniture was practiced, the monarch's natural death did not increase the risk of civil war.

Though the effect is less pronounced than that of primogeniture, Acharya and Lee (2019) thus seem correct in assuming that the availability of living sons made power transitions easier regardless of *de jure* succession arrangements—likely because it seemed natural for many contemporaries that the monarch's eldest son should inherit the throne irrespective of the succession order (Bartlett 2020: 397–402). However, the independent effect of primogeniture indicates that this principle further reduced uncertainty about succession by legitimizing the eldest son's claim. The fact that primogeniture delineates a clear line of succession even when the monarch lacks living sons, as long as he has other living relatives (such as grandsons, brothers, nephews, or daughters, if female inheritance is allowed), may explain why the principle had a positive effect on political stability in the absence of living sons.

Did war cause 'natural' deaths?

Perhaps the most important potential objection against our findings is reverse causality. Could what we term the 'natural' deaths of monarchs have been caused by wars, instead of the other way around? Even though we exclude murders, depositions, and battle deaths, one might still worry that war places increased demands on the monarch and heightens tensions, which could provoke or at least accelerate a natural death. To determine whether this is the case, we do two things. First, we reverse our analysis and make natural leader death in a country-year the dependent variable and variables for ongoing civil and international wars our independent variables, together with all previously used controls. We exclude years in which a war started, since our main analyses already show a positive correlation between a natural death and the outbreak of war and as it is impossible to determine the direction of causality relying only on statistical correlations. However, if war-induced stress is a cause of natural deaths, we should observe an effect in war years, which we do not. The risk that a monarch died a natural death was no higher in years with ongoing civil and international war.

One could speculate that the stress of war is highest at a war's outbreak. We have therefore specifically studied the years in which monarchs died of natural reasons *and* war broke out. What was the order of events and what do the descriptions of the wars in the sources tell us about their causes? Forty civil wars broke out in countries the same year a monarch died of natural reasons. According to the sources we have consulted, the vast majority of wars were related to the succession or the death of the monarch. Only five of the wars were underway when the monarch died and hence completely unrelated to their death. However, it is unsurprising that during natural death years, some wars broke out which were unrelated to succession. Removing conflicts that erupted before the death of the monarch from the analysis would make these years unnaturally peaceful. The expected number of wars in years in which a monarch died would only have been 10, instead of the observed 40, if the probability of conflict had been identical to years in which no monarch died.

For international wars, we have looked at the 32 wars in which a country was attacked the same year its monarch died of natural causes. Twenty-four of these wars erupted after the death of the monarch. In comparison, a country should have been attacked by another country in, on average, 16 of the 441 years in which a monarch died a natural death if the probability of being attacked were identical to years in which no monarch died. Reverse causality does not seem to be an issue.

Conclusions

When Edward the Confessor died childless in 1066, it forever changed the face of England. Before the year had ended, the newly elected king, Harold Godwinson, had fought and killed his own brother Tostig, defeated and killed the invading Norwegian king Harald Hardrada, and lost his life at Hastings, trying to stop an invasion led by the Duke of Normandy, William the Conqueror. Edward's death thus triggered one civil war, two foreign invasions, and the demise of two kings. It also sounded the death knell for Anglo-Saxon rule in England. When the Domesday Book surveyed all English lands 20 years later, only 5 per cent were still in Anglo-Saxon hands (Thomas 2003). The nobles who had elected Harold king in 1066 were either dead or impoverished: 'England in 1075 was a land under occupation' (Bartlett 2000: 1).

The events of 1066 were exceptional, even by the violent standards of the day; but as we have shown in this chapter, they were far from unique in European history. Destructive succession wars haunted the continent with regular intervals up until the nineteenth century. Even with the restrictive definition of 'succession war' used in this chapter, we have identified more than 80 such wars. With a broader definition that also includes wars triggered by violent successions and wars that took some time to break out, the tally increases dramatically. No wonder contemporaries feared the disruptive forces successions unleashed (Bartlett 2000: 123–5).

The root of the problem was that members of the regime found it difficult to coordinate their efforts to uphold the regime if they did not have a designated crown prince to rally around in advance of the succession. Seen from this vantage point, the elective monarchies that dominated Europe early in the period were especially problematic. Primogeniture solved this problem by tying succession to biology. If the monarch was able to produce a son, the regime had an assurance that it would have a crown prince who could guarantee its continuation beyond the sitting monarch's rule. We have also shown that the gradual adoption of primogeniture can explain why the number of succession-related civil wars dropped over time.

In contrast to international wars, civil wars are normally seen as detrimental to state-building efforts. They threaten the very foundations that keep the state together. Moreover, they shorten the time horizon of both the monarch and his regime, which has implications for their incentives to invest in state-building efforts: 'stationary bandits' benefit more than 'roving bandits' from long-term investments, as Mancur Olson (1993) has told us. By reducing the risk of succession wars, primogeniture therefore increased both monarchs' and their regimes' willingness to engage in state-building.

However, commitment problems that are bound to appear *ex post* are usually anticipated by, and influence the behaviour of, the contracting parties *ex ante*. The same is true for the contract between the monarch and his regime: monarchs and their elite groups always lived in the shadow of future successions. The stabilizing effect of primogeniture on successions therefore likely had repercussions for political violence far beyond succession wars. It is to these consequences we turn in the next chapter.

6
Leader Depositions

"The Goths had adopted the reprehensible habit of killing out of hand any king who displeased them and replacing him on the throne by someone whom they preferred." Gregory of Tours, A History of the Franks, Book III:30

(Thorpe 1974).

Writing in the sixth century, Gregory, Bishop of Tours and chronicler of the history of the Franks, offered a scathing indictment of the adjacent Visigothic monarchy. It is today widely acknowledged that the truth-value of Gregory's chronicle is low; indeed, it may be almost completely fictitious (Wickham 2009: 12–18). But in this instance, the simple data that has come down to us on the Visigothic monarchy confirm Gregory's observation. This Romano-Germanic state in modern-day Spain and southern France spectacularly failed to properly institutionalize a stable order of succession (Wickham 2005). When King Amalric died without an heir in 531, a new king was elected, setting a dangerous precedent (Barbero and Loring 2005: 354). Of the 27 kings that followed, nine were deposed, and the average reign was less than eight years (Shaw 1906: 212; Crouch 1994). Without a clear principle of succession, violence became the true decider. Another medieval chronicler, Fredegar, called the frequent depositions in the kingdom the *morbus Gotorum*—the Gothic disease (Esders 2019: 176).

The violent fates of many of the Visigothic monarchs (seven of the nine who were deposed were also murdered, as far as we can glimpse the events based on the surviving sources) highlights the primary objective of any authoritarian leader: to stay in power. Even if a ruler is able to hand on power, the next person in charge could very well eliminate his predecessor, and would in fact be wise to do so, to forestall any attempts to take power back.[1] Democratic leaders know that if they lose an election, they can retire or have another

---

[1] At least in some circumstances (see e.g. Egorov and Sonin 2015).

shot at political office in the future. Authoritarian leaders can never be certain that there will be an 'after' and must always be vigilant, ready to identify and respond to threats against their rule (Svolik 2012).

Even though peasant uprisings were legion in medieval and early modern Europe, popular insurrections hardly ever led to the fall of monarchs (Zagorin 1982). Instead, it was the elite—the dukes and counts, the nobility, the bishops—at whose mercy kings and queens lived or died. Controlling and pleasing this elite was therefore the key to staying in power, as it still is for modern authoritarian rulers. Doing so requires a steady flow of spoils to members of the regime as well as credible threats that disobedience will be punished (Bueno de Mesquita et al. 2005). In the early medieval period of the Visigothic monarchy, these spoils were very concrete. A ruler needed a well-stocked treasury of gold, silver, and other valuables to pay his retainers, and a king who lost his treasure could be sure to lose the throne shortly thereafter, and possibly his life as well (Wickham 2009: 119).

But even if a king managed to keep his treasure, there were many other reasons why the loyalty-for-spoils contract between him and his supporters might break down. Economic crisis (say, successive harvest failures) or foreign threats could make the elite doubt that their interests were best served by loyalty towards the ruler.

However, a more common cause of ruler–elite tension has to do with the principles (or the lack thereof) governing the succession, and the anticipation of what might happen during the next succession. In this chapter, we analyse the way the politics of succession affected medieval monarchs' chances of holding on to the throne. We saw in the previous chapter how moments of succession—upon the deaths of leaders—could spark conflict: this chapter is about what happens during the reign and how fear of a tumultuous succession can shorten it.

How the principles of succession affect leader survival

Chapter 5 dealt with the direct consequences of uncertainty about the succession and the conflicts that can arise from it. When members of the elite are unable to come together around a preferred candidate there might be violence. Civil wars and rebellions were more likely to break out when the issue of succession became acute, on the death of a monarch.

But the fear of such conflict also reverberates during the reign. In the theoretical chapter, we described how the 'shadow of the future' looms over political regimes characterized by vague succession arrangements. In an anthropological study of succession practices around the world, the anthropologist Robbins Burling (1974: 71) summarizes the risks and rewards of moments of leader change: 'Successions ... were times when everyone had to be vigilant, lest he be displaced by others, and at the same time they offered the best possible occasion for each man to advance his own interests.' Apart from the possible violence that could arise from a crisis of succession, a change of leadership might lead to a rearrangement of the ruling coalition, in which members of the elite that are currently 'in' could find themselves 'out'. It was a 'time for changes, when both the dangers and the opportunities of political life were great' (Bartlett 2000: 7).

Prudential actors will anticipate such future conflicts and prepare for them in advance. In general terms, this can create a situation akin to the 'security dilemma' known from international relations, where the efforts taken by one actor to increase his security threatens the security of other actors, who are forced to respond, resulting in an arms race that lessens the security of everyone (Herz 1952). In the same way, the preparations one actor makes for a future succession might cause others to take similar actions. The shorter the time to an expected succession seems to be—for instance, when the ruler is old or ailing—the more necessary are preparations. The ultimate preparation would be to forestall the entire succession and depose the incumbent ruler, catching rivals off guard. But the realization that others may plan a similar takeover increases the urgency of the situation and the threatening circumstances.

Is there a successor?

Several features of the principles of succession affect how the elite will act during the reign. First, it matters whether there is a designated successor or not. The existence of an heir apparent resolves much of the uncertainty of the succession by creating a focal point around which members of the elite can concentrate their efforts to uphold the status quo, thus reducing the threat of a violent conflict later. A designated successor also ensures the elite that the removal of the incumbent ruler will not result in an open contest and gives them a stake in the survival of the regime (Frantz and Stein 2017). As Konrad and Mui (2017) argue, the existence of a crown prince moreover creates a 'barrier effect', at least if he has the resources to fight back (Meng 2021). Potential rivals know that the default outcome if they assassinate the monarch is that power will devolve on the successor, who can and will use his own resources and the resources of the crown to fight back. A designated successor thus means that challengers must upset the status quo to a larger extent than when there is no heir who can fight for his position (Bartlett 2020: 62). If there is a clear line of succession and many potential successors, it becomes even more difficult to stage a successful coup without retaliation.

A further benefit of designating a successor is that the elite can groom him or her, to ensure a favourable disposition once in power. However, members of the elite can never be entirely sure of their prospects, as the incentives of the successor and the elite will diverge as soon as the successor takes the throne. Incumbent rulers thus always have an advantage over challengers: since the ruler is already in power, his supporters can be more certain that they will continue to be favoured, if they remain loyal. A challenger does not have the same track record of loyalty to his supporters (Bueno de Mesquita et al. 2005). In the context of a succession, both a designated successor and potential challengers are in one sense unproven and should thus face similar commitment problems. However, a designated successor will most likely be given some assignments and responsibilities during the reign, which can be used to demonstrate his future preferences—at least if the monarch trusts him. All else equal, being able to spend more time with the future ruler should make it possible for the elite to groom him, at least to a higher extent than they can cultivate someone from the outside.

A monarch famously obsessed with his succession was Henry VIII of England, who did not have a son that survived past infancy until 1537, 28 years into his reign. The need to produce an heir weighed on Henry, and for good reason. In 1521, Edward Stafford, the Duke of Buckingham and descendant of Edward III, allegedly sought out a monk to hear prophecies about the future. According to the indictment in the later trial against Buckingham, the monk told the duke 'that the king would have no issue male of his body' and that were the king to die, Buckingham would succeed him (Henry VIII 1521). Hearing this, the duke started making plans to assassinate the king and take the throne for himself. When Henry was informed, he had Buckingham arrested, tried, and executed for high treason (Harris 1976). Had the king had a designated and credible successor—he could hardly be sure that his daughter, the Princess Mary, would be accepted as heir (Harris 1976)—Buckingham's own claim to the throne would have been much weaker, as would his incentive to dispose of Henry.

The fault here lay not so much with the principle of succession but in the fact that Henry had the misfortune of not having any sons. Nonetheless, the episode illustrates the risks created by an anticipated power vacuum. Of course, had the acceptance of female inheritance been greater, the problem would not have been as serious.

However, the existence of a successor does not fully eliminate the threat against the ruler, as discussed in Chapter 2. A designated heir has a direct interest in the ruler dying and could also have significant power resources to advance that event: 'Heirs might become impatient and fractious' (Bartlett 2020: 109). The threat thus narrows, from the wider elite to an individual person. Gregory of Tours gives a vivid example from the Kingdom of the Burgundians in the sixth century.[2] King Sigismund had a son, Sigeric, whose mother had died. Sigeric resented the new queen and publicly criticized her for taking his mother's place. Furious, she went to the king and convinced him that Sigeric plotted to kill him and take over the country, because '[h]e knows that he cannot realize his plans as long as you live: he cannot rise unless you fall' (Thorpe 1974: 165). The queen's elegant formulation of the crown prince problem has the intended effect: Sigismund subsequently has his son executed, but immediately regrets it and retreats to a monastery to do penance, according to Gregory.

A compromise between the need for a successor and the danger of having one would be to have institutions for selection of a new leader in place during the reign, without designating a specific successor. But the more uncertain the outcome of such a contest is, the more the situation resembles a situation without any procedures for succession. As the losers' security cannot be guaranteed, potential challengers will have an incentive to act preemptively. Additionally, persons in charge of overseeing the transition will be empowered before the succession, potentially enabling them to skew the process in their own favour (Frantz and Stein 2017).

Studying the crown prince problem systematically is difficult, as the designation of a successor (in cases where it is not mandated constitutionally) is endogenous to the risk a crown prince would pose. A ruler who has good reason to fear a power grab by a designated successor will be more reluctant to name one and we will therefore less frequently observe coups led by designated successors than we would have, if all rulers had been forced to name one. Moreover, the rules governing the designation of a successor, which we now turn to, also affects the incentives of the successor to rebel.

---

[2] Again, the details of Gregory's account might be partly or even fully fictitious. But as Wickham (2009: 14) points out, the chronicle—and others like it—tells us about 'the sort of things that could happen' in the world of the early Franks, and we can therefore use the example to illustrate this.

How easily can designations be changed?

The second important feature of the principles of succession that affects the prospects for leader survival is how fixed a designation is. When the principle of succession is designation by the incumbent, it is revocable and dependent on his goodwill. In one way, that could serve to make the successor more loyal and insistent on staying on good terms with the ruler. But it also creates uncertainty, as the heir may fear that he will fall from grace and be replaced by another. In such circumstances, he has an incentive to hasten the succession.

The more personalized a regime is, the harder it is for the ruler to credibly commit to sticking with a designated successor. Formalization of succession rules through institutions helps to tie the leader's hands. Anne Meng (2020: 251) describes this as a paradox: by constraining himself, the ruler is protected against his own caprice, thereby reducing the need for others to stage a coup, protecting him in the long run. The eternal problem in autocratic settings is that the institutions themselves are subject to the same problem. How can the elite, and a designated successor, know that the institutions will be able to constrain the ruler during critical moments?

Meng argues that the institutions need to be self-enforcing, that is, that it is in all parties' interest to uphold them and that deviations can be sanctioned by force. But if the institutions only reflect a more general balance of power, can they be said to have any real power at all? Milan Svolik argues that the main contribution of institutions is to act as coordination devices. For instance, dictators can and frequently do evade term limits but breaking a set term limit—a line in the sand—is more noticeable than prolonging the reign when there is no expectation of when it should end (Svolik 2012; 2013). In our period of study there were few written constitutions that could help to formalize succession agreements. Tradition helped—it is harder to deviate from a practice that has been followed for many successions than a new one.

Succession practices in which the ruler had no say about who was to be the next successor were more constraining than those in which he had. Hereditary systems, especially those with a clear ordering of potential heirs, in theory made the process of selection mechanical. Under primogeniture, the eldest son of a monarch could (in theory) be certain that he would be the eventual successor and could thus afford to wait for his turn. Tying the selection to biology made it more predictable, at least when the monarch managed to produce children.

But no system is foolproof. Even in monarchies with established principles of succession, rulers have been known to disinherit their sons. Peter the Great of Russia in the eighteenth century upended the tradition of primogeniture (which had been established by Michael Romanov after the Time of Troubles) to prevent his own son from taking power. Henry II of England kept his oldest living son Richard (the Lionheart) in suspense about whether he would inherit power, causing tension and eventually war between father and son. However, the power of tradition still held sway: a historian notes that 'as much as Henry may have wished to set aside the son he disliked, he could not bring himself to disavow the principles of "rightful inheritance" for which he had fought from his youth' (Warren 1973: 622).

The more constrained the ruler is in terms of manipulating the succession, the less dangerous crown princes are likely to be. Rulers who can choose whom to designate have more leeway of action and cannot commit credibly to sticking with one. This makes potential successors more dangerous, in turn reducing the likelihood that the ruler will designate anyone at all. Crown princes that are formally designated will therefore seldom challenge the ruler, but that does not mean that the crown prince problem has gone away.

What are the characteristics of the designated successor?

The third important feature of the principles of succession concerns the characteristics of the intended successors. Who tends to get nominated and how does it affect their incentives to challenge the ruler?

The first important characteristic of intended successors is their relation to the ruler. In hereditary systems, heirs will hail from the same family whereas heirs apparent who are designated by the ruler might not. According to the principle of kin selection (Hamilton 1964), behaving altruistically towards near relatives makes sense from a biological standpoint, as their success also increases the probability that a portion of one's own genes will survive. Feelings of love and friendship that arise from growing up in the same family may, of course, also matter (see Chapter 8). While the dynamics of royal families in many ways differ from those of ordinary families, for instance in how children are raised, it is still reasonable to expect that there will be some affinity between parents and children and between siblings. Fourteenth-century Arab historian Ibn Khaldun noted that 'blood relations and other close relatives help each other out, while strangers and outsiders do not,' not because of shared blood per se, but because of the long history of cooperation and affection that comes from close contact (Ibn Khaldun 1958[1377]: 18). Principles of succession that allow more distant relatives, or even non-relatives, to succeed—such

Table 6.1 Relationship of monarchs to their predecessors (per cent)

Relationship to predecessor	Primo-geniture	Elective monarchy	Agnatic seniority
Son/daughter/grandson/great-grandson	61	30	26
Brother	11	10	23
Nephew/uncle	3	6	16
First cousin/spouse/father	4	2	9
More distant relative/no relation	20	52	26
Sum	100	100	100
N	402	282	57

as designation and elective monarchy—do not create the same bonds of loyalty between a monarch and his successor.

We can use our dataset to illustrate these points. Table 6.1 shows that close to two-thirds of the 402 monarchs who came to power under primogeniture were the sons, daughters, grandsons, or great-grandsons of their predecessors, with sons as the absolute majority of those cases. Only 20 per cent of the primogeniture monarchs were unrelated (or at least more distantly related than first cousins) to their predecessors. In contrast, half of the elective monarchs were unrelated, or only distantly related, to their predecessors. In systems with agnatic seniority, we also see that while sons was the most common individual category, there was a much higher degree of lateral inheritance, with brothers, nephews, and uncles succeeding.

A related characteristic of successors is their age. If we compare the two different modes of hereditary succession, agnatic seniority and primogeniture, it is clear that heirs apparent on average will be much older under agnatic seniority where brothers rather than children inherit (until each generation has passed from the scene). Under primogeniture, crown princes might even be underage for substantial parts of the monarch's reign. For obvious reasons, children will be less capable of mounting a challenge against the incumbent monarch—at least one orchestrated by themselves—than adults. But even in adulthood, a large age differential to the heir apparent might be beneficial for the monarch, as the crown prince can be more certain that he will eventually inherit, when the ruler dies. A younger brother cannot be as sure and might therefore be more inclined to take matters into his own hands.

We do not have information on who the intended successor is at each point in time, which would be necessary to determine the true effect of their age. But we can get some idea of the general age differentials by looking at timing of

Table 6.2 Monarch age under different principles of succession

	Primogeniture	Elective monarchy	Agnatic seniority
Age at accession	26.2	30.2	31.6
Age difference to successor	20.9	16.3	10.8
N	402	282	57

births and age differences between outgoing and incoming rulers. In our data, the median age of monarchs at the time of having their first child is 25 years. In contrast, the median age at the time of the birth of the oldest sibling is only four. When monarchs were succeeded by one of their children, the age difference between parent and child was 30 years, on average.

In Table 6.2 we compare ages of monarchs under the different principles of succession. We can see that acceding monarchs were youngest under primogeniture (26.2 on average) and oldest under agnatic seniority (31.6). The difference is even starker if we look at the average age differences between monarchs and their successors: 20.9 under primogeniture, where succession by children is the most common, 16.3 in elective monarchies, and only 10.8 years under agnatic seniority. The implication is that a designated successor in a state practicing primogeniture can afford to be more patient and wait for the natural death of the ruler, normally his father, than heirs in elective monarchies or states practicing agnatic seniority.

There is of course an important downside of having a child as intended successor, which is that the child might become king before reaching adulthood. As we will show in detail in Chapter 7, minorities—meaning that the king is underage—weakened royal power, but from the ruler's perspective, it is an easy choice to buy security in the present for a potential cost borne by the realm after the ruler's death. For the elite, the prospects of being ruled by a child or a regency is less appealing, especially in periods where the ruler was supposed to lead armies into battle, which helps to explain why minorities were less frequent in the early part of the period we analyse, where elective monarchy was still common.

A third important characteristic is how powerful the crown prince is. As discussed in the theory chapter, rulers in the period we study could not rely on the crown's resources alone, but also needed considerable personal landed wealth to hold on to power. Without such private wealth it was virtually impossible to pose as a credible crown prince. However, a too powerful crown prince threatens both the king and the balance of power between the monarchy and the elite. In the best of worlds, the crown prince's private wealth should equal the king's private wealth once the former assumes office. Primogeniture assures this, as the eldest son inherits not only his father's position, but also the bulk of his personal fortune. In addition, the principle guarantees that the crown prince only comes into full control of his father's private wealth after the father's demise, so he cannot use it to rebel. Elective monarchy does not provide similar guarantees, as it is not certain that the new king will have a private fortune that matches his predecessor. And in systems practicing agnatic seniority the new king must cope with the fact that the old king's children will inherit most of his private wealth. None of the latter two systems guarantee that the new king comes into control of his private fortune after the incumbent's death.

No principle of succession can accommodate all desirable features while avoiding all downsides. However, as argued in the theoretical chapter, primogeniture represents a good compromise.[3] The principle provides clarity and predictability in the order of succession (especially if the ruler manages to have children), it ties the ruler's hands, and it produces crown princes that are young and well disposed towards the ruler and have sufficient private wealth to shoulder their father's mantle. The downside is the risk of minorities and of biological uncertainties more generally. Only the latter is salient for the ruler during his reign, but it may then be an important problem.

Hypothesis

The hypothesis we put to the test is therefore: in our sample of monarchies, rulers in states that practice primogeniture were less likely to be deposed than rulers under elective monarchy and agnatic seniority.

Descriptive statistics

In a study of the fates of monarchs in Europe between 600 and 1800, the criminologist Manuel Eisner (2011) found that more than one in five monarchs

---

[3] As argued in Chapter 2, the same applies to partible inheritance when practiced in an orderly manner, as it came to be in Europe in the period we analyse. It is for this reason that we have merged the two categories in our empirical analysis also in this chapter. As mentioned in Chapter 3, because the merged category of primogeniture and partible inheritance in reality consists of 90 per cent primogeniture monarch-years, we simply refer to primogeniture when interpreting the results (all reported results are robust to using a specification that only counts undisputable primogeniture monarch-years).

(out of a sample of 1,513) met a violent end. Most of these deaths were murders (14.6 per cent), followed by battle deaths (5.9 per cent). This corresponds to a death rate of 1,547 per 100,000 ruler years. The murder rate of the world's most violent country, El Salvador, pales in comparison: in 2017, the yearly number of homicides per 100,000 population was 'only' 62. And even though violence was much more common historically than today, monarchs were still more exposed than their subjects—the homicide rate in the general population in Europe rarely exceeded 100 per 100,000 (Eisner 2003).

Death was not the only undesirable outcome: depositions that resulted in the monarch's exile or imprisonment were also common. Medieval and early modern monarchs thus had good reason to watch their back. However, things improved over time. The regicide rate of monarchs in the eighteenth century was 190 per 100,000 ruler years, compared to 2,303 in the seventh century (Eisner 2011). Battle deaths show a similar decline.

In our dataset we have information on 741 reigns in 27 countries. On average, monarchs remained on the throne for 18.2 years, with a median of 15 years. One hundred and ninety-nine reigns—26.5 per cent—ended in a deposition of the monarch. Of these depositions, 133 were forcible removals from the throne, 41 were assassinations, and the rest were deaths resulting from civil war (19 in battle, six of sickness on the campaign trail).

Naturally, reigns which were cut short by a deposition were briefer than those which were not. The median reign for a deposed monarch was six years, compared with 19 for monarchs who were not deposed. Almost half of the depositions happened within the first five years on the throne—a pattern that has also been noted in research on modern authoritarian rulers (Bueno de Mesquita et al. 2005: 293; Svolik 2012: 77). Clearly, rulers are more exposed early in their reign when they have not consolidated their rule and eliminated potential rivals. Figure 6.1 shows the distribution of length of reigns for monarchs in our data who were and were not deposed.

Of the 20 longest-serving monarchs in our sample, all but one avoided deposition. The top three are Louis XIV of France, the Sun King, who remained on the throne for 72 years (1643–1715), followed by James I of Aragon (63 years, 1213–1276) and Christian IV of Denmark (60 years, 1588–1648).

But there are also interesting exceptions to the general rule that depositions happen early in the reign. Among eventually deposed monarchs, Eric of Pomerania, who was king of the three Scandinavian countries in the Kalmar Union, ruled as King of Norway for 53 years (1389–1442) before finally being deposed by the Norwegians. Before that, he had been deprived of his crowns in Denmark and Sweden. In places two and three we find two emperors: Henry

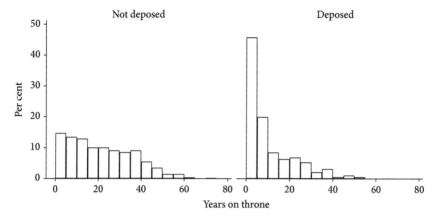

Fig. 6.1 Distribution of length of reigns, depending on whether the monarch was deposed or not

IV of the Holy Roman Empire (49 years) and Andronikos II of the Byzantine Empire (46 years).

Trends in leader tenure and depositions

The monarchs in our sample spent longer and longer periods on the throne. Figure 6.2 shows the average tenure for monarchs that acceded during the period we analyse, in intervals of 50 years. Although the line is far from straight, it trends upward. To some extent the trend is driven by the simple fact that monarchs tended to live longer in the later period, possibly due to general improvements in health. Among monarchs who were not deposed, the average lifespan of those who acceded to the throne in the eleventh century was 45 years, compared to 58 years for those who acceded during the eighteenth century.

But another important factor is that depositions became rarer and rarer, which corroborates the patterns noted in previous research (Eisner 2011; Blaydes and Chaney 2013). Figure 6.3 shows a striking reduction in the risk of being forcibly removed from the throne, from almost 40 per cent for the early monarchs to 20 per cent or less by the end of the period we have data for. This is a pattern that needs explaining. Earlier we have argued that the introduction of primogeniture is important for making sense of this puzzle. We now subject this hypothesis to an empirical test.

LEADER DEPOSITIONS 123

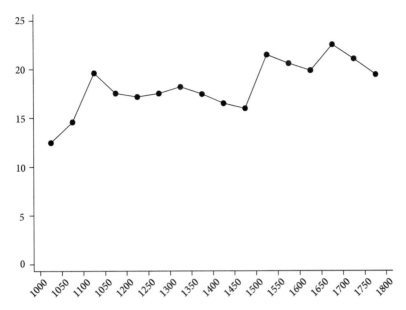

Fig. 6.2 Average tenure for monarchs that acceded during each half-century

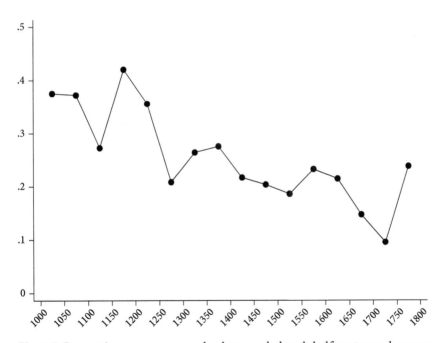

Fig. 6.3 Proportion among monarchs that acceded each half-century who were deposed

The effects of succession arrangements on depositions

As a preliminary analysis, we examine descriptive statistics of how monarchs fared under different principles of succession, in Table 6.3. In the first row, the unit of analysis is monarch reigns, showing the percentage of monarchs under each principle of succession who were deposed, regardless of their length of tenure. In the second row, the unit of analysis is instead monarch-year, meaning that the percentages represent the yearly risk of being deposed. The differences are striking: about 40 per cent of monarchs in states which did not practice primogeniture were eventually deposed, compared to only 14 per cent of monarchs in states practicing primogeniture. Correspondingly, the yearly deposition rate was much lower in states practicing primogeniture: 0.6 per cent, compared to 2.6 and 4.0 in the elective and agnatic seniority categories, respectively. We can also see that the average reign lasted longer for monarchs in states practicing primogeniture: 21 years, compared to 15 and 11 for the elective and agnatic seniority categories, respectively.

These simple descriptive statistics support our hypothesis and they also single out primogeniture; the difference between elective monarchy and agnatic seniority systems is less important than the difference between primogeniture and the two other principles of succession. Adoption of primogeniture explains a substantial part of the observed decrease in depositions over time. If we add primogeniture to a simple regression where deposition is the dependent variable and time of accession is the independent, it takes away a lot of the explanatory power of the time trend. Figure 6.4 shows both the actual proportion of monarchs who acceded each half century who were eventually deposed, and the corresponding numbers, controlled for primogeniture. We also plot linear trends.

Table 6.3 Depositions in states with different principles of succession (per cent)

	Primogeniture	Elective monarchy	Agnatic seniority
Per cent of reigns ending in deposition	14.0	39.0	46.0
Per cent of monarch-years with a deposition	0.6	2.6	4.0
Average length of tenure (years)	21.1	15.3	10.8

Note: Recall that this category includes about 10 per cent de facto partible inheritance monarch-years. However, results are similar if we only use the primogeniture monarch-years.

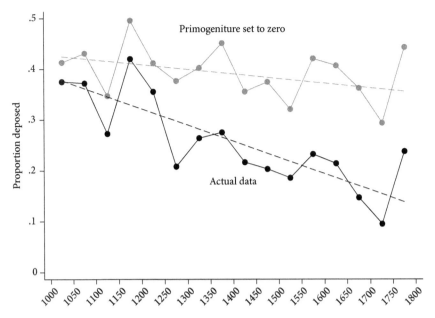

Fig. 6.4 Proportion of monarchs who acceded each half-century who were eventually deposed and predicted numbers from regressions with control for primogeniture

The grey lines show predicted values from a regression that includes primogeniture as a control, with primogeniture set to zero in the resulting regression equation: basically, what the trend in deposition might have looked like had primogeniture never been adopted. The trend with primogeniture set to zero is much flatter, barely registering a decrease over the eight centuries investigated. Although this simple counterfactual obviously does not cover the complexity and nuance of European political history, it indicates that primogeniture might well have been a decisive factor in bringing about greater domestic political stability in the period after AD 1000.

However, there are potential alternative explanations, which call for more sophisticated quantitative analysis. In these analyses, we control for whether a monarch's predecessor was overthrown to account for previous political instability. This variable also addresses Abramson and Rivera's (2016) argument that powerful monarchs were more likely to bequeath a more stable realm to their heirs, as well as to adopt primogeniture. In addition, we control for the presence of parliaments, the monarch's tenure, his age and age squared, and for how large and mountainous countries were (see Chapter 5 for the construction of these variables and reasons for including them).

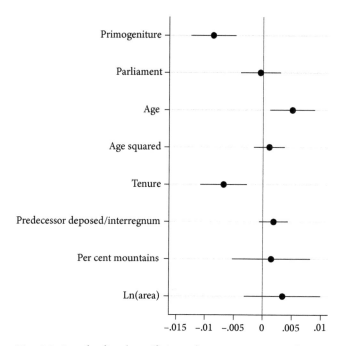

Fig. 6.5 Standardized coefficients from regression analysis with deposition in a year as the dependent variable

Note: 95 per cent confidence intervals. Unit of analysis is monarch-year. The analysis also includes country and century fixed effects. Standard errors clustered on countries.

We perform our analyses using the monarch-year structure of the data, where the outcome of interest is whether a monarch was deposed in any given year. We use linear probability models, estimated with OLS regression, controlling for the factors outlined earlier, as well as country and century dummy variables. Standard errors are clustered at the country level. The standardized coefficients are shown in Figure 6.5.

Primogeniture had a substantial negative effect on monarchs' risk of being deposed, even when controlling for alternative explanations. Monarchs with long tenures were less likely to be deposed whereas older monarchs were more likely to be deposed. The fate of the predecessor seems to have mattered to some extent, as monarchs were slightly more likely to be deposed if their predecessor had been deposed. However, the effect is not significant at conventional levels. Neither the presence of parliaments nor geographical factors seem to have affected the deposition risk.

The alternative explanations thus cannot account for the stabilizing effect of primogeniture. Monarchs who ruled states which practiced primogeniture were less likely to be deposed than their peers in elective monarchies and states practicing agnatic seniority, all else equal. But why? In the following section, we explore the possible mechanisms.

Testing the mechanisms

There are several channels through which primogeniture could reduce the risk of deposition. We outlined earlier how the mitigation of the coordination problem and the crown prince problem could usher in stability. But there are other potential factors that have to do with the monarchs themselves; for instance, we saw earlier that monarchs who came to power under primogeniture were on average younger. This could possibly correlate with being healthier and more able to fend off rivals. Being the son of the previous monarch could also be beneficial, in terms of legitimacy and inheritance of resources.

The coordination problem

The coordination problem states that the elite should be more uncertain about their future when no clear successor is designated. Confirming this expectation, we saw in the previous chapter that civil wars and rebellions were less likely to break out upon the deaths of monarchs in states practicing primogeniture than in elective monarchies. Therefore, members of the elite in elective monarchies had stronger reason to fear successions—and stronger incentive to preempt them in different ways, including instigating a coup against the incumbent monarch.

However, to genuinely test whether the stabilizing effect of primogeniture is due to mitigation of the coordination problem, we need to know whether there existed an heir presumptive at each point in time. Research on Imperial China has shown that emperors who designated sons as crown princes were less likely to be deposed by the elite, which is in line with the theoretical argument we have made (Wang 2018; see also Chapter 9). However, while designation of crown princes in China were major and well-documented events, we do not have access to comparable data for our European sample.

In many instances sons also succeeded their fathers in elective monarchies; more detailed historical knowledge is required if we are to determine whether a son was the heir presumptive or not. But we can reasonably assume that a son was more likely to be the heir presumptive under primogeniture than under

Table 6.4 Percentage of monarchs deposed in a year, depending on principle of succession and son

	At least one living son	No son
Primogeniture	0.62	0.57
Other succession orders	2.43	3.13

elective monarchy, whereas monarchs who did not have sons faced a coordination problem regardless of the principle of succession (if they did not have other male relatives). The beneficial effect of primogeniture should therefore be more pronounced for monarchs who had at least one son.

That is not what the data show. If we simply cross-tabulate whether a country practiced primogeniture or had other succession arrangements with a variable indicating whether the monarch had at least one son and calculate the yearly risk of deposition, there is little or no correlation (see Table 6.4). Monarchs were deposed much less frequently under primogeniture than under other principles of succession. But the difference is not driven by primogeniture monarchs with sons; they are in fact (ever so slightly) more likely to be deposed than primogeniture monarchs without sons. Contrary to what could initially be expected, monarchs in systems with election or agnatic seniority seemingly benefited more from having sons. The patterns are the same when controlling for confounders such as age in regressions.

We see the same pattern even if we include daughters in the equation and thus check whether the monarch had *any* children. Of course, the fact that a monarch was childless did not mean that he or she was bound to remain so forever; the elite could bet that an heir would be born later, which would have solved the coordination problem. Moreover, as previously mentioned primogeniture usually delineates a clear line of succession even when a monarch has no children, insofar as he has other relatives (grandsons, brothers, nephews, etc.).

Table 6.5 presents the relationship of the monarch to his or her successor, depending on the principle of succession and whether the monarch died childless or not, only including monarchs who were not deposed. Monarchs in states practicing primogeniture who had children were almost always succeeded by their direct descendants (88 per cent). Monarchs who had children in other systems were also usually succeeded by their children, but to a lower extent (63 per cent). Only 5 per cent of the monarchs with children in states practicing primogeniture were succeeded by someone of distant or no

Table 6.5 Monarchs' relationship to their successors (only non-deposed monarchs), depending on principle of succession and child at reign end (per cent)

	Primogeniture		Other succession orders	
	No child	Child	No child	Child
Son/daughter/grandson/great-grandson	7	88	13	63
Brother	28	4	20	5
Nephew/uncle	7	1	6	4
First cousin/spouse/father	16	2	2	1
More distant relative/no relation	42	5	59	27
Sum	100	100	100	100
N	88	248	90	100

relation. The corresponding figure for monarchs with children in states with other succession arrangements was 27 per cent.

When monarchs died without being survived by children, the crown was kept in the family to a higher extent in states practicing primogeniture. Only 42 per cent of the childless monarchs in states practicing primogeniture were succeeded by distant relatives or unrelated persons, whereas the same number for childless monarchs in states with other succession arrangements is 59 per cent. In states practicing primogeniture, brothers took over after childless monarchs in 28 per cent of the cases, which is natural given that younger siblings are next in the line of succession after the monarch's own progeny. Sixty-three per cent of the childless monarchs in states practicing primogeniture who had a living brother at the time of their reign's end were also succeeded by one.

There is thus good reason to suspect that members of the elite were less fearful of a succession crisis due to coordination issues in states practicing primogeniture even when the monarch did not have children. Successions in other systems were more likely to lead to radical dynastic shifts, which meant more risks for the elite. However, without data on the elite's perceptions of who the likely successor was, at each point in time, we cannot say for sure.

The crown prince problem

Another important reason why primogeniture should reduce monarchs' risk of being deposed is that the principle provides monarchs with less dangerous crown princes. All designated successors have an interest in the death of the monarch, but a monarch's children can usually afford to wait to inherit the throne due their relative youth. They are also often too young to overthrow the monarch on their own. In contrast, the age difference between a monarch and his younger brothers is usually small, which means that they will be more impatient to inherit the throne and more capable of overthrowing the monarch early in his reign.

Eleven monarchs in our data were deposed by their sons and 19 were deposed by their brothers. The average age of monarchs who were deposed by their brothers was 39.6 years, while the corresponding figure for monarchs who were deposed by their sons was 53.5 years. Threats from children thus naturally materialized later in life than threats from siblings.

The youngest monarch to be deposed by his son according to our coding was James III of Scotland, killed at the age of 37 in a battle against rebels whose (nominal) leader was his 15-year-old son, the later James IV. It is telling that the level of involvement of the younger James is unclear—he may have been a simple figurehead for dissatisfied nobles, who were reluctant to take responsibility for the demise of the king; official accounts at the time say that the king 'happinnit to be slane' (Mason 1987: 147). James IV also made public penance for his role in the death of his father throughout his reign (MacDonald 2003: 150).

It is hard to directly observe the degree to which monarchs were deposed by their intended successors in non-hereditary systems, without data on the identity of the intended successor, if there was one. But as a rudimentary test we can contrast primogeniture with agnatic seniority, under which younger brothers take precedence over sons. Table 6.6 shows that the likely successors under primogeniture (sons) were much less dangerous than the likely successors under agnatic seniority (brothers). In any given year, only 0.02 per cent of monarchs in states practicing primogeniture were deposed by a son, while 0.96 per cent of the monarchs in states practicing agnatic seniority were deposed by their brothers. One could object that monarchs under agnatic seniority were more likely to be deposed by their sons as well, reflecting an underlying instability. However, if we contrast agnatic seniority to election, we see that the yearly risk of deposition by a son was the same but the yearly risk of deposition by a brother was much higher (0.96 compared to 0.19 per cent) for monarchs in states practicing agnatic seniority. This indicates that the intended successor did indeed constitute a greater threat if he was a brother, rather than a son.

Monarchs' age at ascension

A rival explanation of our findings is that monarchs who came to power under primogeniture were relatively young and therefore possibly healthier, more

Table 6.6 Monarchs deposed by sons and brothers under different principles of succession (per cent)

	Primogeniture	Elective monarchy	Agnatic seniority
Yearly risk of deposition by:			
Son	0.02	0.17	0.16
Brother	0.06	0.19	0.96
Share of those deposed that were deposed by:			
Son	3.7	6.4	4.0
Brother	9.3	7.3	24.0

vigorous, and more resilient than their peers in states with other succession arrangements. Younger monarchs also provided the elite with a longer time horizon, which helped postpone the coordination problem.

Old age does appear to have reduced monarchs' chances of surviving in office. Controlling for the length of tenure (monarchs who had ruled for long should have been able to consolidate power—see e.g. Abramson and Velasco Rivera (2016)), age is associated with a higher risk of being deposed. Monarchs who ascended the throne later in life were thus weaker than their colleagues who ascended the throne early in life.

However, age patterns do not explain the primogeniture effect. Controlling for age and tenure in a regression does not diminish the size of the primogeniture coefficient. The reason is that there is an interaction between primogeniture and age as well as tenure: both factors matter more in systems without primogeniture. We can see this in Figure 6.6, which shows coefficients for age and tenure in a simple regression that only includes controls for century. Under other principles of succession than primogeniture, older monarchs were more likely to be deposed, controlling for tenure, and longer-reigning monarchs were less likely to be deposed, controlling for age. Although a similar pattern is evident in states practicing primogeniture, it is much weaker and not statistically significant there.

The fact that rulers tended to ascend the throne earlier in life in primogeniture monarchies thus does not explain the beneficial effect of primogeniture, since young age seemingly only mattered in other systems. One reason may be that the elite did not fear the demise of a monarch as much in states practicing primogeniture since the coordination problem was less severe in such

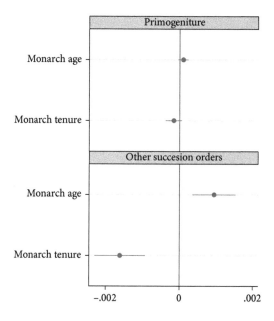

Fig. 6.6 Coefficients for age and tenure on deposition under primogeniture and other principles of succession

states. There were simply not the same incentives to depose an old and ailing monarch to preempt a succession struggle.

Conclusions

Successions threaten to upend the bargain between a ruler and the elite. A well-ordered principle for transferring power reduces uncertainty about such moments and allows the elite to coordinate their efforts to uphold the status quo. At the same time, the ruler needs to make sure that the succession is not hastened; the crown prince must not become too powerful before his time. In this chapter, we have shown that monarchs in states that practiced primogeniture were less likely to be deposed, and that the gradual adoption of primogeniture can explain a substantial portion of the increase in security for monarchs. While we can only perform indirect tests, both the coordination problem and crown prince problem seem to be contributing factors as there were often more dynastic shifts in states with other succession arrangements and as brothers appear to be more dangerous heirs apparent than sons.

Max Weber pointed out the uniqueness of medieval Europe in adopting the principle of primogeniture and noted the benefits it had for political stability:

> Lineage charisma, however, does not assure the unambiguous identification of the successor. This requires a definite rule of succession; hence the belief in the charismatic importance of blood relationship must be implemented by the belief in the charisma of primogeniture. For all other systems, including the system of 'seniority' frequently applied in the Orient, lead to wild palace intrigues and revolts, particularly when polygamy is practiced and the wives' struggle for the succession rights of their children is added to the ruler's interest in eliminating potential pretenders in favor of his own offspring.
>
> Weber (1968: 1137)

In this chapter we have focused on the effects of succession arrangements for the fortunes of the ruler. But if we broaden our perspective to the state, primogeniture can have dual benefits, relating to the ruler's time horizons. Here, we can return to Mancur Olson's (1993) insight that the development of societies to a large extent depend on the ruler's incentives to exploit or invest. Hereditary succession in general and primogeniture in particular lengthens the time horizons for rulers insofar as monarchs care more about the fortune of their children than those of unrelated successors, which there is good reason to believe. But as Olson (1993: 572) notes, it also lengthens the time horizons of the monarch himself. As we have seen in this chapter, primogeniture does so in particular by reducing the risk of deposition. For instance, Abbasid caliphs plagued by political instability (partly brought about by vague succession arrangements, see Chapter 9) focused on the military and neglected investment in irrigation, reducing agricultural productivity in their economic heartlands in southern Iraq (Stasavage 2020: 189).

Furthermore, a stable succession reduces uncertainty for other actors in society, who can reasonably expect current policies to continue even after a change of leadership (Cox and Weingast 2018). Contemporary research has also found a negative association between leader turnover and economic growth, driven by the negative effects of uncertainty (Cox and Weingast 2018).

In the next chapter, we focus on another aspect of the struggle between the ruler and the elite. Successions were, as we have discussed, contentious and uncertain moments, which made power-sharing agreements and institutions more important, especially if the designated successor was underage.

7
The Development of Parliaments

King John Lackland's signing of the charter of liberties that later came to be known as the Magna Carta, the 'Great Charter',[1] on Runnymede, 15 June 1215 is often highlighted as one of the signal events of European history. It has been seen as the cause of the development of the medieval English parliament which, in an unbroken historical sequence, grew into the present British Parliament in Westminster (Fukuyama 2015).

However, King John—supported by his liege-lord, Pope Innocent III—almost immediately annulled the concessions he had given his barons on Runnymede. The main reason that the Magna Carta came to have staying power is that John died soon after, in October 1216. His son and heir, Henry, was a nine-year-old boy, and to further complicate the situation the adult French crown prince Louis (the later Louis VIII of France) had received the English crown from a rival coalition of magnates and controlled London and the eastern half of England (see Carpenter 1990; Bartlett 2000; Maddicott 2010). Only by securing support among the English clergy and the remaining magnates could Henry win the throne. Henry III's protectors—headed by the old but still formidable William Marshall, popularly known as the greatest knight of his day—duly made the Magna Carta a coronation charter for young Henry and consistently called assemblies of nobles and clergy to placate the rebellious English magnates (Vincent 2012: 82; Maddicott 2010, 151–2). In fact, during his long minority, which lasted until 1227, Henry's regency reissued the Magna Carta thrice: in 1216, 1217, and 1225. These reconfirmations took place during assemblies of high clergy and magnates, which Henry (or rather his protectors) regularly convoked.

In this chapter, we analyse how monarchical succession affected the development of parliament-like assemblies in medieval Europe. We first use our theoretical framework to develop a series of hypotheses about succession

---

[1] To distinguish it from the 'Forest Charter' of 1217, which was henceforth normally re-issued together with Magna Carta.

The Politics of Succession. Andrej Kokkonen, Jørgen Møller, and Anders Sundell, Oxford University Press.
© Andrej Kokkonen, Jørgen Møller, and Anders Sundell (2022). DOI: 10.1093/oso/9780192897510.003.0007

and power-sharing institutions in medieval and early modern European monarchies. We then provide some simple descriptive statistics about successions, minorities, and the development of parliamentary constraints in Europe from the emergence of what Marongiu (1968) terms 'pre-parliaments' in the eleventh century until the end of the eighteenth century. Finally, we interrogate these data to better understand the relationship between successions and the convocation of parliament-like assemblies in European monarchies. Our results confirm that successions were conflictual moments where power arrangements had to be stabilized. They also show that over time primogeniture mitigated this problem. The chapter ends by discussing the broader implications of these findings.

Succession and power-sharing institutions

Recent research has documented that autocrats introduce power-sharing institutions to shore up support for the regime by co-opting opposition groups and alleviating commitment and monitoring problems between the autocrat and other members of the regime (e.g. Magaloni 2008; Ghandi and Przeworski 2006; 2007; Ghandi 2008; Svolik 2012; Schedler 2013; Boix and Svolik 2013). Medieval and early modern monarchies were no different in this respect. These were societies where monarchs were weak and where the elites—primarily lay magnates and high clergy—were all that mattered in political terms (Zagorin 1982: 61–5; Koeningsberger 1971: 3–4; Bisson 2009; Wickham 2009; 2016; Oakley 2010; 2012). To stay securely in power, the monarch needed reliable support from members of these groups. According to Svolik (2012: 98–9), in this situation power-sharing is inevitable, but it can occur either via formal or informal arrangements.

But what happens when the ruler dies or is deposed? The recent literature on power-sharing institutions in autocracies has been strangely silent with respect to this situation, which has tended to rattle autocracies throughout history (Tullock 1987). It follows from our theoretical framework in Chapter 2 that the death of medieval monarchs represented a crisis for the political equilibrium, after which power arrangements had to be reconfigured and stabilized, even when downright civil war was avoided (see Chapter 5).

In this situation, power-sharing concessions provided a means for reestablishing the political equilibrium or at least reconfiguring power structures in a non-violent way. To be effective, such power-sharing concessions must 'rest on mutual advantage and respect the power of key participants' (Svolik 2012: 15).

While power-sharing can occur in many ways, the medieval power-sharing institution par excellence was the convocation of parliaments (Van Zanden et al. 2012; Blaydes and Chaney 2013; Boix 2015, 70–1; Stasavage 2016). In our empirical analyses in this chapter, parliamentary convocations therefore function as a proxy for the institutionalization of power-sharing arrangements, similarly to Boix and Svolik's (2013) use of legislatures and parties as measures of institutionalized power-sharing arrangements today (see also Svolik 2012; Ghandi and Przeworski 2006; 2007; Ghandi 2008).[2] However, to signal that we include more assemblies than some prior datasets (see the discussion of the data later), we generally use the term 'parliament-like assemblies' to describe our dependent variable.

The immediate political effects of succession

In theoretical terms, during successions elite groups can credibly threaten to rebel by siding with a rival would-be ruler. Successions are therefore likely to see the introduction or strengthening of power-sharing arrangements as rulers compete for support among members of elite groups. First, such institutions result in greater transparency in transactions between the monarch and the elite. The monarch can communicate his succession plan to the elite at the same time as he offers the elite a forum for approving the plan and coordinating their efforts to realize it, thus reducing the risk for potentially dangerous misunderstandings. Second, the monarch can publicly signal his commitment to the agreed succession plan.

We began the chapter with a well-known example of this, namely the political dynamics surrounding King Henry III's troubled succession after the death of his father, John Lackland, in 1216. Henry's supporters, headed by William Marshall, faced a difficult situation. King John had made himself unpopular among the English nobility and the English Church (as well as in the city of London) by losing wars, forfeiting his ancestral territories in Normandy and Anjou, taxing unlawfully to regain these provinces, fighting several civil wars against the English magnates, and of course by annulling Magna Carta a few months after he had granted it on Runnymede on 15 June 1215 (Bartlett 2000: 27–8). Only by securing support among the English clergy and the remaining magnates could Henry win the throne. This situation understandably

---

[2] See also Boix (2015: 70–1) who argues that medieval parliaments were power-sharing institutions.

required some form of power-sharing concessions to win over especially the magnates that Henry's father had fought against.

Yet, this example also indicates that some successions were more problematic than others. An obvious example of this was when the old monarch had been deposed or killed and the established succession process disrupted. In such circumstances, the succeeding monarch's claim to the throne was often tenuous. He could be a usurper, with little legitimacy among the remnants of the old regime. Even if he was the legitimate heir, he was in a precarious situation, as the groups that had ousted his predecessor had shown that they were able to overthrow a monarch and thus had to be appeased. We therefore expect such 'troubled successions' to have seen more frequent convocations of parliament-like assemblies than 'normal' successions.

Another, more peaceful example of a problematic succession was when the new king was too young to rule on his own and a regency (that is, a group of protectors appointed to rule while the king is underage) was needed. To quote Maddicott (2010: 148–9):

> By comparison with a king who was crowned and of age, even a properly constituted regency had only a slippery foothold on legitimacy. For this reason those governing for the young king had to look for support as widely as possible: to consult the magnates, to see general consent for their actions, and to use the customary machinery of great councils for both purposes.

These royal minorities—meaning that the king had not reached adulthood and was therefore a minor[3] or underage—occurred frequently in medieval and early modern Europe and they virtually always weakened royal power (e.g. Jordan 2001: 87–8; Maddicott 2010: 148–52; Greengrass 2014: 22) and led to rivalries and competition within the elite for influence over the child ruler (Bartlett 2020: 116). The need for control mechanisms is obvious in this situation because royal minorities meant that power had to be redistributed within the regime on a temporary basis. The most acute problem was to assure elites that the regency would hand over power to the child king once he reached adulthood (his 'majority' to use the technical term). Regents could always be suspected of intending to hold on to power, and even to do away

---

[3] Kings could come of age at different points in time, depending on local traditions and the personal character or maturity of monarchs (Bartlett 2020: 120–1). When Henry III's minority finally came to an end in January 1227, he was 19 years old. Alfonso XI of Spain and Louis XIV of France, both of whom we return to later, assumed full regal power at the tender age of 14 and 13, respectively. In our statistical analyses in this chapter, we use linear and squared functions of age to identify the effect of age.

with the young king, or to use their power to enrich themselves at the crown's expense—there are numerous historical examples that members of regencies were self-serving in this way (Bartlett 2020: 119–20). To mitigate these anxieties, the regency needed to consult with the nobility and high clergy on a regular basis. Assemblies provided a forum for this sort of coordination, which is why minorities are likely to have been particularly important for the convocation of power-sharing assemblies.

To illustrate this logic, we can return to Henry III's succession in 1216. As mentioned earlier, Henry was not only the son of an unpopular king (John Lackland), he was also a nine-year-old boy. During his minority, Henry's regency could only govern with consent from the magnates (Carpenter 1990: 54–63). To quote Maddicott (2010: 148) again:

> For the historian of parliament John's death and the accession of his nine-year-old son are important for one main reason: they brought in a ten-year period when magnate assemblies were especially prominent and when political demands were made on their behalf which were to surface again in Henry's majority.

Hypotheses

Two sets of expectations about the consequences of succession in our sample of monarchies follow from this discussion: 1) parliament-like institutions are more likely to be convened when a new monarch succeeds to the throne, especially when the old monarch has been deposed or killed; 2) parliament-like institutions are more likely to be convened during minorities (i.e. when monarchs are too young to govern on their own). These are the main hypotheses that we put to the test in this chapter.

Long-term political effects of succession

These hypotheses raise the question whether successions constitute inflection points where power-sharing arrangements consolidate? As mentioned earlier, both historians and social scientists have emphasized the long-term political effects of the Magna Carta for English constitutional development (e.g. Maddicott 2010; Fukuyama 2015). More specifically, many historians argue that Henry III's troubled ascension had lasting consequences. According to Carpenter (1999: 329), the developments following King John's death in 1216 marked a 'watershed in English politics'. Maddicott (2010: 148) refers to the minority as a period of 'proto-parliamentary government' and observes that '[i]n the eyes of at least some magnates, the effect of the minority was to put the great council at the heart of political decision-making, not by long-standing custom and royal volition, but *de jure*, by legal right' (152).

However, recent work by political scientists on power-sharing institutions indicates that successions (including minorities) are unlikely to have had such lasting effects on representative institutions in medieval and early modern monarchies. Boix and Svolik (2013: 300) argue that autocrats will only agree to power-sharing institutions when the elite can threaten to sanction a ruler who does not abide by the terms of the power-sharing agreement (see also Svolik 2012). This is of course the very reason that successions and minorities are likely to be moments of political concessions. But it also follows from this that agreed-upon institutions will lose their power when the balance of power swings back in favour of the ruler, undermining the credibility of the threat of rebellion.

Based on these arguments, successions in general and troubled successions in particular represent short-term shocks to the political equilibrium and once a new adult monarch consolidates his position, the power-sharing institutions established during the succession are unlikely to be perpetuated. The reason is, first and in general, that these institutions are endogenous to the balance of power between ruler and elites, second and more particularly, that they serve the purpose of solving coordination problems in the face of succession disputes (Svolik 2012). They are therefore no more stable than the temporary weakening of the monarchy during the period where succession becomes a salient political issue (Boix and Svolik 2013).

It also follows from these arguments that when a king who ascended the throne as an underage or minor reached adulthood and took over from his regency, there was little reason to perpetuate the power-sharing institutions that were needed until then. While the effects of minorities can be expected to last longer than those of a new monarch ascending the throne—sometimes, kings would be minors for a decade or more—they, too, are thus likely to disappear over time.

Several case illustrations can be used to bolster these reservations about the long-term impact of succession in medieval and early modern monarchies. For instance, in 1312, the one-year-old Alfonso XI ascended the throne of Castile, following the premature death of his father Fernando IV. To secure support for the infant king, Alfonso's regency called a large number of parliamentary assemblies (of the Castilian *cortes*). At the *cortes* of Palencia in 1313, the regency even promised *biennial* convocations and in fact near-annual convocations took place during Alfonso XI's long minority (1312–1325). Strikingly, this was followed by only three documented assemblies of the *cortes* during Alfonso's ensuing 25-years-long majority (1326–1350) (O'Callaghan 1989: 36).

Three hundred and fifty years later, King Louis XIV took note of and emphatically defended a similar political development. Louis spoke about the power of the French *Parlements*, which despite their name were not parliaments in our sense (in France, that role fell to the Estates General and Provincial Estates, see Stasavage (2010)) but courts of law. However, these courts of law had a veto on registering laws and the right to ask for revisions, meaning that many historians have seen them as a functional equivalent of genuine parliaments. From the position of strength of his majority, which had begun on 7 September 1651, two days after his thirteenth birthday, Louis noted that during his early reign the Parlements had been in 'possession and enjoyment of a usurped authority' and explained:

> The too great prominence of the Parlements had been a danger to the whole kingdom during my minority. It was necessary to humble them, less for the evil they had already done than for what they might do in the future. Their authority, in so far as people regarded it as being in opposition to mine, produced very mischievous effects, however good their intentions may have been, and thwarted all my greates and most useful measures.
> (Blanning 2007: 215–16)

However, there is also some reason to doubt that institutional concessions are as ephemeral as these two empirical illustrations seem to show, and as Boix and Svolik seem to suggest. Boix and Svolik's perspective clashes with the ubiquitous path-dependency models of political science, the premise of which are that, once introduced, institutions tend to be sticky or at least to change in a sluggish way (Mahoney 2000; Pierson 2000; Capoccia and Kelemen 2007). The most recent historical institutionalist literature argues that reality is likely to be situated somewhere in-between the scenario where institutions are endogenous to power relations and the scenario where they are sticky, come what may. As Kathleen Thelen has argued, path-dependency perspectives have tended to ignore that institutions are often altered in a piecemeal fashion: changing and fixed aspects of institutions interact so that change is calibrated or mitigated by the stable elements (see Mahoney and Thelen 2010).

Shifts in the balance of power that weakens the elite groups who forced through power-sharing concessions need not mean that these institutions are removed. Rulers will often prefer to alter institutions to suit their needs rather than do away with them. From a position of strength, they will attempt to reform the institutions which were created to constrain them to serve their interests. The result is a form of 'bounded change'—what Mahoney and Thelen (2010: 16) refers to as 'conversion' or 'the changed enactment of existing rules due to their strategic redeployment'—which goes a long way to explain why institutions are frequently perpetuated in autocracies (including medieval monarchies).

The key reason for this endogenous persistence via subtle changes is that power-sharing concessions tend to become rallying points for the elites that extracted them in the first place. By calling together the elites at power-sharing assemblies, the ruler de facto lowers the future costs of collective action for these elites. This means that only a direct showdown with elite groups will enable the autocrat to dismantle the new power-sharing arrangements. Even if rulers have the power to do this, it seems unlikely that it will be worth the bother, not least because they will often come to realize that power-sharing institutions can be used to facilitate at least some aspects of their power in a situation in which they are dealing with elite groups from a position of renewed strength. Rather than reneging on power-sharing concessions, rulers will attempt to mould the institutions in a way that better serves the exercise of power or simply to use the existing power-sharing arrangements in this way.

If nothing supervenes in this process, the result is that the ruler, though more hemmed in by institutions, may actually become more powerful in certain respects. A good way of understanding this point is via Mann's (1986) distinction between despotic power, which power-sharing institutions curb, and infrastructural power, which the same institutions might well augment, especially in the long run (see also Meng 2020). Empirically, this is reflected in a form of tacit or hidden change, which adapts institutions to a new context.

To illustrate this, we can once more return to Henry III's reign. Even after entering his majority, Henry repeatedly called assemblies to raise taxes to regain the territories that his father had forfeited in France (Maddicott 2010; Møller 2017: 191–4). Of course, this means that the political developments during his majority were confounded by warfare, which might explain why parliamentary activity stayed high. But the pattern was extremely robust, and Henry's successors, too, henceforth relied on parliament, which had struck roots in England in the century following Henry's troubled succession in 1216 (see Møller 2017).

In sum, it is theoretically difficult to predict the longer-term effects of successions on parliament-like institutions in our sample of monarchies: arguments for and against long-term institutional persistence can be deduced from the literature, based on our general theoretical framework. We therefore have no strong expectations but we will scrutinize the long-term relationship between monarchical succession and power-sharing institutions empirically.

Succession arrangements and parliament-like assemblies

One final theoretical aspect of the relationship between succession and representative institutions in medieval and early modern monarchies merits interest. We know from previous chapters that primogeniture[4] reduced the number of troubled successions (i.e. successions brought about by coups, assassinations, and deaths in civil war). Such successions usually weakened a new monarch's position, regardless of whether he had usurped the throne himself or had been given the throne by other, rebellious, forces. It therefore put pressure on him to bring about new power-sharing arrangements, and/or to formalize already existing power-sharing arrangements.

To bolster their own position, monarchs who succeeded peacefully also had to acquaint themselves with their elites and assure them of their status – but not to the same extent. Primogeniture is therefore likely to indirectly reduce the need for calling parliament-like assemblies during successions. There is also some reason to expect primogeniture to reduce the need to call parliaments during peaceful successions, as we know that monarchs in states practicing primogeniture sat safer on their thrones than their counterparts in elective monarchies and monarchies practicing agnatic seniority (see Chapter 6).

It is not that primogeniture removed all uncertainty about the succession. First, the principle tended to increase the frequency of minorities because sons would inherit even if they were underage, which as already mentioned is likely to have amplified the need for power-sharing concessions (see also Wang 2018). Second, early in the period we study in this book, primogeniture was often a vague principle that was open to interpretation. Could daughters inherit if the king did not have a living male heir? Could the throne be inherited by a male in the female line? What happened if the eldest son of the king

---

[4] As argued in Chapter 2, the same applies to partible inheritance when practiced in an ordered manner, as it came to be in Europe in the period we analyse. It is for this reason that we have merged the two categories in our empirical analysis in this chapter. Because the merged category of primogeniture and partible inheritance in reality consists of 90 per cent primogeniture monarch-years, we simply refer to primogeniture when interpreting the results (all reported results are robust to using a specification that only counts undisputable primogeniture monarch-years).

predeceased his father but left a living son? Did the king's second eldest son or the deceased son's eldest son inherit in such circumstances?

Questions such as these were legion, and they caused numerous succession disputes in countries where the eldest son normally inherited his father's throne. The tumultuous start of Henry III's minority in 1216 is again illustrative. The widespread opposition against John Lackland's son inheriting the throne owed not only to Henry's tender age and John's misrule, but also to the fact that the deceased king's own claim to the throne had been tenuous, as his nephew, the underage Arthur of Brittany (son of John's late older brother Geoffrey), should have inherited the throne in 1199 based on primogeniture. As mentioned in a previous chapter, John was able to sideline and later defeat and murder Arthur but this 'wicked uncle' behaviour clearly weakened his legitimacy in the eyes of many contemporaries (Bartlett 2000: 25–6; 2020: 211–14), as well as the downstream legitimacy of Henry's claim in 1216. These events show that the rules of succession were still vague and, as related earlier, even the French pretender, Louis, was able to put forward an inheritance-based claim on the English throne upon John's death in 1216 (Bartlett 2020: 23).[5]

It follows from our description of medieval power relations that such ambiguity was likely to create a perilous situation both for the ruler and for elite groups who would prefer stability to a dangerous succession struggle that might dispossess the losing side. The ruler, on the one hand, and the nobility and other members of the elite, on the other hand, therefore had a mutual interest in diminishing the ambiguity of extant succession rules. The principle of primogeniture consequently became more detailed and unambiguous over time as it was amended to deal with the circumstances that had given rise to succession disputes in the past. Some observers point to the thirteenth century as a period when the details of primogeniture were chiselled out in more detail (e.g. Bertocchi 2006; see also Broms and Kokkonen 2019). During this period,

---

[5] Partible inheritance was also often open to interpretation early in the period (though not to the same extent as under the Merovingians and Carolingians, where it was practiced in a chaotic way). What happened if a son who was designated to inherit a certain part of the realm died? Did the next son in line take over his lands while passing his own intended lands to a younger brother? Or did he take over his older brother's lands while retaining his own? And what happened when a new son—possibly a 'late lamb'—was born and the plans for the partition suddenly had to be altered? The former issue was what Henry II and his son Richard fell out over when Richard's older brother Henry the Young King died in 1183. Richard, who had been the second eldest son of Henry and heir to the Duchy of Aquitaine (the matrimony), now suddenly found himself the eldest surviving son and heir to the English throne and Normandy (the patrimony). In return for his new status, his father wanted Richard to concede Aquitaine to his younger brother John (Lackland) and refused to acknowledge his claims to England and Normandy if he did not make this concession. However, Richard, having been duke of Aquitaine for several years, felt Aquitaine was his and refused to concede it. Father and eldest son spent the remainder of Henry's life in conflict (Bartlett 2000).

the principle of primogeniture was codified in a series of landmark succession laws, such as the Norwegian Law of Succession of 1260 and the Siete Partidas that was compiled during the reign of Alfonso X of Castile.

This development increasingly made parliaments powerless against rightful claimants, as they could not deny them their lawful right. Hence, there was little reason for lawful heirs to call parliaments to strengthen their claim when succession rules had become less vague in primogeniture monarchies. If our argument that primogeniture mitigates the relationship between succession and power-sharing is correct, we should therefore expect to see a further weakening of the association between successions and the convocation of parliament-like institutions over time in monarchies practicing primogeniture.

However, disputes over the interpretation of primogeniture persisted, or popped up due to unforeseen circumstances, in many monarchies long after the thirteenth century. To illustrate this, we can turn to the twist and turns of English King Henry VIII's succession policy. Henry negotiated with parliament to issue no less than three consecutive Succession Acts during his reign, as he changed his mind about his preferred heirs (Ives 2008). The First Succession Act of 1533 (passed by Parliament in 1534) declared his oldest daughter Mary illegitimate and made the yet unborn Elizabeth heir. The Second Succession Act of 1536 removed Elizabeth from the line of succession on the ground of illegitimacy, whereas the Third Succession Act of 1543 reinstated the sisters in the line of succession behind their brother Edward. One of the first acts of Henry's successor Edward VI (or rather of his regency) was to have parliament issue the Treason Act of 1547, which made it high treason to break the line of succession stipulated in the Third Succession Act. Other famous examples include the Pragmatic sanction of 1713, which was issued to ensure the succession of one of Emperor Charles VI's daughters to the Habsburg hereditary lands, and the negotiations after the death of the childless Charles XII of Sweden that ensured the succession of his sister Ulrika Eleonora.

Hypothesis

In summary, we expect a weakening of the association between successions and parliamentary activity over time in medieval and early modern monarchies practicing primogeniture; but we do not expect the need to call parliament-like assemblies during successions to go away entirely in such states.

Successions and parliament-like institutions: the empirics

The emergence of parliament-like institutions is shrouded in the mists of history. In medieval Europe, gatherings of nobles and prelates probably took place long before we have reliable records of them. For example, in the Frankish realm leading nobles gathered regularly with their men to campaign at the king's request, at so-called *Heerbanns*. It is likely that the king took advice from—and negotiated with—his nobles on such occasions. This kind of advice and negotiations also occurred in what later became the Holy Roman Empire at diets (often called *Hoftage*, as the nobles usually gathered at the emperor's court) long before the turn of the first millennium. In northern and eastern Europe similar gatherings primarily seem to have taken place at a local level (as for example the Norse *things* and the Slavic *veche*), at roughly the same time.

Wickham (2005; 2009: 101–5; see also Stasavage 2020) refers to this as an assembly model of politics where the freeborn would gather at regular public meetings. Assembly politics has deep historical roots, going back to the breakdown of the Western Roman Empire in the fifth century. In the early Middle Ages, we thus find assemblies—often known in the Latin sources as *placitum* (plural *placita*)—all over Western and Central Europe. Over time, assemblies started to become more institutionalized at the level of the realm. It is difficult to draw a clear distinction between more informal gatherings, such as the above-mentioned *Hoftage* and *Heerbanns*, and the more institutionalized parliaments that appeared later, and it is not certain that contemporaries would see clear breaks where we see them today (Møller 2017)—just as the first generations of townsmen practicing urban self-government probably did not clearly realize the difference (Wickham 2015).

The development of representative institutions was thus a gradual process and attesting when an assembly turns into a representative institution, normally defined by townsmen attending as representatives of town councils, is very difficult (Procter 1980: 1; O'Callaghan 1989; Møller 2017). We are mainly interested, first, in power-sharing institutions regardless of which groups they included and which formal powers they had (many of the earlier assemblies did not have formal written rules) and, second, in the frequency with which they met once they had been adopted/invented, not why they were adopted/invented in the first case.

To deal with the first issue we have chosen an inclusive definition that also denotes what Marongiu (1968) terms 'pre-parliaments': assemblies where townsmen either did not participate or, if they did, were not called as genuine representatives. We thus register assemblies insofar as they were realm-based in character and included substantial parts of the elite (i.e. nobles and prelates). With respect to the second issue, we code polities from the first year we have been able to identify such an assembly. Polities varied in how fast they adopted assemblies, but the quality of sources also varies between countries, particularly early in the period. Statistics up until the thirteenth century should therefore be taken with some caution, as they only build on a few countries and scarce historical sources.

We have coded or enlisted existing data on parliament-like assemblies for the 26 polities in our sample that adopted such institutions (the only state that did not was the Byzantine Empire). Figure 7.1 describes the frequency of assemblies for the polities in our sample that at some time adopted such assemblies.

The figure shows that the few countries that adopted parliament-like assemblies in the eleventh and twelfth centuries had relatively high meeting frequencies right from the start. The eleventh-century sample primarily builds on data from the Holy Roman Empire and is thus difficult to compare to the rest of the data. The dip in meeting frequency in the thirteenth century cannot be ascribed to a dip in meeting frequency in those countries which already had

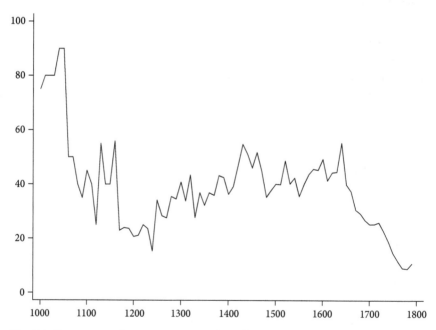

Fig. 7.1 Percentage of country-years with parliamentary meetings over time

parliament-like assemblies at the beginning of the century, but rather to the fact that new polities—with lower meeting frequencies—adopted parliament-like assemblies during this century. From the mid-thirteenth century onwards, we see a gradual increase in meeting frequency in most countries up until the seventeenth century, when the frequency drops drastically in most countries.

These aggregate trends are neither obviously correlated with aggregate trends in the frequency of successions in general nor with aggregate trends in the frequency of successions caused by natural monarch deaths. Likewise, aggregate patterns of minorities (here defined as monarchs who were younger than 16 years old) do not track aggregate trends in parliament-like assemblies, at least not judging by Figure 7.2. The spikes in minorities in the eleventh and twelfth centuries are due to the low number of countries in the sample, which gives more weight to individual minorities.

But Figure 7.2 clearly documents that minorities were a common feature in medieval and early modern European monarchies. During several periods, around 20 per cent of the sample is characterized by polities ruled by underage monarchs. Royal minorities and the associated regencies were thus a recurrent aspect of the power-relations in Europe in the period we analyse. Add to this

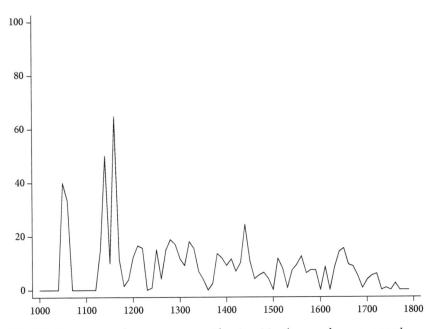

Fig. 7.2 Percentage of country-years with minorities (years when a monarch was under age 16) over time

Table 7.1 Percentage of country-years with parliamentary meetings

	No minority	Minority
No natural succession	35	43
Natural succession	47	58

that we are dealing with an era where mortality rates were high, even for men in their prime, and it is clear that successions and minorities were important aspects of power-relations of these states. Did this matter for the convocation of parliament-like assemblies in our sample of monarchies? To what extent do we find successions and minorities to be occasions of power-sharing concessions, as we have hypothesized?

Our data strongly support the expectation that successions and minorities affected power-sharing arrangements. Table 7.1 compares the frequency of parliamentary assemblies in years in which natural successions took place (i.e. successions which were caused by natural monarch deaths) with years without natural successions, as well as years in which monarchs were too young to rule on their own with years when they were old enough to do so.

The table shows that years with natural successions saw about 12 percentage points more parliament-like meetings than years without natural successions when monarchs were adults. We can also see that non-successions years in which monarchs were too young to rule on their own saw about 8 percentage points more parliament-like meetings than non-succession years when monarchs were old enough to rule on their own. Finally, the highest meeting frequencies are found in succession years where an underage monarch ascended the throne.

This supports our argument that both successions and minorities placed monarchs in a relatively weak position where they needed to consult their elites and often give them power-sharing concessions. Another piece of evidence supporting our theoretical arguments about the destabilizing character of succession is that years with successions caused by coups, assassinations, and deaths in civil war saw even higher rates of parliament-like assemblies (about 25 percentage points higher than normal years). This indicates that troubled successions increased parliamentary activity. Considering that parliament-like assemblies met in about a third of the years without natural successions when monarchs had come of age, the observed differences are substantial, though not overwhelming.

Regression analysis

These patterns can of course be confounded by other factors. We therefore next explore the effect of successions (in general), natural successions, and minorities in a regression framework. In addition to our main variables (successions, natural successions, age, and age squared), the models also include controls for country size, mountainous terrain, and time trends (year and year squared). The controls for country size and mountainous terrain account for the fact that previous research has shown that geographical factors affect parliamentary activity in the period we study (Stasavage 2010; 2016). In addition, the models include a variable that measures the number of years that have elapsed since the last time there was a parliamentary meeting in the country (and a square function of the same variable) to account for trends in parliamentary activity.[6]

We perform our analyses using the monarch-year structure of the data, where the outcome of interest is whether a parliament met in any given year. We use linear probability models, estimated with OLS regression, controlling for the factors outlined earlier, as well as country fixed effects. Standard errors are clustered at the country level.

Figures 7.3 and 7.4 show how successions and natural successions, respectively, affected the likelihood that parliament-like institutions met. The figures show parliamentary activity in years where successions took place, as well as in years leading up to, and following, successions, compared to years in which successions did not take place.

Figure 7.3 shows that parliament-like institutions were 17 percentage points more likely to meet in years with successions (regardless of how successions were brought about) than in years without successions, whereas Figure 7.4 shows that parliament-like institutions were 13 percentage points more likely to meet in years with natural successions than in years without natural successions. Hence, there is empirical support for both our expectation that successions increased parliamentary activity and that troubled successions increased it more than smooth successions.

Years following both ordinary and natural successions saw about 10 percentage points more parliamentary-like meetings than other years without successions. The lagged effect probably reflects that parliament-like meetings

---

[6] In contrast to our models in Chapters 5 and 6 we do not include a control for monarchs' tenures, as the lags of the natural succession variables that we include in our models in this chapter are to a large extent co-linear with monarchs' tenures. We also use time trends (year and year squared), instead of century fixed effects, to get a smoother function of time.

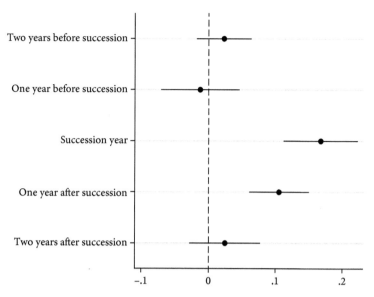

Fig. 7.3 Successions and the likelihood that parliament-like institutions met

Note: The figure shows the effect of succession years, and lags and leads of such years, on parliamentary activity with 95 per cent confidence intervals.

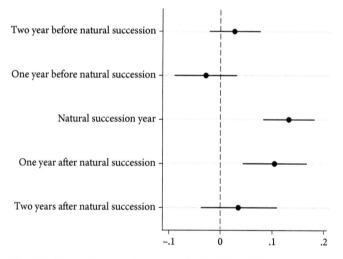

Fig. 7.4 Natural successions and the likelihood that parliament-like institutions met

Note: The figure shows the effect of natural succession years, and lags and leads of such years, on parliamentary activity with 95 per cent confidence intervals.

took time to organize—especially in large realms where distance slowed communication and travel (Stasavage 2010)—and hence sometimes spilled over to the year after the succession and/or that monarchs and elites on some occasions needed more than one meeting to come to terms. However, after two years parliamentary activity was back to normal both following successions in general and natural successions.

There is no sign of increased parliamentary activity preceding successions in general or natural successions, which assures us that the increased activity in the wake of both types of successions reflects a succession effect and not other factors.

Figure 7.5 shows that monarchs' age also mattered for parliamentary activity. Parliament-like institutions met almost every second year when a monarch was an infant (more often if the pure succession effect is considered). Activity then decreased until it stabilized shortly after the monarch had turned 20 and thenceforth parliament only met every third year. There is no indication that the effect of minorities lingered on in the long run. When the monarch was old enough to rule on his own, parliamentary activity went back to normal.

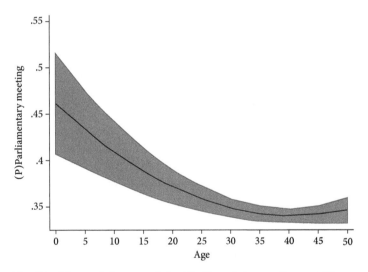

Fig. 7.5 Monarchs' ages and the likelihood that parliament-like institutions met

Note: The figure shows the probability of parliamentary activity over monarch ages with 95 per cent confidence intervals.

Institutional persistence?

Our data thus clearly confirm our main expectation: that succession had immediate effects on power-sharing in the form of convocations of parliament-like institutions in our sample of monarchies. Minorities and succession appear in the data as politically unstable periods, where rulers had to chain themselves to power-sharing arrangements that were unnecessary in 'normal' years. What can we say about the long-term consequences of the politics of succession in medieval and early modern monarchies? On the one hand, the immediate effect of successions and minorities disappears rather quickly. This can be taken to support Boix and Svolik's (2013) notion that power-sharing concessions become less important when the balance of power swings back in the monarch's favour—for instance when monarchs come of age and take over from their regencies.

On the other hand, parliament-like institutions obviously had staying power in Western and Central Europe. If succession affected some of the crucial developments of representative institutions, then we might see it as creating precedents that would have downstream importance, especially during future succession crises. Much supports this interpretation. We have already mentioned the circumstances which made Magna Carta a political rallying point for English elites, and which are clearly related to Henry III's tumultuous minority. Another example comes from the Crown of Aragon, where we find the first documented convocation of a genuine representative institution at Lérida in August 1214 (see Møller 2018). This assembly was called to sort out the succession after count-king Peter II had been killed at the battle of Muret in September 1213. His eldest son, later known as James the Conqueror, was only five years old (and in the enemy's custody), and the assembly at Lérida was called to get clergy, nobles, and townsmen from the kingdom of Aragon and the duchy of Catalonia to recognize James's claim to the throne. This would have long-term consequences as genuine representative institutions became a fixed part of the body politics of the Crown of Aragon during the thirteenth century (Møller 2017). Much the same happened at approximately the same time in England, where parliament developed into a permanent political institution under Edward I, the son of Henry III (Møller 2017; Stasavage 2020: Chapter 5).

The logic often seems to have been one of two steps forward, one step back. In other words, the concessions given during troubled successions and minorities were partially withdrawn when monarchs had consolidated their position. But the monarchs tried to alter the rules of the game on the new playing field, rather than switch playing field completely. So, instead of ridding themselves of earlier power-sharing arrangements, they would try to finesse these to better suit their interests. The next time a troubled succession occurred, previous concessions would matter because they had become a focal point—in an age where precedent conferred legitimacy in a way that is difficult to fathom today—for elite groups.

If we return to the Crown of Aragon, we find a good illustration of these dynamics in the decades following the death in July 1276—after a reign spanning more than 60 years—of the above-mentioned count-king James the Conqueror (see also Møller and Doucette 2022: 163-74). The next 15 years saw no less than three ascensions: first by James's son Peter III (1276–1285), then by two of Peter's sons, Alphonso III (1285–1291) and James II (1291–1327). This period was confounded by warfare, just as Henry III's majority. But we nonetheless find an interesting development, which seems to be associated with the frequent successions. In this period, all three kings had to commit themselves to very strict power-sharing arrangements, including charters of rights and fixed convocations of the representative institutions of the Aragonese and Valencian *cortes* and the Catalan *corts* (annually, biennially, or triennially) (see Kagay 1981). After James II had consolidated his position, he continued to observe most of these concessions, but he gradually learned how to use the power-sharing arrangement to project public power rather than to be neutered by them (Kagay 1997: 32).

In that sense, successions probably mattered for the long-term institutional trajectory, which made monarchs in the Latin west depend increasingly on representative institutions, at least up until the sixteenth-century military revolution (Downing 1992; Parker 1996). But the point remains that successions were most important as short-term political destabilizers, which required power-sharing arrangements to smooth over the transfer of power.

Succession arrangements, successions, and parliamentary-like activity

We finally turn to our last theoretical expectation, which concerns the way primogeniture moderated the relationship between succession and power-sharing. Figure 7.6 shows that, as expected, successions in general—including depositions—increased parliamentary activity less in monarchies practicing primogeniture than in elective monarchies.

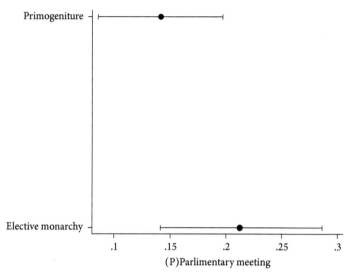

Fig. 7.6 Succession arrangements, successions, and parliamentary activity

Note: The figure shows the effect of succession years on parliamentary activity with 95 per cent confidence intervals.

In the latter set of polities, successions increased the likelihood that parliaments met with 22 percentage points, whereas successions only increased them with 14 percentage points in the former. In contrast, there is no evidence that primogeniture reduced the need to call parliaments to handle natural successions (the interaction between the two is not even close to being significant).

One plausible interpretation of these results is that successions (in general) in elective monarchies saw more parliamentary activity because they were more troubled than successions in monarchies practicing primogeniture and that monarchs therefore had a greater need to co-opt elites in the former countries. Hence, primogeniture indirectly reduced the need to call parliaments in the wake of successions because the principle reduced the risk that monarchs were deposed by domestic enemies. Peaceful successions saw similar levels of parliamentary activity, even though monarchs in elective monarchies were more likely to be deposed than their counterparts in states practicing primogeniture.

Can we also see a weakening of the association between successions and parliamentary activity over time in states practicing primogeniture, as the principle (presumably) became more chiselled out and less open to different

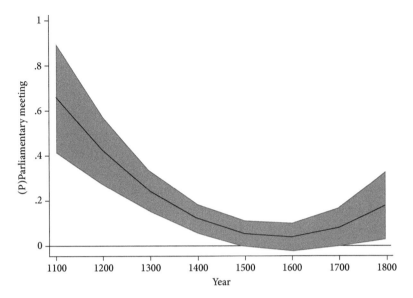

Fig. 7.7 Natural successions and parliamentary activity over time

Note: The figure shows the effect of natural succession years on parliamentary activity over time in states practicing primogeniture with 95 per cent confidence intervals.

interpretations? Figure 7.7 reports the effect of natural successions between AD 1100 and AD 1800 in states practicing primogeniture (the approximate period for which we have evidence of parliamentary activity in these kinds of states).

The figure shows that the effect of natural successions diminished over time and ceased to be significant around AD 1500 (even though it increases somewhat again at the end of the period). This indicates that as primogeniture became less susceptible to rival interpretations, it mitigated the need to call parliamentary assemblies to oil the wheels of succession.

There is no evidence of a similar development in elective monarchies over time. If anything, there is a tendency towards increasing parliamentary activity in natural succession years, perhaps because monarch elections increasingly took place in parliament-like assemblies and not in the popular assemblies preceding them. However, this tendency is not statistically significant so we should be careful about reading too much into it.

Conclusion

Our analysis sheds new light on the political consequences of succession in medieval and early modern monarchies. In the fragmented power context of late medieval Europe, rulers needed power-sharing institutions to facilitate bargaining and coordination with elite groups. We have argued that parliament-like assemblies were more likely to be called in the immediate aftermath of a new monarch ascending to the throne, especially following troubled successions and when monarchs were too young to govern on their own. However, it is less clear whether successions in general and succession disputes in particular are expected to have had lasting effects on political institutions.

The immediate effect of succession and minorities was confirmed in all analyses. While there is little direct evidence of long-term effects of either successions or minorities, we have argued that the institutional concessions granted during moments of succession are likely to have created precedents that would become focal points during future moments of weakness for monarchs, including future successions. We also showed that successions in general saw fewer parliamentary-like meetings in monarchies practicing primogeniture than in elective monarchies, and that this pattern can be explained by the fact that the former saw fewer troubled successions than the latter. In addition, the effect of successions also decreased over time in monarchies practicing primogeniture, presumably because the principle became more refined, and less prone to different interpretations which would need to be settled in parliament.

In the longer term, primogeniture therefore strengthened the hand of monarchs and decreased their reliance on formalized power-sharing arrangements. England again provides a stirring example. We described in Chapter 4 how in 1272 Henry III's son Edward I, away on crusade, did not even bother to go straight home to England upon his father's death but postponed his crowning for two years, without this causing any political instability of note in England. It is hard to imagine a bigger difference to the troubled circumstances that faced Henry (or rather his protectors) 56 years earlier, and with which we began this chapter.

However, there are some important nuances here. As pointed out in the empirical analysis, it was during the reign of Edward I that the English Parliament first became a permanent political institution. This probably reflects that, as we argued in the theoretical section, English kings came to realize that the institutions that were created to constrain their power could be used to augment it, especially in the long run. In the European context where power constantly begat countervailing power, primogeniture might here have struck a golden balance, at least seen from the perspective of state-building. The English case is a perfect example of this: the representative institutions that were often called during succession conflicts survived, even when the hand of monarchs was strengthened, and they ultimately aided the building of the English territorial state because they allowed English kings to project power, even at the local level. This happened precisely because English rulers were strong enough to harness these institutions to royal power (Boucoyannis 2015; Stasavage 2020: Chapter 9). The same development can be observed in the composite primogeniture monarchy of the Crown of Aragon, as described earlier. Where rulers had a weaker hand vis-à-vis representative institutions, as in the elective monarchies of Hungary and Poland, they instead became the hostages or even stooges of parliament; where they were too powerful for their good, they got rid of parliamentary constraints altogether, as in early modern Prussia.

8
Family and Dynasty

An old Bedouin proverb goes, 'Me against my brother, my brother and I against my cousin, and all of us against the stranger.' Though the saying is rather bleak, suggesting ever-present conflict, even of brother against brother, it is very different from Thomas Hobbes's 'war of all against all'. There are different circles of loyalty: each person is closest to him—or herself, but closer to relatives than to strangers.

In the previous chapters, we have argued that hereditary succession in the form of primogeniture is conducive to political stability. An important reason is its predictability, which enables elite coordination. But we cannot disregard the fact that primogeniture also ties the succession to descendants of the monarch, to the family. When hereditary succession works, it creates dynasties.

That is, of course, if the vagaries of nature allow it. In a world of dynastic politics where even high office was a family affair, biology mattered much more for political life than it does today (Bartlett 2020). King Henry VIII in 1509 inherited the throne of England as the son of a rebel, Henry Tudor, who had taken power on the field of battle (Bosworth) where his predecessor Richard III had been slain. Henry VIII was thus only the second monarch of the Tudor dynasty and was not even meant to inherit in the first place. His older brother Arthur had been groomed for succession but died at 16 before he could take the throne. In Hilary Mantel's award-winning novel about the era, *Wolf Hall*, one of the king's most powerful supporters describes the situation as follows:

> The old king bred, and by the help of Heaven he bred sons. But when Arthur died, there were swords sharpened in Europe, and they were sharpened to carve up this kingdom. Henry that is now, he was a child, nine years old. If the old king had not staggered on a few more years, the wars would have been to fight all over again. A child cannot hold England.
>
> (Mantel 2009: 210).

The dialogue is invented, but the situation it describes is not. As an adult, Henry was acutely aware of the need to produce heirs to give both allies and enemies a guarantee of stability and continuity. However, his marriage to Catherine of Aragon only resulted in miscarriages and sickly babies that died shortly after birth, except for one daughter, Mary. Blaming Catherine for their misfortunes, Henry sought a divorce and when the Pope refused to grant him one, he broke with the Catholic Church. Then followed a succession of queens, more miscarriages, and only one son that survived infancy, Edward.

Edward eventually succeeded Henry, but just as his uncle Arthur, the young king died at 16, leading to a disputed succession which saw Mary, Henry VIII's oldest daughter, elevated to the throne. When she died without children, the throne passed to her half-sister Elizabeth. Elizabeth unusually refused to marry, much to the dismay of the English Parliament, whose leadership continuously implored her to find a husband and ensure the succession. When Elizabeth died after a very long reign, the Tudor dynasty, haunted by the spectre of succession from beginning to end, came to a close.

If Henry, Mary, or Elizabeth had had more children, the Tudor dynasty would surely have been more secure and entrenched. But, as illustrated by the Bedouin proverb earlier, kinship is no guarantee against strife. It is not hard to think of examples from European royal families of brothers fighting brothers, sons fighting their fathers, or nephews fighting their uncles (see Bartlett 2020: 109-10).

As we discussed in Chapter 6, a monarch's most trusted supporters also represent the biggest threat against his position. No one is better placed to take power than another member of the royal family, who will often control men-of-arms and other resources, have an ancillary hereditary claim on power, and know more about the ways of the ruler than outsiders. However, primogeniture alleviates this by passing on power to the monarch's children in a clearly delineated order, thus reducing the risk of conflicts between them.[1]

Dynasty also matters for relationships in time, between a ruler and his predecessors, as well as his descendants. Monarchs of established dynasties saw themselves as caretakers of a heritage, stretching back in time (Bartlett 2020: 285). Individual members of the dynasty normally cooperated in aggrandizing the family name. Writing about what is perhaps the most famous royal dynasty

---

[1] As argued in Chapter 2, the same applies to partible inheritance when practiced in an ordered manner, as it came to be in Europe in the period we analyse. It is for this reason that we have merged the two categories in most of our empirical analysis in this chapter. The exception to this rule is the models that focus on how the introduction of primogeniture affected states' ability to grow territorially, where we separate between periods in which primogeniture and partible inheritance were practiced as the two principles differ in how they allocate the inheritance between sons.

of them all, the Habsburgs, Andrew Wheatcroft said that each member of the family embodied the essence of the 'House of Austria',[2] transmitting it to future generations, regardless of present fortunes (1995: 49). Solidarity with the lineage meant that monarchs had greater incentive to build up the strength of the kingdom, to leave a bigger inheritance.

In contrast, the world of the agnatic seniority succession orders of the Polish Piasts and Rus Rurikids was one characterized by political instability, in which relatives constantly fought each other over slices of the royal domain (Dvornik 1962; Davies 2005: 60; Stokes 1970; Kollman 1990). Similar patterns were evident in the elective monarchies of Scandinavia, especially in the high Middle Ages where even monarchs often lost their lives in family infights (Bartlett 2020: 246). So did other family members. For example, all three sons who survived the Swedish king Magnus III (r. 1275–1290) were killed in conflicts with each other (and each other's supporters), leaving the throne to Magnus's three-year-old grandchild (Schück 2003).

In this chapter, we use our dataset to show that monarchies practicing primogeniture generally produced longer-lasting dynasties than monarchies that practiced agnatic seniority or election. We also show that individual monarchs with larger families—more children, siblings, and paternal uncles and aunts—were less likely to be deposed, irrespective of the succession order. The results demonstrate the importance of family, and how primogeniture helped create political stability by uniting dynasties towards a common goal, thereby prolonging their hold on power. Finally, we show that the switch from partible inheritance to primogeniture is associated with an increase in state size, which can probably be explained by the fact primogeniture leaves the inheritance intact to the eldest son whereas partible inheritance splits it between the monarch's surviving sons.

Why trust kin?

Throughout this book, we have described how, as all other autocratic rulers, medieval and early modern monarchs needed the support of individuals and groups who could back them with force and influence. The key to controlling these elite groups is the sharing of power and spoils (Bueno de Mesquita et al. 2005; Svolik 2012; Boix and Svolik 2013). But we can also think of the

---

[2] One senses this dynastic self-consciousness in the Habsburg's famous motto: *Austria Est Imperare Orbi Universo/Alles Erdreich ist Österreich untertan* ('the whole world is subject to Austria').

relationship as a problem of delegation. How can the ruler be sure that his entrusted agents act in his best interests? One way is to monitor their behaviour, and a large surveillance apparatus is therefore an integral part of any modern authoritarian state. The medieval and early modern monarchs we focus on also employed informants and spies, but the amount and quality of information that could be gathered was of course not on par with what modern rulers can obtain.

However, if the principal chooses an agent with the same preferences as the principal direct monitoring or detailed instruction become less important. One of the central results from the delegation literature is therefore that the principal is wise to follow the *ally principle*—that is, that the principal picks the ideologically closest agent (Bendor, Glazer, and Hammond 2001; Huber and Shipan 2006). The problem is to identify these allies; individuals who can be expected to work in the interests of the autocrat, without having to constantly be threatened to do so.

This is where relatives come in. There are several reasons why it makes sense for authoritarian leaders to trust their family more than non-relatives. First, there are biological reasons. A large body of observational and experimental evidence confirms that humans behave more altruistically towards close kin than towards distant kin and strangers (Essock-Vitale and McGuire 1985; Daly and Wilson 1988; Madsen et al. 2007; Henrich 2020). Genes that encourage altruism towards close genetic relatives have a higher likelihood of surviving and will therefore have an evolutionary advantage. Humans are simply evolutionarily hardwired to care for their relatives. Even though there might be reason to suspect that people act abnormally in the cutthroat world of authoritarian politics and power struggles, studies show that near relatives are less likely than strangers and more distant relatives to kill each other over political office and also less likely to break up political alliances (e.g. Johnson and Johnson 1991; Dunbar et al. 1995).

Second, there are social reasons for trusting relatives. Apart from the innate biological factors that predispose us to help close relatives, being related means that you are more likely to have grown up together, thus forming strong social ties (Blau 1977; Verbrugge 1977; 1983). As mentioned in Chapter 6, fourteenth-century Arab historian and sociologist Ibn Khaldun based a whole political theory on tribal solidarity and cohesion, having lived for years among desert tribes in Northern Africa. But he did not ascribe kinship any innate properties; it mattered because it helped to foster contact:

> The consequences of (common) descent, though natural, still are something imaginary. The real thing to bring about the feeling of close contact is social intercourse, friendly association, long familiarity, and the companionship that results from growing up together, having the same wet nurse, and sharing the other circumstances of death and life. If close contact is established in such a manner, the result will be affection and cooperation. Observation of people shows this to be so.
>
> (Ibn Khaldun 1958[1377]: section 18)

A ruler could rely on his clan for help and support and use them as soldiers and officials. However, over time, growing accustomed to the spoils of ruling, the group solidarity of the ruling tribe would wane, and they would eventually be deposed by another clan with stronger group solidary, according to Ibn Khaldun. Due to modern genetics, we now know that the consequences of descent are not entirely imaginary. But the social contact mechanisms identified by Ibn Khaldun are still relevant.

In the influential selectorate model by Bruce Bueno de Mesquita and colleagues (Bueno de Mesquita et al. 2005), the most important factor determining the loyalty of the ruler's support coalition is the size of spoils. But the model also incorporates affinity, an unspecified like or dislike between the ruler and supporter that potentially stems from several different factors (including family ties). However, neither the ruler nor the supporter can be sure of the level of mutual affinity before they have had a chance to interact. Affinity is revealed over time, allowing the ruler to select supporters with the greatest affinity. If we apply the same intuition to our case, we can see that even if there is no guarantee that all relatives will be well disposed towards the ruler, he will be better able to identify those who are in a group of relatives than in a group of strangers.

Third, there are external reasons for trusting family, stemming from how the leader and his family are viewed by others. Blood relations can be important simply because others believe them to matter. Given the widespread view that families care for each other, that 'blood is thicker than water,' people will generally assume that the ruler's relatives will support him. This is especially true when they are positioned in the line of succession and can function as potential rallying points for the ruler's supporters in the case that he dies or is imprisoned. When a ruler is deposed, the successful challenger will try to eliminate all possible threats to the new regime, and relatives of the old ruler are high on the list (cf. Palmstierna et al. 2017). According to Niccoló Machiavelli, only two things are necessary for rulers who have taken over a new principality and wish to hold it: leave taxes and laws unaltered and extinguish the family of the former prince (Machiavelli 1988[1532]: 24).

Regardless of whether there is any real affection between the ruler and his relatives, their destiny is simply tied together. They will hang together, or hang alone, in the words of Benjamin Franklin's famous one-liner. Dynastic solidarity thus becomes a self-reinforcing institution (cf. Greif 2006). It is in the interest of all members of the dynasty to advance it, even if for selfish reasons.

Functions performed by family

These general reasons are likely to have applied throughout history. But as indicated earlier, they have often been weakened or even offset by competition among relatives in political systems where there are no clear mechanisms for elevating one family member at the expense of others, illustrated by blurred lines of legitimacy. Not so in the European context that we analyse in this book; or at least much less so than in early medieval times or in many regions beyond Europe (see Chapter 9). As described in Chapter 4, after AD 1000 the European setting came to be characterized by nuclear families based on the monogamous marriage, illegitimacy of children from liaisons, and eldest-son-takes-the-patrimony inheritance rules. Against this backdrop, we proceed by detailing the more specific functions that family members played in medieval and early modern European monarchies.

The most important function in which relatives (especially offspring) played a part was of course the succession. In Chapter 2, we discussed why sons are better suited as designated heirs than other relatives or strangers; we will not repeat those arguments here. But to designate a son as crown prince, a ruler of course needed to have at least one son, and in a world of high mortality levels preferably more as backups—'an heir and a spare' in the words of Bartlett (2020: 71). A large pool of children, especially male, creates stability in the line of succession, insofar as the principle that determines their order is clear. The existence of multiple children and siblings, who, in turn, could have offspring of their own, also meant that a rival could not dislodge the dynasty from power by assassinating the monarch, as the crown would simply pass on to one of his relatives who would have an ancillary claim to the throne. In such cases, a full-scale coup would be necessary, whereas the assassination of a monarch without heirs would open the way for rival claimants. Using a modern term, the existence of a large family means that it is not a 'one-bullet' regime (Herb 1999: 237).

Trusted agents

In a world without efficient communications, geographical distance made it difficult to project power and to monitor the behaviour of agents (Stasavage 2010). The lack of impersonal bureaucracies also increased the importance of interpersonal ties between the ruler and elite groups, especially after the spectacular collapse of public authority in the ninth and tenth centuries. In this situation, the personal presence of the monarch was often required to bolster his power (Bartlett 2000: 13). Medieval and early modern monarchs spent a lot of their time travelling around the realm, making sure to be seen and maintaining relationships. It was an age of 'lordship on the march' (Bartlett 2000: 143).[3] However, rulers also often used members of the immediate and extended family as representatives (governors, viceroys, commanders, ambassadors, etc.), as they could be trusted more than others and could be believed to speak with the authority of the ruler. Illustrating this reasoning, Habsburg emperor Charles V in 1549 directly instructed his son, the future Philip II, that it was 'his duty to sire offspring who would be a ready supply of royal governors and viceroys' (Fichtner 1976: 245).

This was of course not unique to medieval and early modern Europe. For instance, in a study of Imperial China, Wang (2019) finds that family networks to some extent substituted for state capacity. However, using relatives as agents was especially logical where primogeniture had removed competing claims on the throne by, inter alia, uncles and younger brothers, meaning that the monarch did not risk nurturing a potential pretender by entrusting kin with offices or men-of-arms.

A clear illustration of how rulers can use family ties to their advantage can be found in the reign of Edward III of England, who created the title of Duke for his sons, assigning them different parts of the realm. The crown prince, Edward, known to history as the Black Prince, successfully commanded English armies in the Hundred Years' War, including in the victories of the Battles of Crécy (1346) and Poitiers (1356) (Green 2007). Of course, the new arrangements proved to be the source of great instability further down the line (see also Bartlett 2020: 198–200). Edward III's younger sons founded houses of their own, including those of York and Lancaster, the main belligerents in the War of the Roses—but by then, Edward III was long dead. A later example can be found in Prussia, where Frederick the Great—himself

---

[3] As Bartlett (2000: 133) documents, the court (including the king) of John Lackland on average moved 13 to 14 times a month.

a brilliant general—let his younger brother Henry command armies in other theatres of war.

Similarly, the German emperor Frederick II, who hardly set foot on German soil after 1220, preferring to stay in his native Sicily, had his eldest son Henry govern in his stead as King of Germany (until the two fell out in 1234–1235, illustrating the crown prince problem). However, as the examples indicate, not all family members were suited to work as trusted agents. Political office was usually a male privilege in medieval and early modern Europe (Wickham 2016: 191–5; Acharya and Lee 2019). Although research shows that reigning queens were as likely to go war as kings (Dube and Harish 2020), queens normally only came to power when there were no male heirs, as bravery and battle prowess were seen as manly qualities (Bartlett 2020: 52). Hence, it was only a monarch's male relatives that could occupy formal positions in the military and administration. However, women could fill another important role, in diplomacy.

Marriage alliances

Given that medieval and early modern politics were dynastic and interpersonal in nature, commitments were often made credible by sealing them with a marriage. Children and younger siblings could therefore be used as commitment devices—a 'pledge of peace' (Bartlett 2020: 13)—when entering alliances with either royal and noble families in other realms or noble families in one's own realm. In-married relatives (i.e. wives and husbands and their relatives) are likely to have offered support to the monarch, as they had become allies due to the marriage and as they shared an interest in protecting the progeny that arose from the marriage that united the royal family with theirs (cf. Burton-Chellew and Dunbar 2011).

In this respect, female relatives are likely to have been more valuable than male relatives, as they could be married to men, who in context of the gendered roles of medieval and early modern Europe had a formal monopoly on exercising power.[4] A prominent example is Rudolf of Habsburg's marriage politics. As the first Habsburg king of Germany, Rudolf strategically married four of his daughters to prominent princes who supported his election (Fried 2015: 318). Rudolf thereby laid the foundation stone of a dynasty that managed to hold the throne of Austria for six centuries and which, over the years, excelled

---

[4] 'Marriage could even be classed, along with warfare, as one of the two things necessary for the state' (Bartlett 2020: 9). Needless to say, homosexual marriages were not a possibility in this period.

in the game of marriage politics, reflected in the famous early modern saying *Bella gerant alii, tu felix Austria nube* ('Let others wage war: thou, happy Austria, marry').

Married members of the family would often function as the lineage's advocate abroad. Female relatives normally possessed their own material resources because of the practice of queens, princesses, and noblewomen controlling at least part of their dowry, and they would often wield influence with both their husband and, most importantly, their sons (Earenfight 2007; 2017).[5] Queens and countesses often dominated royal or noble regencies when their husbands had died while their sons were still underage. A network analysis of marriage ties and war in Europe shows that states that were connected in this way were less likely to go to war with each other (Benzell and Cooke 2021).

Sons or younger brothers of the monarch, while less important as marriage partners, would sometimes be married to an heiress, possibly a dowager who had earlier been married to a king or high noble or a daughter of a house that had died out in the male line. In this way, additional resources in the form of land and men-at-arms would fall under the direct control of the lineage. A monarch might even successfully install a younger son or a brother as monarch in another realm due to openings created by dynastic politics, in a situation where female inheritance enabled royal cadets to become monarchs via marriage (Sharma 2015: 167–8; 2017).[6]

Hypotheses

Summing up, there are several reasons why a large pool of legitimate offspring and siblings was an important asset for medieval and early modern monarchs, in a situation where central power was weak and personalized and where heirship practices were centred on the monogamous family in general and primogeniture in particular. Monarchs had better reason to trust close relatives, both because they knew each other well and because they had a shared interest in keeping the lineage at the helm of power. A large reserve of relatives thus meant an ample supply of agents/representatives, heirs, and material for marriage alliances. We therefore expect larger families to be associated with a lower risk of deposition.

---

[5] Again, this logic was not confined to medieval and early modern Europe. For instance, it has been shown that Ottoman sultans' whose mothers hailed from Europe were less likely to go to war against European polities than sultans whose mothers hailed from other Muslim states (Iyigun 2013).

[6] These cadet houses would then normally ally with the senior branch (Bartlett 2020: 275).

However, we can specify our expectations further, along two dimensions: which family members mattered most and what kind of political instability they mitigated. As pointed out earlier not all relatives could fulfil the outlined roles in a similar manner. Men could fulfil all three, whereas—in normal circumstances—women could only fulfil the third role (as marriage partners) but with the important stipulation that they were more important than men in this respect (Bartlett 2020: 15). Using family members as trusted agents and to ensure future succession is particularly likely to reduce the risk of depositions against challengers from outside a monarch's inner circle. We would therefore expect male relatives to be more useful than female relatives when it comes to preventing coups from outside the family. However, male relatives, especially brothers and uncles, also increase the monarch's risk of being deposed from within the family, as argued earlier.

We also expect primogeniture to be conducive to the founding of longer-lasting dynasties. Even though children would often succeed in elective monarchies, a clearer line of succession makes it easier for them to do so, increasing the likelihood that the dynasty is perpetuated. Add to this that monarchs are less likely to be deposed under primogeniture, as shown in Chapter 6. We should thus expect dynasties in primogeniture monarchies to last considerably longer, due to both the ease of succession and the low likelihood of deposition.

By disinheriting younger sons, we also expect primogeniture to have helped states consolidate and expand their territories. The main difference between primogeniture and partible inheritance is the fact that primogeniture leaves the inheritance intact to the eldest son, whereas partible inheritance in the period we study often meant that the eldest son had to share the inheritance with (some of) his younger siblings (at least when territorial conquests and acquisitions through marriage were available). This crucial difference is likely to have made it easier for monarchies practicing primogeniture than for monarchies practicing partible inheritance to keep and expand their territories, with the consequence that the former outgrew the latter. As the impartibility principle usually also applied to elective monarchies and monarchies practicing agnatic seniority, we only expect a difference between primogeniture and partible inheritance in this respect.

Descriptive statistics on royal families

The primary duty of a queen in medieval and early modern monarchies was to bear children, and the royal couple was expected to produce children as soon

168   THE POLITICS OF SUCCESSION

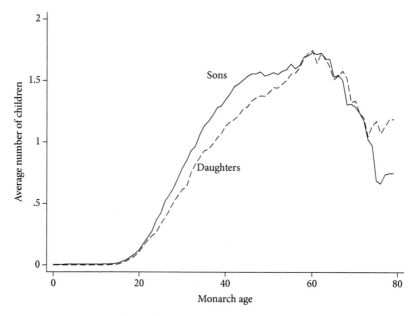

Fig. 8.1 Average number of living sons and daughters over a monarch's lifetime

as possible to secure the succession. However, high infant mortality kept the total number of surviving children down, which meant that many monarchs never stopped having children. In Figure 8.1, we plot the number of living sons and daughters the monarchs in our sample[7] had over the course of their lives (not only during their time on the throne). We can see that the total number of children starts to rise around the age of 20, continuing all the way up until the age of 60.[8]

Figure 8.1 shows that monarchs in general had slightly more sons than daughters, which is what we would expect, biologically. The difference should not be exaggerated: for 40-year-old monarchs, it is 0.2 sons more. But it is slightly larger than contemporary sex ratios at birth, which could either suggest underreporting of women, for instance those who were stillborn or died at a very early age, or that an individual was more likely to reach the throne if he had more sons.

In contrast, we see an opposite pattern when looking at the number of brothers and sisters in Figure 8.2. Monarchs consistently have more sisters than

---

[7] Data on monarch's families are coded from the Medieval Lands database (Cawley 2006) and Europäische Stammtafeln.
[8] The graph has been cut off at age 80 as the number of older monarchs is very small.

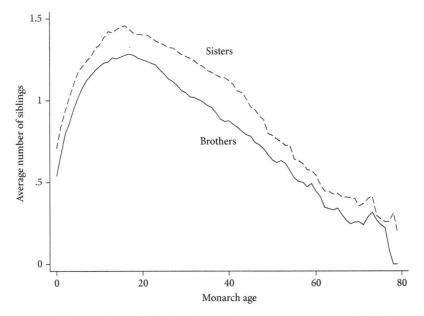

Fig. 8.2 The number of living brothers and sisters over a monarch's lifetime

brothers. This is however natural, as monarchs most of the time are men and thus comes from the same 'pool' of children as their brothers. The number of siblings goes up until the age of 20 and then declines during the monarch's life.

Finally, in Figure 8.3 we plot the number of living paternal uncles and aunts that monarchs had. It starts at a high level but then decreases rapidly. The gender difference is also evident here, for the same reasons as the one between brothers and sisters. Given that we only have data for paternal uncles and aunts, one man (the monarch's father) is always subtracted from the number of sons in a family.

Monarchs were expected to marry, even though there were a few who did not, such as the 'Virgin Queen' Elizabeth of England. In our data, we can see that the proportion of monarchs who were married starts to rise well before the age of 20, going up to almost 70 per cent at the age of 40 (Figure 8.4). That the figure is not higher is due to high attrition rates among queens, stemming mainly from the dangers of childbirth. But kings normally replaced queens who passed away with younger queens. When a monarch in our sample was 20, the average age of the spouse was also 20. Forty-year-old monarchs on average had 32-year-old spouses, and 60-year-old monarchs had 43-year-old spouses.

If we combine the different figures to a sum total—children, siblings, and paternal uncles and aunts—we find that the size of the family increases from

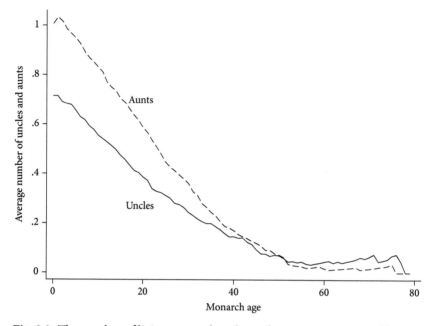

Fig. 8.3 The number of living paternal uncles and aunts over a monarch's lifetime

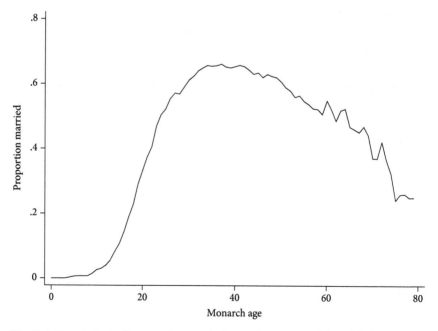

Fig. 8.4 Proportion of monarchs married over the course of their lifetime

childhood to middle age and then starts to decrease rapidly after the age of 60. Monarchs around the age of 40 statistically had the largest families.

Were monarchs with larger families more secure?

Medieval and early modern European monarchies were characterized by weak institutions, in which personal relationships were the means through which power and influence was wielded. We have argued that there are good reasons to believe relatives to be more trustworthy than others. But was a large family a bulwark against deposition? The simple analysis presented in Figure 8.5 suggests that the answer is yes: rulers with more children and siblings were deposed less frequently than others. Childless monarchs faced an annual 1.7 percentage risk of being deposed, whereas monarchs with five children only faced a 0.6 per cent risk. Similar patterns are evident for siblings.

However, there are numerous omitted factors of relevance, such as age and time on the throne. If we instead run a regression analysis where the unit of analysis is monarch-year and the dependent variable is deposition, we can include the number of living relatives each year, as well as controls for age, length of tenure, time period, and country. Results from three such models are presented in Figure 8.6. In the first model, the main independent variable is total number of relatives; in model 2 we divide the variable according to relations; in model 3 we split it with respect to gender as well.

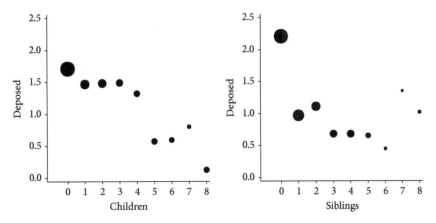

Fig. 8.5 The percentage of monarchs deposed in a year, depending on family size

Note: Circle size indicate the number of observations.

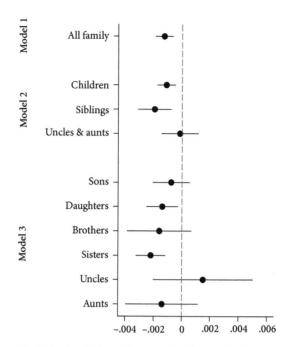

Fig. 8.6 Coefficients from regression analysis (OLS), dependent variable deposition

Note: Controls for age, tenure, century, and country. Standard errors clustered on monarch.

The coefficient for family size has a significant and negative relationship with the risk of deposition. For each additional family member, the yearly risk decreases with 0.13 percentage points, which may sound trivial, but is in fact substantial given that the average yearly risk of deposition is 1.4 per cent. Model 2 shows that it is primarily children and siblings who are responsible for this decrease, whereas uncles and aunts have a weaker and insignificant relationship with deposition. Finally, in model 3 we divide the variables according to gender. Here it is necessary to keep in mind that the gender pairs are correlated—monarchs with many sons tend to have many daughters as well, which means that the confidence intervals are wider. Nevertheless, we can see that despite the patriarchal nature of societies of the day, female relatives—especially sisters—have stronger negative effects than male relatives.

A possible interpretation is that while women could be used to cement alliances as marriage partners, they constituted little threat of their own. As expressed by Greengrass (2014: 304): 'There was a political paradox in Christendom's dynastic states. They were patriarchies, but women were essential to their dynastic strategies.' Male relatives had greater claims to power, which perhaps offset their protective value to some extent. An indication that this might be the case is the coefficient for uncles, which is positive, albeit statistically insignificant. Could there be some truth to the 'evil uncle' trope?

Deposition from inside and outside the family

> 'O bitter consequence, That Edward still should live! "True, noble prince!" Cousin, thou wert not wont to be so dull: Shall I be plain? I wish the bastards dead; And I would have it suddenly perform'd.'
> Shakespeare, Richard III, Act IV, Scene II.

These sentences are spoken by Richard, Duke of Gloucester, imploring Lord Buckingham to kill Richard's nephews, King Edward V, and Richard, Duke of York. They were the sons of Edward IV, placed under the protection of their uncle Richard upon their father's death, as they were both children (ages 12 and 9). He had them imprisoned in the Tower of London, from where they later mysteriously disappeared, which cleared the way for Richard to take the throne, as Richard III. Were they murdered? It has not been conclusively proven, though an excavation of the location in the seventeenth century unearthed a wooden box with two small skeletons, buried under a staircase (Diehl and Donnelly 2006). Regardless, Richard III clearly profited from their death, and his guilt is widely assumed, as is evident from his characterization in Shakespeare's play.

Paternal uncles constitute a threat to rulers because they have both motive and opportunity to usurp the throne. Under primogeniture, they and their descendants are normally excluded from the direct line of succession, but their close association with the previous ruler gives them both a relatively legitimate claim and a power base from which to mount a challenge. At the same time, they have an interest in protecting the dynasty from outside threats. To separate the positive and negative effects of relatives, we have coded the identity of perpetrators of depositions, specifically whether the perpetrator was a member of the family—meaning parent, child, sibling, uncle, aunt, nephew, or first cousin. When the sources gave no indication that the monarch and the deposer were related or when they were more distantly related than outlined earlier, the 'perpetrator' of the deposition has been coded as unrelated.

Table 8.1 shows that two-thirds of depositions are led by persons with no or distant relation to the monarch. When a member of the family is behind

Table 8.1 Successors and perpetrators of depositions (per cent)

	Successor (monarch not deposed)	Successor (monarch deposed)	Perpetrator (monarch deposed)
Son/grandson	56.7	19.2	5.3
Brother	11.2	11.7	11.7
Uncle/nephew	3.4	10.1	9.6
Other relative (cousin, spouse, father)	4.0	4.8	6.4
Unrelated	24.7	54.3	67.0
Total (N)	100 (526)	100 (188)	100 (188)

the coup, it is most often a brother, followed by uncles. It is interesting to note that deposed monarchs are frequently followed on the throne by their sons, even though sons are seldom the perpetrators of the coup. In those cases, the reasons for the coup might be due to dissatisfaction with a particular ruler, rather than the regime or dynasty itself.

To further gauge the effect of having few or many relatives, we conduct a multinomial logit analysis with three potential outcomes: no deposition, deposition by a relative, and deposition by a non-relative, using the same covariates as in the analysis earlier, excluding country fixed effects (due to the low number of depositions in each category). The results are presented in Figure 8.7, where dark dots represent coefficients for deposition by nonrelatives and grey dots deposition by relatives.

The main result of the analysis is—unsurprisingly—that relatives protect better against depositions from outside than from inside the family. All categories of relatives have a negative coefficient for depositions from the outside, but while female relatives have similar effects for depositions from the inside, all categories of male relatives have a positive coefficient for depositions by family members (none of them are, however, statistically significant). We have run additional analyses where we interact family with primogeniture, but found no statistically significant interactions, meaning that family seemed to have helped monarchs, regardless of principle of succession.

The strongest positive effect for depositions from the inside is found for uncles, giving some empirical support to the 'evil' or 'wicked' uncle stereotype. However, depositions from within the dynasty are rarer than those from outside. The positive effects of the male relatives thus seem to outweigh the negative. A strong dynasty with many relatives on average does more to shield

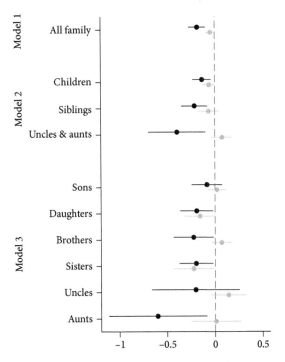

Fig. 8.7 Coefficients from regression analysis (multinomial logit), dependent variable deposition from non-relatives (black) and relatives (grey)

Note: Controls for age, tenure, and century. Standard errors clustered on monarch.

the ruler than to threaten him—but the monarch is wise to keep an eye on his uncles and to a lesser extent his brothers.

Marriage and family

We saw in the analysis that daughters, sisters, and even aunts seem to help protect monarchs from deposition. While they generally did not hold important political offices themselves, they could tie dynasties together in marriage. Unfortunately, we do not have reliable data on the marriages of monarchs' family members, but we have coded the marriages of all the monarchs in our dataset, including the noble house of the spouses. By looking at the ancestry of royal spouses, we can get a sense of the 'placement record' of dynasties, which could say something about their diplomatic influence.

176   THE POLITICS OF SUCCESSION

Table 8.2 Noble houses that produced the most royal spouses

House	Origin	Spouses from dynasty (excluding in-marriage)
Habsburg	Austria	40
Wittelsbach	Palatinate	26
Piast	Poland	24
Barcelona	Aragon	22
Hohenzollern	Brandenburg/Prussia	21
Rurik	Russia	20
Luxembourg	Bohemia	15
Bourbon	France	14
Savoy	Savoy	14
Bourgogne-Comte	Castile	13

Throughout the period under analysis, one dynasty stands out in terms of their ability to place their offspring in other royal houses: the Habsburgs. Sixty-two of the royal spouses in our data are from the Habsburg dynasty. Partly this is due to the Habsburg practice of marrying within the dynasty, which over time caused genetic defects to spread in the family, most famously the protruding 'Habsburg jaw'. But even if we exclude marriages within the family, the Habsburg dynasty was by far the most successful on the marriage market, followed by the German Wittelsbachs (the most common combination of houses in marriage is also Habsburg/Wittelsbach) and the Polish Piasts, as seen in Table 8.2. The Origin column displays the state in our dataset with most monarchs from the house.

How are the dynasty's marriage prospects affected by the availability of different relatives? For each monarch in our dataset, we count the number of marriages in the 100 years following the monarch's accession in which a member of the monarch's house was married to another monarch. That is, if a Wittelsbach takes the throne in 1650, we count the number of times other Wittelsbachs marry monarchs in the period 1650–1750. We then regress this number on the current monarch's family size (controlling only for time), again excluding marriages within dynasties. The results are presented in Figure 8.8.

All female relatives have positive and statistically significant coefficients. The coefficient for sisters is for instance 0.19, meaning that each additional sister a monarch has is associated with 0.19 additional marriages in the century following the monarch's accession. The coefficient for sons is positive but not as strong as that for female relatives. A likely explanation is that our data only

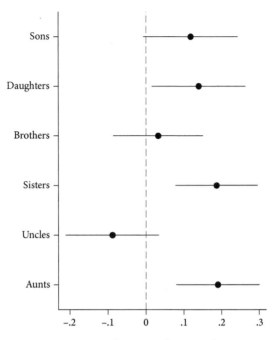

Fig. 8.8 Association between the size of a monarch's family and the dynasty's marriages to other monarchs in the following 100 years

consider marriages of monarchs (or individuals who later became monarchs), who are therefore almost exclusively male. Princes were attractive marriage partners but married off to princesses or even just to noble heiresses. A similar logic applies to brothers and uncles. What we can take away from the analysis is that larger numbers of female relatives resulted in better future connections to other royal houses, which could be an indication of diplomatic strength.

Family and the length of dynasties

Next, we look at the length of dynasties, not just the survival prospects of individual monarchs. Rulers who had good reason to suspect that their descendants would enjoy the fruits of office for longer were incentivized to invest in long-term state-building. While elective monarchies did sometimes see long dynasties—it was not uncommon for sons to be succeed their fathers—the transfer of power between fathers and sons was not institutionalized in the

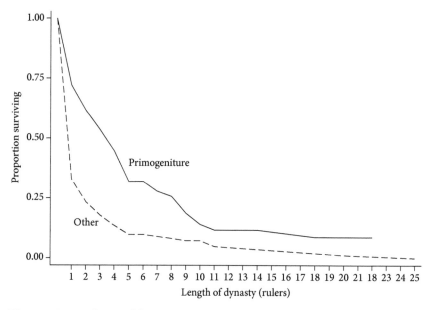

Fig. 8.9 Survival rate of dynasties

same way as in primogeniture monarchies as it obviously depended on the vagaries of election. Figure 8.9 presents a survival graph of the length of dynasties, where a dynasty is counted as an unbroken line of rulers from the same house. The *x* axis shows the number of rulers, and the *y* axis the proportion of dynasties that survived past that number of rulers. The two curves represent states that practiced primogeniture at the start of the dynasty (solid line) and those that did not (dashed line).

The difference is stark: about half of all dynasties in states that practiced primogeniture survived past the fourth ruler, whereas less than a fifth of the dynasties in other states did the same (even though the longest-lasting dynasty, the Piasts, ruled in a monarchy practicing agnatic seniority, Poland). Even so, the graph understates the stability of states practicing primogeniture. We saw in the chapter on leader depositions that monarchs in primogeniture states ruled for longer periods of time, as they were deposed less frequently. If we instead count the number of years each dynasty occupied the throne (see Figure 8.10), the pattern is therefore even clearer, and the longest-ruling dynasties can now be found in states practicing primogeniture. The Piast dynasty, though it had a long line of successive monarchs from the same family, saw frequent depositions and ruler changes. The many rulers from the same house thus did not mean that the political situation was stable.

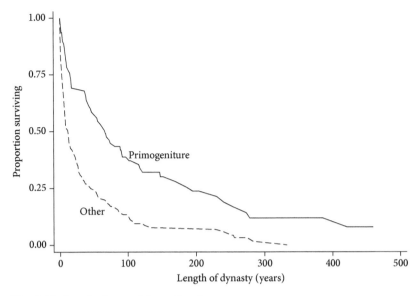

Fig. 8.10 Survival rate of dynasties, in years

If we regress dynasty length on family size, we find that sons are the best determinant of long life for a dynasty, followed by brothers. Female relatives do not have an effect.

Primogeniture, partible inheritance, and the size of states

Finally, we examine how the introduction of primogeniture in monarchies previously practicing partible inheritance affected the ability to agglomerate territory. It may sound obvious that states that are left intact to the eldest son will outgrow states that are occasionally split up between several sons. However, as we discussed in Chapters 2, 3, and 4 partible inheritance often defaulted to primogeniture in the time period we study, because of the Church's regulation of family affairs and because partible inheritance mainly tended to be practiced when there were large territorial acquisitions from conquest, marriage, or inheritance. We have already mentioned that kings were often survived by one son only, which meant that the holding would not be divided. But reconsolidation was also a possibility down the line, for instance if one brother did not leave a surviving male heir or if one of several branches of a royal family was strong enough to put Humpty Dumpty back together again. Partitions in one generation were thus often followed by a reconsolidation of

Table 8.3 Primogeniture, partible inheritance, and state size

	(1) No lagged dependent variable	(2) Lagged dependent variable
Primogeniture	1.12**	0.69*
	(0.36)	(0.27)
Lagged (log)area		0.38*
		(0.14)
Observations	90	76
Countries	22	22
Adjusted R^2	0.873	0.928

Note: Standard errors in parentheses * $p < 0.05$, ** $p < 0.01$, *** $p < 0.001$. All models include country and century fixed effects with standard errors clustered on countries. The models only include country-centuries when primogeniture and/or partible inheritance were practiced the whole century.

the realm in the next generations—as in the case of Leon-Castile in 1230—or even in the very same generation that the territory had been divided, as happened when all King Henry II's legitimate sons save one (John Lackland) died during a short time span. Hence, it is interesting to see how much difference the introduction of primogeniture made.

Table 8.3 presents models that compare centuries when primogeniture was practiced to centuries when partible inheritance was practiced (excluding centuries when elective monarchy or agnatic seniority was practiced). As no monarchy switched from primogeniture to partible inheritance and as the models include country (and century) fixed effects, the coefficient of primogeniture can be interpreted as taking stock of how the switch from partible inheritance to primogeniture affected states' territories.

The models show that the introduction of primogeniture is associated with a significant increase in state size, even when controlling for a state's size in the century preceding the introduction. The effect is rather substantial (0.69–1.12 logged units increase), showing that a transition from partible inheritance to primogeniture definitely helped states consolidate and expand their territories.

Conclusion

The empirical analyses presented in this chapter point to the central role played by kin relationships in medieval and early modern monarchies (see also Haldén 2020). Monarchs with larger families were less likely to be deposed, with both male and female relatives contributing to security. While having many male relatives increased the risk of being deposed by family members somewhat, this risk was more than offset by the protection relatives provided against outside deposition. We also saw that having many female relatives increased the chance that members of the dynasty would marry into other royal houses in the future, which could be an indication of the role marriage alliances played in shoring up political support for dynasties. Large families also helped perpetuate the dynasty in time. Finally, primogeniture is associated with longer durations of rule for dynasties.

However, our analyses do not indicate that the role of family was different in monarchies practicing primogeniture than in other monarchies. On the one hand, this result is surprising, given that the greater clarity of succession and the greater age difference between monarch and crown prince offered by primogeniture should reduce conflicts within the dynasty. On the other hand, a more uncertain political environment, created by the absence of primogeniture, could well mean that the trust stemming from kinship increases in importance. In his account of the development of political order, Francis Fukuyama contrasts tribal organization, based on personal relationships, with the more impersonal state: the state as the 'exit out of kinship' (Fukuyama 2011: 81).

Primogeniture thus represents a paradoxical development. It made the monarchy more formalized, and succession more mechanical and predictable, but it did so by making it more biological. Other institutional developments of the period, such as the construction of increasingly professional bureaucracies and more powerful representative institutions only point in one direction, towards impersonal relationships and rule by law. Hereditary succession in this way appears as an anomaly. But the often visceral images evoked by hereditary succession practices—blood, birth, death—mask a political philosophy that is more impersonal and rule-bound than that associated with election and personal qualities. Summing up the contradictions, Ernst Kantorowicz wrote:

> The perpetuity of the head of the realm and the concept of a *req qui nunquam moritur*, a 'king that never dies,' depended mainly on the interplay of three factors: the perpetuity of the Dynasty, the corporate character of the Crown, and the immortality of the royal Dignity. Those three factors coincided vaguely with the uninterrupted line of royal bodies natural, with the permanency of the body politic represented by the head together with the members, and with the immortality of the office, that is, of the head alone. It has to be stressed, however, that those three components were not always clearly distinguished.
>
> Kantorowicz (1957: 316)

The continuity of a dynasty promoted the idea of an immortal body politic, an institution that goes beyond the identity of the individuals currently wearing the crown. Hence the counterintuitive conclusion that personal relationships in some ways might matter just as much in an elective political system that does not formally build on kinship connections. Nevertheless, even though they might have been more institutionalized than their elective counterparts, the hereditary monarchies of medieval and early modern Europe were still a far cry from the constitutional and bureaucratic modern states of today. Throughout the period, blood was thicker than water.

Primogeniture also helped states consolidate their territories, by leaving the inheritance intact to the eldest son. The contrast to how states were sometimes split up when partible inheritance was practiced is stark. This feature of primogeniture not only assisted states in retaining old and acquiring new territories, but probably also helped them build more stable institutions that contributed to fostering a sense of common identity among people and elites in the long run.

9
The Politics of Succession in Comparative Perspective

In 1271, the Mongol great khan, Khubilai, completed the conquest of China that his grandfather, Chinggis, had begun 60 years earlier. Khubilai founded what has become known as the Yuan dynasty, which lasted until 1368. He himself enjoyed a long reign, ruling as Yuan emperor until his natural death in 1294. But after his passing, the short-lived Yuan dynasty was plagued by political instability and short reigns that often came to a violent end. In this respect, the Yuan dynasty fares badly compared with the Chinese norm. As Wang (2018) has demonstrated, Chinese rulers typically governed for long periods and leader deposition was relatively uncommon. Indeed, in many periods Imperial Chinese dynasties were more stable than the European monarchies we have analysed in previous chapters (see also Scheidel 2019).

What explains the stark difference between the normal Chinese imperial stability and the Yuan instability? In this chapter, we apply our theoretical framework on China, as well as a string of other, non-European regions of Eurasia. We first present narrative historical evidence that the politics of succession mattered in Europe before the period we analyse and outside of Europe up until and during this period. We then present a statistical comparison—couched in a narrative analysis—between our sample of European Christian monarchies, where primogeniture was gradually introduced, and a sample of polities in the Middle East, where we find different succession principles. Finally, we further place this difference in relief via a statistical analysis of the 'within-case' importance of what we term 'father-to-son' succession practices in Imperial China.

Europe before the introduction of primogeniture

In preceding chapters, we have analysed the politics of succession in European monarchies in the period AD 1000–1800. Delving further back in

European history, we can start by noting that neither the Roman Empire nor its Byzantine offspring devised a constitutional mechanism for solving the problem of succession. In the Roman Empire, succession worked best under what Machiavelli termed the five 'good' emperors, who ruled from 96 to 180. These emperors (starting with the sexagenarian Nerva who had been appointed by the Senate) would legally adopt an heir, chosen based on skills and loyalty, who the Roman elite would then hail as new emperor upon the old emperor's death. For almost a century, this system worked smoothly, and on Nerva's death in AD 98 it produced what is arguably the most successful Roman emperor—the *optimus princeps*—of all times, Trajan, known for his administrative and military skills as well his personal modesty. By the fourth century, new Roman emperors would be hailed in the Senate with the stirring formula 'Felicior Augusto, melior Traiano' ('be more fortunate than Augustus, better than Trajan') (Kershaw 2013: 174–83).

However, in other periods, the Roman system proved very inefficient in dealing with the problem of succession. On numerous occasions, there were rival claimants, often generals who controlled sections of the Roman army or different members of an imperial family fighting it out, or by the Pretorian Guard 'auctioning' the emperorship to the highest bidder. This repeatedly created spikes of political instability and some periods saw very short ruler spells, which often came to a violent end. Two famous examples are the instability following the deaths of Nero in AD 68 and Commodus in AD 192. In Roman historiography, 69 is known as the 'year of the four emperors' (Galba, Otho, Vitellius, and Vespasian) and 193 as the 'year of the five emperors' (Pertinax, Didius Julianus, Pescennius Niger, Clodius Albinus, and Septimius Severus) (Kershaw 2013). In both cases, it took civil war to decide who would wear the purple, with Vespasian and Septimius Severus, respectively, emerging as victors, and imposing a new stability.

Numerous historians have associated this Roman instability with the recurrent problem of how to tackle the succession. As Kulikowski (2020: 25) summarizes this view in a recent review of John Drinkwater's *Nero: Emperor and Court*, the autocracy established by Augustus was born with an inbuilt problem: 'if Augustus wasn't king ... how was power to be transferred when he died. Much care was taken to fudge the answer.' In 293, Emperor Diocletian, who ruled 284–305, tried to provide an answer by devising a model where two senior emperors (each titled Augustus)—one for the Western and one for the Eastern half of the empire—co-ruled with each their junior emperors (titled Caesar), the idea being that the junior emperor would be groomed to eventually succeed as senior emperor. This 'tetrarchy' (rule of four) did create some political stability. But it broke down in 306, and it took civil war to decide that Constantine the Great would become emperor. The situation repeated itself after Constantine's long rule, which ended in 337. Again, the politics of succession was to blame. 'Constantine had no plans for avoiding the perennial problems of succession' (Davies 1997: 210). He had his eldest son killed due to rumours of plotting, and his other sons, nephews, and brothers—as well as some of his associates—would fight it out after his death. Subsequently, some aspects of Diocletian's model were re-adopted, primarily the regular grooming of junior emperors. But down to the end of the Western empire in the fifth century, the Romans continued to struggle with frequent usurpers and frequent civil wars during successions.

In the Byzantine Empire, succession worked best in periods of de facto hereditary monarchy, such as during the Macedonian dynasty from from 867 to 1056 (Gregory 2005). But these periods were the exception, as only about half of the Byzantine emperors were related to their predecessors by blood and as multi-generational dynasties were uncommon (Finer 1997a: 702; Marsham 2009: 5). If we extend the period back to the fall of the Western Roman Empire in the fifth century and look more narrowly on patrilineal successions, the numbers are even more striking:

> a credible approximation is that, of about sixty-five imperial successions between 476, the date of the abdication of the last western Roman emperor, and 1204, only eighteen or so were simple father–son transfers of power, that is, not much more than one in four. All the others involved transmission by marriage, collateral inheritance or, very frequently, usurpation.
> (Bartlett 2020: 3)

Indeed, during this 700-year period, only two Byzantine dynasties—the above-mentioned Macedonians and the Heraclians—managed to produce five successive generations of emperors (Bartlett 2020: 3).

For much of its existence, succession in the Byzantine Empire was therefore a very violent business, settled by palace intrigues (including maiming or outright murder) or civil wars (Bartlett 2020: 243–4). One of the worst such periods was between AD 602 and AD 820—an age where the Byzantine Empire was much pressed by the forces of Islam—when only five of 22 Byzantine emperors died natural deaths while in office (Wickham 2009: 257). More generally, Byzantine emperors on average ruled for only half the number of years of the Capetian kings of France (Bartlett 2020: 243).

Samuel P. Finer (1997a: 633) has attributed this instability to ambiguity in the succession. The Byzantines had retained the Roman principle that an emperor was elected by acclamation but they had no clear institutional mechanisms for election (Gregory 2005: 5). It was often the support of the army, or parts of it, that decided the succession. Might was right, and the Byzantines even devised a theory of a kind of heavenly mandate, according to which the one who triumphed in the battle for purple was the one favoured by God Almighty; the—*ex post*—divine acclamation was what ultimately mattered. This was a recipe for instability because it constantly invited would-be emperors to make a violent grab for power, which, if successful, would legitimize itself. While we find a similar notion of a heavenly mandate in Imperial China, as we shall see later it was here mitigated by a hereditary principle that was conducive to longer-lasting dynasties (Finer 1997a: 633).

This fundamental weakness of the Byzantine state led to constant leader depositions. In Finer's (1997a: 636) summary: 'I do not know of any comparable polity in which the throne was so precarious: I count sixty-five emperors between 518 and 1204, and of these no fewer than twenty-eight had usurped the throne.' This fluidity of ruler tenure was placed in relief by the remarkable stability of the regime, in the form of the imperial autocracy.

The Germanic kingdoms of Western Europe saw similar instability unleashed by succession during the early Middle Ages. As mentioned in Chapter 6, the Visigothic realm in Spain and Southern France is a good example. Here succession was based on an elective principle where the king's successor was chosen by bishops and the nobility (Barbero and Loring 2005: 354). Ruler tenures were generally short and usurpations rife (Bartlett 2020: 246). A similar instability characterized the Franks under the Merovingians, where the realm was constantly divided in unpredictable ways between brothers due to the combination of de facto polygyny, which produced numerous heirs, and unregulated partible inheritance (early on worsened by the lack of sub-polities with fixed borders within the realm that would have made divisions easier). As reported in Chapter 4, between 511 and 679, we only find 22 years of unity of the Frankish realm (Wickham 2009: 114). Disputes over these divisions would result in numerous succession wars between brothers, uncles, nephews, and cousins (Bartlett 2020: 192).

In Chapter 4, we narrated how the 'Carolingian wonder' of leaving only one male successor meant that the Frankish realm virtually remained united from the ascension of Pepin III in 751 to the death of Louis the Pious in 840. But from the 830s onwards, the great empire created by Charlemagne was in the grip of vicious succession struggles. The result was the large-scale collapse of public authority that we mentioned in Chapter 1 and described in detail in Chapter 4. Recent historical research argues that the 'real catalyst' for the ninth-century Viking raids often singled out as a cause of the decay of public power in West Francia (Bloch 1971) are to be found in the politics of succession (Price 2020). The Viking pirates seeped in where state power had buckled, and this, in turn, was due to the succession conflicts that were first unleashed between Charlemagne's grandsons.

Succession in Islamic states

Going beyond Europe, we find a similar pendulum movement between periods of relatively stable transfers of power and periods of unstable successions in many of the other great Eurasian civilization areas. Prior scholarship has often privileged the comparison between ruler tenures in Europe and the Islamic Middle East (e.g. Blaydes and Chaney 2013) and this, too, is where we start. We end this section by reporting some simple statistical results of a comparison between European and Islamic polities. However, we first try to contextualize this comparison by describing the approaches to the problem of succession tried out in early Islam, as well as their consequences for ruler tenure and political stability more generally.

Discussing how the belief in heredity as a legitimate form of political selection greatly affects the structure and persistence of polities, Max Weber (1968: 1138) points to the fact that Muhammed died without heirs as one of the great historical accidents, a chance event with enormous implications. After his death in AD 632 (according to tradition), the first generation of Muslims were faced with the practical problem of how to deal with the succession to this charismatic founder. This problem was to echo through the centuries, down to the present day (Madelung 1997: 1). It was this issue that spawned the division that would harden into today's distinction between Sunni and Shia Muslims, as well as a long history of more specific succession struggles.

The succession conflict initially revolved around whether to go for a form of hereditary succession, centred on Muhammed's son-in-law and cousin Ali and his descendants, or a more general model where the Caliph (the word is derived from the Arabic word for 'successor') was selected from among Muhammed's tribe, the Quraysh. The former model for appointing the Caliph was the one favoured by those who became known as the Shia branch ('followers of Ali'), the latter the one favoured by the Sunni branch.[1] The most

---

[1] The Sunni and Shia traditions were not fully formed until the tenth and eleventh centuries (Silverstein 2010: 25–6).

188   THE POLITICS OF SUCCESSION

important bone of contention was whether Muhammed had nominated Ali as his heir, as Shiites claimed, or whether he had intended the community of believers to elect his heir, as the Sunnis claimed.

We have virtually no hard historical facts about what happened during the life of Muhammed and in the decades following his death (Silverstein 2010). It is only from the 680s onwards that evidence about the caliphal succession starts to accumulate (Marsham 2009: 86), and contemporary written sources only really begin in the eighth and ninth century. However, what mattered for the historical actors was of course their interpretation of early Islamic history, not the real thing. In this sense, the rival interpretations of succession in the early Caliphate were hugely important for later Islamic history (Silverstein 2010).

The Caliphate established in the seventh and eighth centuries would be based on what became the Sunni tradition or approach. The first three successions (the caliphates of Abu Bakr, Umar, and Uthman) were all non-hereditary. According to tradition, they were based either on some form of election or consultation, *shura*, (Abu Bakr and Uthman) or on designation by the prior Caliph (Umar). Then Ali was—again, according to tradition—elected as the fourth Caliph in 656, but in 661 he was assassinated and replaced by the second[2] Umayad Caliph after the first Muslim *fitna* or civil war. The Umayads (661–750) were of the Qurayshi tribe but they were relative latecomers to Islam, and they were not part of Muhammed's Hashemite clan (the Banū Hāshim) (Silverstein 2010: 15).

Henceforth, the succession came to combine elements of the three modes used to appoint the first four Caliphs, namely designation by the prior leader, election by the followers, and heredity (Finer 1997a: 685). As the Sunni theory of the Caliphate needed to distance itself from the claims of the followers of Ali, the distinction from kingship with its hereditary succession was emphasized. This opposition to traditional Arabic kingship (*mulk*) was needed to justify the Sunni Caliphate, and as such the Sunni theory is obviously 'posterior to the succession' to Muhammed (Madelung 1997: 5).

After 661, the main model was that the Caliph would designate his successor from within the Umayyad family, usually one of his sons. This began when the first Umayyad Caliph of Damascus, Muawiya, designated his son Yazid as his successor, thereby inaugurating a tradition of hereditary succession (Silverstein 2010: 16). But the designated successor still needed some

---

[2] Uthman was also an Umayad but he had converted early and had marriage ties with Muhammed, as opposed to the branch of the Umayads who would take over the throne in 661.

form of popular acclamation by religious scholars, the *ulema*, normally in the Umayyad capital of Damascus (Finer 1997a: 697). Later, a similar model was used by the Abbasid Caliphs (750–1258), who came to power in 750 and moved the capital to Baghdad. Indeed, the Abbasids may be said to have strengthened the hereditary element as they were not only part of the Qurayshi tribe but descended from Muhammed's paternal uncle, Abbas.[3]

Compared to Byzantium, the early Caliphate had much more stable ruler tenure, 'partly reflected in, and partly explained by the hereditary principle in the Caliphate' (Finer 1997a: 702). According to Finer's (1997a: 702) tallies, between 632 and 944, only six out of 65 Caliphs were deposed, compared with 64 out of 107 Byzantine Emperors in the period 395–1453. Moreover, discounting the Abbasid juncture, after the Umayyad takeover of power all of the 51 Caliphs that ruled for the next six centuries were blood relatives, usually sons, of their predecessors (Finer 1997a: 702).

However, while the de facto hereditary principle decreased the frequency of depositions, the lack of clear rules about *which* relative would take the throne and *how* this relative was to be recognized as heir, recurrently created problems. This was a consequence of the fact that genuine hereditary kingship ran afoul of the Sunni theory of succession, described earlier. As caliphs tended to prefer one of their sons over the others, the result was conspiracy and civil war (Finer 1997a: 697). Other close Umayyad or Abbasid relatives would sometimes harbour their own ambitions, knowing that a successful power grab could be legitimized, *ex post*, by acclamation. Stasavage (2020: 187–9) shows how ruler tenures in the early Abbasid Caliphate (750–946)—on average around eight years—were much lower than in Capetian France (987–1328) or Plantagenet England (1066–1399) (see also Chapter 6). Ruler tenure then increased during the later Abbasid Caliphate (946–1258), where caliphs in Bagdad had become figureheads (Silverstein 2010: 24), meaning that they had less to fear from other power holders.

The original Caliphate in the 'Islamic Golden Age' ended abruptly with the extinction of the last Baghdad Abbasid Caliph in 1258, following the Mongol conquest of Baghdad. But vague succession rules would resurface in many of the Islamic successor states. Stasavage (2020) describes this with respect to one of the earliest 'other' Islamic polities, the Caliphate in *al-Andalus*, centred around the great city of Cordoba. Here, we find the opposite patterns as in the Abbasid Caliphate. After an initial period of political stability, this polity in the

---

[3] For this reason, several Shiite groups supported the Abbasid Revolution of 750. But the Abbasids themselves adhered to the Sunni tradition.

tenth century came to be characterized by very short leader tenures. Stasavage shows how in the period 929–1031, rulers in Cordoba held on to power for less than seven years on average. This instability culminated in the fragmentation of the realm after the last Umayyad Caliph of Spain lost power in 1031. Islamic Spain broke into a set of competing statelets or emirates, so-called *taifas*, which were vulnerable to the Christian *Reconquista*. Without pursuing the point, Stasavage (2020: 178) speculates that the Northern Spanish 'Christian forces were more cohesive because they had better solved the problem of leadership succession', an argument that dovetails with the one we make in this book.

Mamluk Egypt (1250–1517) presents an even starker example of ruler instability. Like the Byzantine Empire, the Mamluk regime was entirely stable for a very long period, but ruler tenure was very precarious because there was no procedure for dealing with the succession as sultan and as all attempts to insert hereditary principles were resisted by the Mamluk community of 'slave' soldiers. This created an almost implausibly high frequency of ruler rotation, with reigns generally lasting less than five years. A sizeable portion did not even reach the one-year mark (Finer 1997a: 734).

The Ottoman sultanate was also repeatedly plagued by political instability sparked by succession. Here, rule passed in the family, but as in the early Caliphate there was no institutionalized mechanism for choosing between the sons of a previous sultan, other than sheer violence (Alderson 1956; Peirce 2003; Quataert 2005; Imber 2009: 75). As a result, civil war frequently broke out on the death of a sultan. The victor would then often execute his siblings to avoid future challenges to his rule. A book of law (probably falsely) attributed to the sultan Mehmed II stated that 'To whichever of my sons the sultanate shall be granted [by God], it is appropriate that he should kill his brothers for the good order of the world' (cited in Imber 2009: 83). The book was compiled in the reign of Mehmed III, who after his accession executed 19 of his brothers. Needless to say, the expectation that the future sultan would murder his siblings would have been a cause for concern for all of them during the reign of their father. The elite, who had to choose which brother to place their bets on, also had much to fear from ending up on the losing side. Later, the succession system moved towards agnatic seniority, though it took generations before this principle—itself hardly a recipe for stability, as we have seen in preceding chapters—was fully accepted (Alderson 1956; Peirce 2003; Quataert 2005).

There is thus convincing evidence that the politics of succession haunted most Islamic states. As we have seen, during the early Caliphate, a de facto hereditary succession did mitigate this problem, but even here we find a relatively vague model of hereditary succession. It always made the top spot a precarious place to be, at least compared to the model offered by primogeniture. The same would—to an even greater extent—be the case in the Ottoman Empire, and in cases such as Mamluk Egypt there was virtually nothing to stabilize succession, because all hereditary elements were resisted.

We proceed by carrying out a general statistical comparison of succession arrangements and ruler tenures in Western Europe and Islam. As a stepping stone, we take Lisa Blaydes and Eric Chaney's (2013) data and models on how ruler tenures in Western Europe (including crusader states in the Middle East) and Islam came to diverge over the medieval era. We first replicate their results, and then test to what extent the adoption of primogeniture can explain the patterns they identify. When coding succession arrangements for Western European polities, we primarily rely on our own coding of succession arrangements (and the coding in Kokkonen and Sundell 2014), whereas, based on the discussion earlier, we assume that Islamic polities never adopted primogeniture.

For Western European polities that are *not* covered by our main coding, we rely on general observations of patterns of succession. Most of the literature points to the conclusion that dynasties originating in subnational polities in West Francia and smaller polities in the Iberian and Italian peninsulas started to adopt primogeniture or orderly partible inheritance in the eleventh century. We therefore code them as being 'halfway' towards the adoption primogeniture by the eleventh century (assigning them a value of 0.5) and fully after that.

Many princely families in the Holy Roman Empire never fully adopted primogeniture in the period Blaydes and Chaney study but stuck to versions of partible inheritance well into the fifteenth century and sometimes even longer (Wilson 2016: 424–7). However, as related in Chapter 4 there were tendencies towards primogeniture in the German area, especially from the twelfth century onwards. For example, Emperor Frederick Barbarossa declared all honorary fiefs to be hereditary and indivisible in 1158 (Wilson 2016: 424)—a decision that was reaffirmed by his grandson, Emperor Frederik II, in the thirteenth century (Starr 2019: 45) and codified for the secular Electorates in the Golden Bull of 1356. Many noble families also adopted the principle between the thirteenth and the fifteenth centuries (Wilson 2016: 425). The emperors were not always able to enforce these rules, but Christian family norms created a high likelihood that only one son survived to inherit (see Chapter 4). Polities that were guided by partible inheritance thus often came to default to de facto primogeniture. Regardless, our theory predicts that, when practiced in a regulated and orderly manner, partible inheritance is as conducive to political stability as is primogeniture (though it creates territorial fragmentation). We therefore treat dynasties originating in the Holy Roman Empire that are not covered by our own hand-coding as having adopted primogeniture or orderly partible inheritance from the twelfth century (assigning them a value of 1). In the eleventh century many fiefs had not yet become hereditary and were given to nobles by the emperor, which is why we treat dynasties as having only adopted primogeniture or orderly partible inheritance halfway (i.e. we assign them a value of 0.5).

Anglo-Saxon, Irish, early Pict, and early Welsh polities never adopted primogeniture (Beverly Smith 1986; Biggs 2005; Boyle 1977; Jaski 2000); nor did the old Germanic kingdoms that dominated Europe before the eleventh century (Grierson 1941; King 1972: 45–50; see Chapter 4). The same goes for the crusader states in the Middle East. Though established by nobles who often adhered to primogeniture (or other forms of hereditary succession) in their ancestral lands, succession arrangements never really stabilized in the new conquests at the other end of the Mediterranean. For natural reasons, rulers were initially elected or chosen, and the elective character of monarchy remained strong, as none of the newly established states had a clear rule of succession to fall back upon.[4] The first kings—Baldwin I of Boulogne and Baldwin II of Bourcq—of the Kingdom of Jerusalem were, for example, elected by the nobility in the high court, and it is telling that they hailed from two different noble families (Murray 1988: 118–53). The dynastic principle later strengthened as testamentary succession and different hereditary principles became increasingly important. However, the high court continued to play an important role in deciding the succession, especially when monarchs were killed or captured in battle and new regents had to be elected. There was also often disagreement over which hereditary principles applied, as family members that resided in the Middle East argued that their hereditary claims should take precedence over closer relatives who resided in Europe (e.g. Riley-Smith 1973: 101–21).[5]

Using this—admittedly rough—coding, Table 9.1 reports analyses based on Blaydes and Chaney's (2013) models. Model 1 replicates their findings for

---

[4] The only exception is the Latin Empire in Constantinople (1204–1261), which viewed itself as a continuation of the Byzantine Empire and acknowledged the imperial aristocracy's role in appointing new emperors (van Tricht 2017).

[5] The possible exception is the Kingdom of Cyprus, in which the succession was seemingly guided by primogeniture from 1205 onwards (Edbury 1991: 23–38).

Table 9.1 Ruler Duration in Western Europe and Islam

	(1) WE-Islam	(2) WE-Islam	(3) WE-Islam	(4) Iberia	(5) Iberia
Eighth century	−0.87 (3.09)		−0.87 (3.09)	−8.22 (7.81)	
Ninth century	1.63 (2.48)		1.63 (2.48)	−2.30 (8.56)	
Tenth century	4.65* (1.96)		4.65* (1.96)	−14.54 (8.69)	
Eleventh century	3.73* (1.52)		−0.16 (1.59)	9.59*** (2.84)	
Twelfth century	5.84*** (1.60)		1.12 (1.46)	21.64*** (4.73)	
Thirteenth century	9.69*** (1.54)		3.73* (1.53)	10.65 (6.03)	
Fourteenth century	10.34*** (1.38)		3.09* (1.59)	12.26** (4.06)	
Fifteenth century	8.82*** (1.47)		1.40 (1.72)	20.61*** (4.02)	
Primogeniture		10.19*** (0.73)	8.35*** (1.07)		14.37*** (1.84)
Observations	3047	3047	3047	278	278
Adjusted R^2	0.582	0.589	0.591	0.659	0.651

Note: Standard errors in parentheses. Century dummies that measure the general time trend are included in the models but are omitted in the table for representational purposes. The included century dummies represent the difference in tenure between Western European Christian dynasties and Islamic dynasties. * $p < 0.05$, ** $p < 0.01$, *** $p < 0.001$.

the whole dataset. The century dummies, which represent the differences in ruler tenures between Christian and Islamic rulers, show that rulers of Western European polities started to sit longer on their thrones than their Islamic counterparts from the tenth century onwards, and that this divergence is accentuated from the thirteenth century (when, on average, they sat 9.7 years longer on their thrones than Islamic rulers).

In model 2 we substitute the specific time trend for Western Europe with our primogeniture variable, which explains almost precisely as much of the variation in ruler tenures as the specific time trend dummies for Western Europe did in model 1. The dummy variable representing primogeniture indicates that, on average, rulers in these states had tenures about 10.2 years longer than rulers in polities with other succession arrangements. This difference declines to a still hefty 8.4 years in model 3 where we include our primogeniture variable simultaneously with the dummies measuring the time trend in Western

Europe. Meanwhile, the dummies for the eleventh, twelfth, and fifteenth centuries in Western Europe become insignificant, at the same time as the still significant effects of the thirteenth and fourteenth centuries are reduced to about three years (compared to 10 years in the models without primogeniture).

In models 4 and 5—repeating another of Blaydes and Chaney's analytical steps—we rerun the models on data from the Iberian Peninsula, where Christian and Islamic states coexisted for several centuries and where we can keep many other factors relatively constant (geography, historical legacies, etc.). The finding from the first models repeats itself: our primogeniture variable explains almost precisely as much of the variance over time as the century dummies for Western Europe (the adjusted R^2s are 0.66 and 0.65, respectively). On average, rulers in Christian states that practiced primogeniture had tenures 14.4 years longer than rulers of Islamic and Christian states that had other succession arrangements.[6] This seems to corroborate Stasavage's (2020) more specific argument about the causes of different ruler tenures in Christian and Muslim Iberia, mentioned earlier.

In sum, our models show that the adoption of primogeniture largely coincides with—and might well explain—the emergence of the gap in ruler tenures between Western Europe and Islamic states that Blaydes and Chaney (2013) identify. It is true that this gap starts to open somewhat earlier than the formalization of primogeniture as the succession order. But we would do well to remember that the adoption of primogeniture was a gradual process that probably had roots further back in time than it is possible to trace with the available sources. As argued in Chapter 4, there was a de facto tendency towards primogeniture in the Frankish areas of Western Europe, probably due to new norms about heirship and family structures, long before the formalization of this new succession order in the eleventh century. This de facto tendency thus coincides with the initial opening of the gap whereas the formalization of primogeniture corresponds with the widening of the gap.

Imperial China

Going back to Chapter 4, part of the reason for the instability of ruler tenures in the Islamic world (including the Ottoman Empire) probably lies in the practice of polygyny. This made it more difficult to establish clear rules of succession, even when hereditary monarchy was practiced. Polygyny produced

---

[6] Unfortunately, we cannot run a model that includes both our primogeniture variable and the century dummies for Western Europe as they are co-linear.

numerous potential male heirs, with different mothers, and it made it difficult to distinguish between legitimate and non-legitimate male heirs. All of this inhibited the adoption of primogeniture as the succession order.

However, there is at least one, very important, exception to the notion that polygyny destabilized the politics of succession. As Wang (2018) shows, average ruler tenures were long in Imperial China (AD 1000-1800), where polygyny was also practiced. Indeed, Wang attributes this stability, which for some periods was even more pronounced than in medieval and early modern Europe, to Chinese emperors having an abundance of male heirs due to polygyny—and contrast this with the European pattern of monogamy which, he argues, created an undersupply of legitimate male heirs.

Of course, China makes for a difficult comparison because it is in any case the most spectacular historical example of a stable polity (Finer 1996: 442; Scheidel 2019; Wong 1997). Despite some prolonged periods of internal division, the Chinese Empire existed for more than 2000 years, beginning long before anyone thought about the territorial states of France and England. The Chinese case is furthermore interesting because it seems to have developed in virtual isolation from the other civilization areas of Eurasia, or at least the European and the Middle Eastern cases we have discussed earlier (Watson 1992: 22, 85; Finer 1996: 442). China also had a much more developed state and bureaucracy than medieval European States. As David Stasavage (2020: 10–13, 159–64) notes, Chinese emperors were for a long time able to extract up to 10 times the revenues (as a proportion of GDP) that their European colleagues did, even though the gap eventually narrowed during the Ming and the Qing dynasties.[7] We therefore treat China as a separate universe and do a within-case analysis of the politics of succession in China rather than an empirical comparison with other areas.

To understand the normal Chinese politics of succession, we first need to say something about the so-called Mandate of Heaven. This idea, which goes all the way back to ancient China, had important consequences for succession: 'The proof that Heaven had withdrawn its mandate was the overthrow of a ruler. So, rebellion was justified—provided it succeeded' (Finer 1996: 449; see also Mote 1999: 10).

We have already seen how a similar notion destabilized ruler tenure in the Byzantine Empire. The difference is that in Imperial China, hereditary succession among the sons of the emperor was the norm and that this provided

---

[7] This fact means that political offices were much more important for political power in Imperial China than in medieval Europe, and it indirectly allows us to test whether father-to-son successions also have a stabilizing effect when private (landed) wealth matters little politically.

stability. This was the case in the first Chinese dynasty of long standing, the Han (BC 206–AD 220), and it was still the case more than one thousand years later under the Ming Dynasty (1368–1644) (Finer 1996: 483; Finer 1997a: 852).

The very meaning of dynasty for the Chinese has been defined as 'the continuous rule within successive generations of males in one patriline' (Mote 1999: 564) and many Chinese dynasties lasted for centuries. But what exactly did hereditary succession involve in this context? Chinese culture has historically been characterized by a very strong tradition of patriarchy and ancestor worship, which, for instance, infuses Confucianism (Finer 1997a: 811). This tradition almost logically leads to some form of primogeniture because it inserts a hierarchy among sons based on their biological age. As Mote (1999: 587) explains, '[l]egitimacy in the role of successor could only mean legitimacy by norms of Chinese family rules, that is, to be senior in the line of the eldest son by a proper consort.' The Chinese family pattern thus 'recognized *zu* [lineage] leadership based on primogeniture' (Mote 1999: 75). In the case of the imperial succession, it was the eldest son of the empress who was senior heir and as such primogeniture was a common practice, despite the abundant male heirs that emperors had due to their numerous consorts and concubines (Mote 1999: 100).

However, the practice of primogeniture never consolidated or formalized itself to the same extent as in medieval and early modern Europe. In principle, a Chinese emperor was usually free to nominate any of his sons as successor (Finer 1996: 483; see also Wang 2018), with nominations based on (perceived) merit being more common in some dynasties than others. While this would represent a break with Chinese family rules about seniority in some sense, it would normally be accepted as legitimate at court. It therefore seems most correct to talk about 'father-to-son' succession orders with a tendency towards primogeniture.

In some periods, these somewhat vague principles of succession did create instability. For instance, we find examples of influential factions at court deciding which son would succeed (Finer 1997a: 790). But in many other periods, the father-to-son successions were remarkably stable, and measures were taken to mitigate the vagueness of succession rules by appointing an heir-apparent— normally the eldest son of the empress—at an early stage and then banishing other male heirs to the provinces. For instance, this was done during the Ming Dynasty. The Ming Dynasty did see an early succession struggle between the designated heir of the first Ming emperor—his grandson, who was the eldest son of the predeceased eldest son of the emperor—and his uncle, the eldest living son of the emperor, who succeeded in usurping the throne after a bloody civil war. But after this incident, which underlines the normative power of primogeniture (the eldest son of a predeceased eldest son up against the eldest living son), Ming rule was characterized by a remarkable dynastic stability (Finer 1997a: 852; Mote 1999: 586–7).

Nonetheless, we do find periods of precarious ruler tenures in Imperial China. Wang's (2018) Chinese data thus reveal that here, too, we see an oscillation between periods with short and unstable ruler tenures and periods with long and stable ruler tenures, with a long-term upward secular trend. So, what explains these oscillations, or more particularly that China also saw periods of political instability in ruler tenures?

As Wang (2018) notes, these oscillations seem to track the difference between 'native' or 'Han' Chinese dynasties and dynasties established by conquering nomad people from the Central Asian steppes, of which the Mongol Yuan dynasty is probably the most famous example. It is important to note that differences between Han and nomad political stability cannot be explained in terms of the legitimacy provided by the celestial mandate, as non-Chinese rulers could also receive the Mandate and thereby be recognized as legitimate (Mote 1999: 10). The explanation must lie elsewhere. We proceed by applying our theoretical framework to understand why nomad dynasties would normally have shorter ruler tenures and see more frequent depositions.

We have already described Chinese father-to-son succession practices, in the context of hereditary monarchy characterized by abundant male heirs but with a strong tendency towards primogeniture. On the basis of our theoretical framework this model provided a recipe for dynastic and political stability.[8] The succession practices of the steppe nomads differed significantly. There is a limit to how far back in time we can go if we wish to enlist historical sources to describe these differences. But we can start with the so-called Khitan Empire or Liao Dynasty. This empire arose in what is today Mongolia and north-eastern Russia in the eighth century, and during its heydays in the tenth and eleventh century—where its Han Chinese competitor, the Song Dynasty, grudgingly accepted sharing the celestial mandate (Fernández-Armesto 1995: 44–56)—it

---

[8] While the standard Han succession model did cause an impreciseness about the identity of the heir that genuine primogeniture avoids, as Wang (2018) argues it also had advantages that we do not find in European primogeniture monarchies, in the form of an abundant supply of male heirs. A good example of the flexibility this provided is found in the case of the (aforementioned) first Ming emperor. Recent historical investigations indicate that his empress was barren but that the court simply pretended that the emperor's five oldest sons by other consorts were biological children of the empress, and hence legitimate heirs (Mote 1999: 594–5).

came to control the sixteen northern prefectures of China (including present-day Beijing).

The Khitan great khans were elected among members of a particular lineage but the elective element gave other clans a chance to legitimately claim power (Mote 1999: 40). In 907, a Khitan named Abaoji succeeded in such an outside takeover and founded a new line of great khans/Liao emperors. Abaoji tried to hinder future repeats of his own feat by getting rid of the Khitan version of elective monarchy, instead borrowing the Chinese practice of primogeniture. In 916 he named his eldest son, prince Bei, his successor. But Abaoji underestimated the power of Khitan tradition, which caused subsequent succession crises when the old elective principle clashed with the new hereditary system (Mote 1999: 49). Prince Bei was usurped by his younger brother; later, Bei's son retook the throne after a civil war. Succession crises thus continued to plague the Liao dynasty due to the rift between traditional Khitan succession practices and the model imported from China (Mote 1999: 54–6). However, 'father-to-son' successions increasingly became the Liao norm over time.

This theme was to recur every time a dynasty was established from the steppes. Large empires needed stable political institutions, but tribal societies found it difficult to establish them, creating recurring succession crises (Mote 1999: 54). A good example is the Jurchen or Jin Dynasty, 1115–1234, which replaced the Khitans/Liao Dynasty in AD 1125, proceeded to conquer Northern China, and to share the celestial mandate with the Song (Fernández-Armesto 1995: 128). The Jurchen people were only semi-nomads (based in today's Manchuria). Their Jin dynasty was established by Aguda, who died in 1123, to be succeeded by his younger brother. In the next century, several succession conflicts erupted, fuelled by traditional Jurchen succession practices, which made younger brothers within each generation the legitimate heirs of their deceased older brothers (Mote 1999: 237); the succession order that we in this book have termed 'agnatic seniority'. As the Khitans before them, there was some attempt to introduce Chinese-inspired 'father-to-son' succession arrangements, but the old Jurchen family patterns remained a hindrance and down to the end of the Jin dynasty succession conflicts were the norm rather than the exception (Mote 1999: 243). A similar development can be found among the so-called Xi Xia dynasty, a polity ruled by Buddhist Tangut people that encompassed parts of Northern China in the period 1038–1227. Here, too, we find repeated attempts by rulers to adopt primogeniture to facilitate a smoother transfer of power, which ultimately failed because they conflicted with established tribal norms of succession. The results were numerous succession conflicts, including an outright war of succession in the period 1048–1061 (Mote 1999: 179, 187).

As we return to later, similar or even worse instability due to vague succession practices characterized the Mongol Yuan Dynasty. The only nomad dynasty that clearly succeeded in adopting Chinese-inspired succession practices was the Qing, in which father-to-son succession triumphed over tribal customs of brother-inheritance and election as early as during the reign of the Shunzi emperor (r. 1643–1661), the first Qing emperor to rule China proper (Rawski 1998: 98–9). The Shunzi emperor and his son, the Kangxi emperor (r. 1661–1722), initially followed Ming tradition and named their heirs publicly. However, the Kangxi emperor came to regret having appointed his eldest son crown prince and removed him from the succession as he feared that he intrigued against him. In the wake of his decision, factions formed at court that tried to have another of his sons appointed crown prince. The emperor responded by refusing to name an heir until he lay on his death bed.

To prevent a repeat of this situation, where factions formed around the crown prince or potential crown princes, the emperor's son and the eventually appointed successor, the Yongzhen emperor (r. 1722–1735), adopted a system of 'secret succession' that continued to guide succession in the Qing dynasty down to its very end (Rawski 1998: 101–3). According to this system, the emperor informed his Grand Council that he had appointed an heir among his sons and sealed the name in a box that was not to be opened and made public until shortly before his death (or abdication). Thus, the nomination could be kept secret from the public at the same time as the elite was assured a crown prince that they could coordinate around some time before the incumbent emperor's death (or abdication). Hence, the system tackled both the crown prince problem and the coordination problem. As only the emperor's sons could be appointed crown princes and as emperors often prepared their intended crown princes by bestowing important administrative positions on them, the court would often be well placed to guess who the intended crown prince was. This system served the dynasty well until it was overthrown in the twentieth century.

To get at how succession patterns affected political instability in a more general sense, Table 9.2 presents simple descriptive statistics of how common depositions were in different Chinese dynasties in the period we have analysed in previous chapters (data from Wang 2018).

The empirical patterns are striking. In dynasties with nomad succession arrangements, emperors were on average deposed in 5 per cent of ruler years. In dynasties practicing father-to-son succession only 1 per cent of ruler years

Table 9.2 Depositions in Chinese dynasties AD 1000–1800

Dynasty	Type of succession	Deposed per year
Bei (Northern) Song	Father-to-son	0.00
Jin	Nomad	0.03
Liao	Nomad	0.00
Ming	Father-to-son	0.01
Nan (Southern) Song	Father-to-son	0.02
Qing	Father-to-son	0.00
Xi Xia	Nomad	0.04
Yuan	Nomad	0.08
Mean deposed father-to-son:		0.01
Mean deposed nomad:		0.05

Note: If the period before AD 1000 is included the Liao dynasty increases to 0.02 deposed per year, whereas the Bei (Northern) Song dynasty still have no depositions. Data from Wang (2018).

saw depositions. However, the table shows that there is plenty of variation within the former category. The Liao dynasty, in which father-to-son succession became increasingly common over time, did not see any depositions after AD 1000 (though as related earlier the period before 1000, not included in Table 9.2, was more unruly), whereas the Jin and Xi Xia dynasties saw depositions in 3 and 4 per cent of ruler years, respectively. The dynasty that without doubt experienced most political instability was the Mongol Yuan dynasty, which saw emperors being deposed in 8 per cent of ruler years.

To better understand the instability that characterized the Yuan dynasty—and hence the problems caused by nomad succession arrangements more generally—we proceed by carrying out a narrative historical analysis of Mongol succession practices and their consequences. The Mongol Empire emerged out of nowhere around 1200 as Chinggis Khan unified the nomadic Mongol tribes on the steppe northwest of China. Chinggis and his sons and grandsons proceeded to conquer the greatest territorial agglomeration ever, stretching from Russia and Syria in the west to China and Korea in the east. Indeed, the Chinggisids would dominate Eurasian history in the next two centuries (Mote 1999: 403).

The Mongol tribes historically had mixed rules for the succession, including agnatic seniority (eldest brother) succession and ultimogeniture (youngest son) succession (Rossabi 2012: 34–5; Mote 1999: 425–35). But Chinggis had himself been 'elected' or perhaps more accurately 'acclaimed' as Great Khan by the most important Mongol chieftains in 1206. Chinggis and his heirs quickly established a model of hereditary succession in the sense that future Mongol rulers had to come from the Chinggisid line, meaning the descendants of Chinggis's four sons with his principal wife, Börte. As the Mongols practiced polygyny, each of these sons would spawn numerous male heirs. However, neither Chinggis nor his heirs succeeded in establishing a ranked order between these male relatives. Chinggis allegedly attempted to make his eldest son Jochi his heir in 1219 but had to backtrack due to opposition from his other sons by Börte (Mote 1999: 442). Eventually, he instead appointed his third eldest son Ögödei as heir. Ögödei (r. 1229–1241) accordingly became Great Khan after him, but he did not similarly appoint a successor.

The immediate result was a five-year interregnum after Ögödei's death (Mote 1999: 439). The eventual solution to the problem of succession was based on chieftains selecting future Great Khans, in the same way as Chinggis had been in 1206. Meanwhile, the influence of previous norms of succession affected these elections. The venerated practice of ultimogeniture[9] thus helped the heirs of Chinggis's youngest son by Börte, Tolui—first Möngke Khan (r. 1251–1259) and then Khubilai Khan (r. 1260–1294)—secure election as great khans.

But there was no consensus on how to select great khans and different branches of Chinggisids quickly came into conflict with each other when they supported different candidates (Rossabi 2012: 34–5). Indeed, the end of the unified Mongol Empire is normally dated to Möngke's ascension in 1251, as several other Chinggisid lines failed to renounce their claims, and it was clearly a fact when Kubulai took the throne in an even more disputed succession in 1260 (Mote 1999: 443).

The Mongol realm effectively splintered into four: the Golden Horde ruled by descendants of Chinggis's eldest son Jochi, the Central Asian Khanate ruled by descendants of his second eldest son Chagatai, the Great Khans and later Yuan emperors descended from Khubilai, and the il-Khanate ruled by descendants of Möngke's and Khubilai's brother Hulagu. Not only were there frequent conflicts between these realms, each of them was also characterized by repeated succession crises and by short ruler tenures.

We have already seen the Yuan deposition numbers. They are in fact even starker than they initially appear when we consider the brevity of the Yuan

---

[9] This Mongol practice did not necessarily mean that all other sons were disinherited. But it meant that the youngest son would normally take over the main patrimony whereas older sons were supposed to make a living elsewhere (as mentioned in Chapter 2, a similar practice was found among some peasantries in Western Europe, where the youngest son would stay at the farm and care for his parents while older sons would seek occupation elsewhere). Tolui, as the youngest of Chinggis's four sons with Börte, therefore inherited the Mongolian homeland or heartland (Mote 1999: 434–5).

Dynasty, coupled with the fact that the founder, Khubilai, enjoyed a long reign. But even Khubilai was a victim of the Mongol succession arrangements. He thus had to fight and win a civil war against his brother Arigh Böke, as both had convened gatherings of Mongol chieftains that had declared them Great Khans in 1260. After winning this fratricidal conflict, he sat safely on the throne and eventually died a natural death. Yet new instability soon followed. After the death of Khubilai's grandson Temür in 1306, a period of frequent murders of emperors and claimants followed (Rossabi 2012: 114). During the 1320s and 1330s, the Yuan Dynasty was riven by prolonged succession crises and by the 1350s, the dynasty had lost control of much of China (Mote 1999: 470–2, 517–21). Down to its very end in 1368, Yuan emperors tended to come to the throne through intrigue and these repeated succession conflicts have been singled out as 'a critical factor in the dynasty's fall' (Rossabi 2012: 115; see also Mote 1999: 519).

We find similar dynamics in the other Mongol states ruled by the Chinggisids, indicating that the Mongol succession order (or lack of it) is to blame for the Yuan instability. The il-Khanate centered on Iran in fact proved even more brittle, for much the same reason. After the death of Hulagu's son Tegüder in 1284, the subsequent two il-khans were murdered. The dynasty lasted less than eighty years and—tellingly—during this period only one of its chief ministers died a natural death, the rest losing their lives in the incessant factional infighting among potential Chinggisid heirs. The Chagatai Khanate in Central Asia was also unstable, lasting only until 1347. The partial exception is the Golden Horde, ruled by Jochi's branch of Chinggisids, which had a much longer staying power. But it, too, was constantly riven by succession struggles. For instance, in the period 1359–1380, there were 21 different Golden Horde khans, most of whom came to a violent end. As Rossabi (2012: 121) concludes in a history of the Mongols, '[t]he lack of a regular, orderly system for succession to the Great Khanate resulted in devastating struggles for power, often weakening the victors.'

Hence, it is unsurprising that we see more emperors deposed during the Yuan dynasty than during all other Chinese dynasties, nomad ones included.

Conclusion

In his *History of Government*, Samuel P. Finer (1997a: 752) casually remarks about the Chinese Tang Dynasty (618–907) that '[s]uch plots as there were concerned the succession, the weak spot in all monarchies not adhering strictly to the rule of primogeniture.' This chapter has very much borne out Finer's 'weak spot' observation. Using narrative historical evidence, we have shown how the problem of succession created political instability in great empires such as the Roman and the Byzantine ones and how Muslim states never solved this problem either. The result was that, after the spread of primogeniture, Western European rulers began to enjoy longer tenures than rulers in both Muslim states and the Byzantine Empire. Specifically, this difference sheds new light on the reversal of fortune we find in the Iberian Peninsula, where after AD 1000 the Christian states of the north proved less brittle than the Muslim states of the south.

We have also used our politics of succession framework to capture an important variation between Chinese imperial dynasties: namely the variation between 'nomad' dynasties and 'Han' or native Chinese dynasties. Whereas the latter practiced 'father-to-son' hereditary successions with a tendency towards primogeniture, the others started out with succession orders based on election/acclamation or agnatic seniority and conflicts frequently erupted as 'nomad' emperors attempted to secure the throne for their (eldest) sons, partly inspired by 'Han' succession practices. This was the case in the Khitan Liao dynasty as well as in the Jurchen Jin dynasty that replaced it, and we also find evidence of it in the Tangut Xi Xia dynasty. However, instability due to rules of succession was most pronounced among the Mongol dynasties spawned by Chinggis Khan. The Chinese Yuan Dynasty, the il-Khanate of Iran, and the Central Asian Chagatai Khanate all proved short-lived, at least in part due to repeated bouts of instability sparked by succession. We find a similar instability in the one Chinggisid polity that had more staying power, namely the Golden Horde centred on Southern Russia.

As this chapter has documented, the mechanisms of political instability during successions that we have studied in medieval and early modern Europe can thus be found in other areas of Eurasia as well. We could also have looked elsewhere. For instance, an important reason for why Pizarro was able to conquer the Inca empire so easily was that the empire was weakened by a war of succession between two brothers, which Pizarro used to his advantage (Rowe 2006). Going much further back in time, the mighty neo-Assyrian Empire (972-612 BC) that dominated the Middle East for centuries 'was ultimately undone not by a foreign power but by a series of civil wars between rival heirs to the throne' (Podany 2014: 111). These succession wars were fought out by two successive generations of royal brothers, and they weakened Assyria so much that the Medes and Babylonians were able to attack and destroy the capital city of Nineveh in 612 BC, effectively ending the once so formidable Empire. The problem of succession is in fact inherent to all political systems which concentrate power into the hands of one individual, and the way it is handled determines both the character and success of the polity.

Our comparative perspective therefore goes some way towards explaining why European monarchies ended up as more successful than polities elsewhere; with the important exception of Imperial China under native dynasties, probably the most stable polity known to human history. The gradual adoption of primogeniture—first in practice in the ninth and tenth century, then in a more formalized way from the eleventh century onwards—placed European state-builders in a better position because it decreased political instability and lengthened time horizons.

10
Conclusions

Human life is short, and until the advent of modern medicine, even men in their prime would often die unexpectedly. Throughout history, autocracies have therefore regularly been rattled by the problem of who will succeed in power. Authoritarian successions are often violent moments where power relations must be reconfigured. For elite groups this is a dangerous situation. Which would-be ruler has the better chance of securing the top job? Who to bet on to end up on the winning side? And, even if the bet is correct, who will be the insiders under the new ruler, and who will be left out in the cold?

The result of these calculations, machinations, and clashing interests are often devastating for the elites of the polity. Although a contest between rival contenders opens opportunities for personal advancement, it comes with enormous risks, as violence is the ultimate arbiter of conflicts in autocracies (Svolik 2012: 2). Ending up on the losing side in a succession struggle can result in a violent death, or at least forfeiting property and income. But the elites are certainly not the only potential victims. Ruler depositions and wars of succession often destroy or enfeeble the state apparatus, and they can bring times of troubles for the population if they are caught between warring factions or if anarchy prevails. The wars of the Spanish (1701–1714) and Polish succession (1733–1735) are but two examples on a very long list, which—if complete—would have to start in the era of the first states in the Fertile Crescent (Scott 2017).

In preceding chapters, we have shown that ruler depositions and power-sharing institutions are other corollaries of uncertainty about the succession, at least in the medieval and early modern European monarchies we have analysed in this book. Succession, and the anticipation thereof, governed the fortunes of individual monarchs as well as their dynasties, caused revolts and wars, affected the character of ruler–elite relations, was the reason for territorial expansion or contraction, and ultimately determined which states would survive and thrive.

Authoritarian succession is so difficult because—as opposed to democracies—autocracies by definition lack independent institutions that guarantee an orderly power transfer from one leader to the next. Succession arrangements that allow for many contenders are problematic because they leave the elites uncertain about where to place their loyalties. Members of the elite therefore normally prefer to avoid a brutal succession struggle to keep what they have. However, to do so they need to agree upon a successor and to coordinate their efforts to get him installed. Solving this 'coordination problem' is notoriously difficult. The best way of doing so is by designating an heir, supported by law and tradition, who can provide a focal point for the elite. While powerful members of the elite might be unhappy not to get a shot at the top job for themselves or their children, the existence of an undisputed heir will enable them to keep their position, provided they groom the successor sufficiently.

A designated successor thus decreases the risk that potential pretenders will rebel against the ruler as he grows weary and tired. However, while an appointed successor or 'crown prince' underwrites the dictator's rule, he can at the same time be the ruler's most dangerous enemy. After all, the crown prince's route to the throne goes over the dictator's grave. And, as the elites begin to vie for position in the future court of the crown prince, the ruler can become increasingly isolated, a 'lame duck'. This 'crown prince problem' is especially acute when the appointed successor belongs to the same generation as the ruler and cannot be sure to eventually inherit.

To create authoritarian stability, it is therefore necessary to develop some sort of arrangement that handles this dual problem of succession. In this book, we have argued that such a solution was devised in medieval Europe, and we have demonstrated that it was to shape European patterns of political stability and state-formation in the period 1000–1800.

The fall of Francia and the birth of France

We began the book with the coronation of Charlemagne as Roman Emperor in St. Peter's Basilica in Rome on Christmas day AD 800. The new emperor's power was then at a pinnacle. The Carolingian realm comprised what are today France, the Netherlands, Belgium, Switzerland, Northern Spain, and large parts of present-day Germany, Austria, Slovenia, and Italy, and it was arguably stronger—at least in military terms—than the much more culturally refined and administratively sophisticated Byzantine or Eastern Roman Empire, centred on Constantinople (Wickham 2005: 145).

One reason for the spectacular state-building success of the Carolingians seems to have been a biological coincidence. For several centuries, the Carolingian monarchs regularly left only one male heir at their death, as all other legitimate sons predeceased their fathers. This meant that the realm remained intact, a complete volte-face from the days of their predecessors, the Merovingians, where the territories of the Franks were constantly subdivided among several royal claimants, normally the sons of the deceased king.

However, by the death of Charlemagne's son Louis the Pious in 840, the Carolingians' biological luck had run out. Louis left three grown sons, and just like the Merovingians before them, the Carolingians subscribed to the norm of partible inheritance, meaning that the realm was to be divided among these sons. Louis originally intended his eldest son and co-emperor, Lothair, to have suzerainty over his younger brothers' kingdoms. But after the death of their father, the brothers fell upon each other's necks, as they could not agree on how to divide their father's lands between them, nor whether Lothair would rule the roost.

Indeed, they had already fought a war against their father a decade earlier in anticipation of the succession struggle, in part because Louis constantly reshuffled his lands between them (and other brothers who predeceased their father), confusing everyone about how the inheritance was to be divided. A ferocious civil war ended with the Treaty of Verdun of 843, which established the kingdoms of West, Middle, and East Francia, ruled by the three brothers Charles II, the Bald, Lothair I, and Louis II, the German. This division was to have long-term historical consequences as the western and eastern realms developed into France and Germany, respectively. In a shorter-term perspective, the civil wars and partitions after 840 produced a virtual breakdown of public order—with anarchy and lawlessness as the consequence—in West Francia, ruled by Charles the Bald and his successors (Jordan 2001: 60; Wickham 2009).

It was at the nadir of this ninth- and tenth-century collapse of state power that a Frankish nobleman, Hugh Capet, in 987 took the throne of West Francia as the first non-Carolingian since the Merovingians. In the eleventh century, the Capetians were hardly able to rule their native area around Paris—the Île-de-France—in any effective sense, and had to battle robber barons for control of territory close to the capital (Bartlett 2000: 17).

But the Capetians had one thing in their favour. Even before taking the throne, they had broken with the old Frankish tradition of partible inheritance. The patrimonial lands of the Capetians passed undivided to the eldest son, based on the principle of primogeniture. Moreover, the Capetians also had biological luck. For more than 300 years, until the death of Charles IV in 1328, Capetian kings managed to produce at least one surviving male heir, who—based on primogeniture—took over the core Capetian possessions.[1] This allowed the family to slowly consolidate their hold on the throne of West Francia, or France (*Regnum Franciae*) as it was first called in 1205, under the Capetian King Philip II Augustus.

Officially, tenth- and eleventh-century France was an elective monarchy, as were many other kingdoms in Western and Central Europe at that time. This did not mean that the French people elected their monarch, it meant that the French magnates did so, just as the—lay and ecclesiastical—'electors' across the Rhine in the Holy Roman Empire were to do for centuries henceforth. To avoid surprises at these king-elections, eleventh- and twelfth-century Capetian kings normally took the precaution of having their eldest son elected as successor during their own reign. However, during the calm waters of Capetian rule[2] this tradition developed into a mere formality and the aforementioned Philip II Augustus, who ruled from 1180 to 1223, was the last French king to be elected by the magnates. By the early thirteenth century, the Capetian tradition of primogeniture had thus become the official succession order of what was now known as the Kingdom of France.

The ability to impose primogeniture instead of elective kingship helped the Capetians to stabilize and augment their power. After they had achieved effective control of the entire Île-de-France, royal authority gradually radiated to regions of West Francia that had for centuries been outside of the sway of French monarchs. This development culminated in the first decades of the thirteenth century; tellingly the very period where Capetians were strong enough to do away with the formality of king-elections and to proclaim the *Regnum Franciae*. In 1202, Philip II Augustus confiscated the Angevin possessions of Normandy and Anjou from John Lackland and then, in 1214, defeated the English king in the Battle of Bouvines to establish this fact on the ground, and in the 1220s, his son, Louis VIII, retook the areas south of the Loire and in Languedoc (Jordan 2001: 228).

---

[1] This dynastic stability contrasts with the instability of the Capetians main competitors, the Norman and later Angevin kings of England, who in the period 1075–1225 were only able to complete two successions from father to oldest surviving son. But this instability was a prelude to a remarkable stability, as the English crown saw an 'unbroken chain of father-eldest son inheritance from 1216 to 1377' (Bartlett 2000: 4–5).

[2] '[N]o French king suffered a violent death at the hands of assailants between the death of Robert I in battle in 923 and the assassination of Henry III in 1589, a record that has no parallel in medieval Europe' (Bartlett 2020: 245).

Thus 'France' was created, a realm that was destined to become the strongest state in Continental Europe. In this process, dynastic politics figured prominently. Many of the lands south of the Loire were thus first secured by Capetian cadet lines via marriage and then later consolidated with the royal lands (Moore 2000: 166). This was the backdrop of the remarkable French state-building and centralization of power begun by the Capetians, intensified under the Valois and the Bourbons, and emphasized by Alexis de Tocqueville (1955[1856]) in his work on *The Old Regime and the Revolution*.

Primogeniture and European state-formation

This book has shown that the French development under the Capetians captures a more general pattern in the Latin west. The above-mentioned ninth- and tenth-century collapse of public power or royal authority affected most of Western and Central Europe (Wickham 2009; 2016; Bisson 2009; Oakley 2010). This breakdown had several different causes. But key among these were the problems regularly unleashed by succession. Conflicts over succession created spikes of political instability and unrest, potentially culminating in civil wars.

A core reason for this is to be found in the succession orders of the day, which were vague and ambiguous, or even designed to allow for clashes between rival contenders. The best example of this is elective monarchy. Though monarch elections were often a mere formality, they made it possible for several members of a royal or princely family to reach for the throne, and this possibility always loomed, even if fathers in the normal case were succeeded by sons.

Similar problems were created by succession orders that allowed a monarch to appoint his own successor. These royal appointments often led to controversy and strife, either because the king never appointed an heir or because he was free to change his mind. People who had access to dying monarchs would regularly assert that they had been appointed heir.

Even hereditary monarchy could spark such conflicts if succession rules were vague. The fate of Louis the Pious's empire is telling. There was no established rule on how to divide the realm between the Emperor's sons. It was not even clear whether all sons would inherit or how lands should be redistributed between the sons when a new son was born, or an old son predeceased his father. Neither was it clear whether other male relatives were entitled to their share of the inheritance (such as Louis the Pious's nephew, Bernard, who ruled as king in Italy in the name of his uncle). In essence, the partition was decided ad hoc by Louis himself, who used his discretionary powers to reshuffle his lands, and the titles that came with them, between his sons on several occasions. This sowed seeds of distrust and discord both between himself and his sons and among the sons.

Indeed, even when the inheritance was left intact unforeseen situations could arise. For instance, what happened if the eldest son of the king predeceased his father but left a living son? Did the king's second eldest son or the deceased son's eldest son inherit in such circumstances? Could daughters inherit if the king did not have a living son? Might the throne even be inherited by males via marriage into the female line if there was no male issue?

In other words, all the succession arrangements of the day fell short of solving what we have termed the 'coordination problem' and the 'crown prince problem', respectively. Primogeniture, as it was developed under the Capetians, provided a compromise solution to both problems as the principle clearly identifies an heir around whom the elite can rally, but also ensures that this heir is considerably younger than the monarch. The crown prince can thus afford to bide his time, and the aging monarch and his eldest son has a common interest—possibly biologically hardwired—in perpetuating their dynasty. The fact that he will inherit his father's private wealth also guarantees that the balance between the monarch and the regime will remain intact when he assumes office.

Primogeniture was gradually introduced by enterprising monarchs not only in Capetian France but across Western Europe. By the mid-sixteenth century, primogeniture had become the principle of succession in formerly elective monarchies such as France, England, and Sweden.

The empirical analyses we have presented in this book have shown the value of this transformation, as succession was a violent business that regularly unleashed political instability. The advent and spread of primogeniture went quite some way towards solving or at least mitigating many of the problems of succession: it decreased the incidence of civil war, meant that fewer monarchs were deposed, lessened monarchs' dependence on power-sharing institutions, prolonged dynasties and individual ruler tenures, and it ultimately allowed the consolidation of territories which culminated in the modern European territorial states. Indeed, the effects on ruler deposition and civil war are rather spectacular. We have demonstrated that medieval and early modern monarchs who operated under principles of succession other than primogeniture were about three times more likely to be deposed, and when they died of natural causes, civil wars were about three times more likely to break out.

The stabilizing effects of primogeniture in Western Europe were to have global geopolitical consequences. Around AD 1000, Western and Central Europe had been by far the least developed of the great Eurasian civilization areas, an economic, cultural, and political backwater compared with the flourishing Byzantine Empire, which was in the midst of its great flowering under the Macedonian Dynasty; and even more so in comparison with the Abbasid Caliphate in its golden epoch in the ninth century or with Imperial China, which around AD 1000 was the economic powerhouse of the world (McNeill 1982; Wickham 2009). Fast-forward to the nineteenth century and hitherto backward countries on the Atlantic seaboard such as England and France had grown powerful enough to colonize most of the world.

The late American sociologists Charles Tilly (1992) famously explained this historical process—which meant that 1000 European polities around AD 1000 became 25 territorial states around 1900—with his observation that 'war made the state, and the state made war' (Tilly 1975: 142). The gist of Tilly's argument was that what he termed 'nation states' such as France and England were better able to wage war than city-states such as Florence or Venice, or empires such as the Holy Roman Empire. This meant that they eventually triumphed in the Darwinian struggle for survival that characterized medieval and early modern Europe.

However, as recent scholarship has noted, a closer look at the European experience reveals that there is in fact little evidence for this Darwinian model of territorial consolidation via conquest: European wars seldom had the do-or-die character that Tilly's model seems to be premised on (Spruyt 2017; Gorski and Sharma 2017; Abramson 2017; Haldén 2020). Our work suggests an alternative, or at least modified, interpretation, based on the observation that Tilly's nation states were monarchies with primogeniture succession. At the dawn of the nineteenth century, Europe's elective monarchies were a distant memory, as they had either been conquered by rivalling primogeniture monarchies or had changed their succession order to primogeniture (as happened in Capetian France). In contrast, half of the monarchies in our sample that practiced primogeniture throughout their existence still survived on the eve of the French Revolution, and almost none of those that had disappeared had been conquered by other states. Instead, they had coalesced with other primogeniture monarchies via dynastic unions because this succession order, coupled with female inheritance, allowed a peaceful mechanism for territorial agglomeration in situations where a ruling family had died out in the male line. The introduction of primogeniture therefore sheds light on what Samuel P. Finer (1997b: 1269) identified as a unique feature of European state formation:

that it was only here states regularly changed shape via marriage alliances or via testament, rather than (as elsewhere) via war and conquest.

The politics of succession beyond Europe

Our empirical analyses have by and large been confined to European Christian monarchies, AD 1000-1800. But Chapter 9 did apply our politics of succession arguments in comparative perspective, centred on the old civilization areas of Eurasia. We here documented how we find similar dynamics beyond our European sample: outside of Europe, successions were also precarious moments, which often saw conflict, sometimes culminating in war. Moreover, the lack of clear succession rules made for short ruler tenures and frequent usurpations, reaching grotesque proportions in polities such as the Byzantine Empire and the Mamluk Sultanate. Our comparative investigation thus showed that the absence of primogeniture created political instability in authoritarian states outside of Europe in the period we have analysed, just as it had done in Europe before that time.

The rarity of this succession order outside of Europe can at least partly be explained by the fact that its advent depended on a large-scale transformation of family structures and heirship practices, which began in late antiquity and received an important impetus following the so-called Gregorian Reforms of the eleventh century. In Chapter 4, we used a narrative historical analysis to show that the main engine behind this social transformation was the medieval Catholic Church, which first transformed marriage and heirship practices and after the eleventh century even campaigned actively for primogeniture. We also argued that it was the ninth- and tenth-century state collapse that allowed the Church to assert itself as an independent international organization.

However, we did identify one important exception to the claim that the institution of primogeniture was conditional on nuclear and monogamous family structures and the Church-sponsored heirship practices that had brought these about. This was Imperial China, which practiced a form of hereditary monarchy that combined an ample supply of male successors (due to polygyny) with a tendency towards primogeniture that was a result of strong 'Confucian' norms about hierarchy or seniority within families, even if emperors could forego their first-born and choose another if the eldest son was deemed unsuitable for the succession. We termed this model 'father-to-son' successions and showed how Chinese ruler tenures were much more stable in periods where native 'Han' dynasties practiced this succession order than in periods where 'nomad' dynasties ruled parts or all of China and practiced other succession orders, including versions of elective monarchy and agnatic seniority.

The Chinese father-to-son succession order might help explain the remarkable stability of the Chinese imperial state, which can be traced in an unbroken line all the way back to ancient China. Wang (2018) goes so far as to argue that Chinese successions orders were more stable than European ones because the latter—even under primogeniture—were hampered by an undersupply of male heirs (due to monogamy and strict rules about legitimacy). The fact that appointments were usually made early in emperors' reigns and proclaimed officially, at the same time as they were almost never revoked, made them credible.

The Chinese practice bears some similarity to what characterized the period of transition from elective monarchy to hereditary monarchy in many European countries. So, it is true that China in this respect resembled Europe, and in fact may have had a more stable succession given the ample supply of heirs. However, this may partially have to do with the fact that Chinese emperors were more powerful than European rulers and were better able to enforce their appointments (for example, they did not need the elite's consent for their chosen heir). European history is fraught with examples of similar practices failing because monarchs were too weak to force the elites to elect their eldest son as co-rulers. In contrast, the Chinese polity is historically unique in its remarkable stability and settled identity over time, based on strong norms and institutions, and in the fact that for extended periods, it faced few or no threats from foreign enemies who could unseat Chinese emperors.[3] The strength of the central government and the political stability it gave rise to is probably part of what allowed Chinese emperors to, as Wang shows, credibly nominate a crown prince from among their multiple male issues and thereby avoid that the heirs would have to fight it out.

This remarkable political stability may also explain why China never developed many of the power-sharing arrangements that appeared in Europe in the period we study—often during, or following, troubled successions (see Chapter 7). Indeed, China was perhaps too stable for its own good, at least in world-historical perspective. The absence of recurring succession crises may have robbed elites of the opportunities to participate in government that were regularly offered their European counterparts—just as the absence of a

---

[3] As documented in Chapter 9, in some periods China was internally divided and/or faced formidable enemies, normally from the nomadic people on its Northern frontiers (Mote 1999). But these periods were still the exception, not the norm.

multiplicity of competing political units may have made rulers more conservative when it came to the adoption of economic and bureaucratic technologies (Scheidel 2019). If so, Europe's luck—in a development perspective—may have been that it managed to find a balance between too little and too much stability.

We leave it to future research to systematically probe these claims about the difference between Europe and China. But we did carry out one cross-regional comparison: between Europe and the Middle East. Enlisting data on ruler tenure from Blaydes and Chaney (2013), we demonstrated how the transition to primogeniture corresponds with—and possibly explains—the divergence in ruler tenures they find between these two areas. After the transition to primogeniture that began in the Frankish heartlands around AD 1000, European polities became more stable than polities in the Middle East. This dovetails with one of the second-order claims of this book: that in the high Middle Ages Europe came to differ from the other great civilization areas of Eurasia (save China) with respect to the politics of succession, and that this helps us understand the staggering 'Rise of Europe'.

History thus shows that states can make or break depending on how they are able to cope with leadership transitions. This reflects a simple fact. At any given time, state-building is about winning wars, subduing or motivating people, controlling territory, and raising the revenue needed to do this. But in a long-term perspective, effective state-building requires institutions that ensure that the state's destiny does not depend upon a particular individual. In other words, it requires institutions that enable power to be transferred in an orderly way from ruler to ruler, generation after generation.

Our findings can be illustrated with a metaphor used by an eleventh-century Armenian writer. Noting the frequent coups and deposition in Constantinople, he remarked that while 'patrilineal succession is like iron … the Byzantine custom of intrusion by outsiders is like mere brick' (quoted in Bartlett 2020: 4). In this book, we have shown how primogeniture monarchy allowed European rulers to increase political stability and forge strong states. Figuratively speaking, the advent of this succession order allowed Western European rulers to make political structures of iron, replacing the political structures of clay that had so often collapsed in the past.

This does not mean that primogeniture removed all political uncertainty over the inheritance. As we have shown in this book, biological luck also played a part. Dynastic fortune could be very capricious, and childlessness could spell the end of dynasties. There are cases of kings who left several male heirs at their death but whose male lines nevertheless quickly went extinct. A good example is the end of the Capetian 'miracle', after three hundred years of uninterrupted father-to-son successions and augmentation of French royal power. This end came very suddenly and unexpectedly, following the successive deaths of French king Philip the Fair, his three sons, and his grandson in 1314, 1316, 1322, and 1328; collectively known as *les rois maudits*—'the accursed kings' (Bartlett 2020: 77). These sudden deaths were to spark (or were at least used to motivate—see Chapter 5) the Hundred Year's War which devastated the Kingdom of France. This illustrates one of the main points of this book: the calm waters of Capetian rule gave way to tempestuous waters of all-out succession war. In a world of monogamous marriages, rulers might win or lose in the genetic lottery. But this element of reproductive chance (and the high mortality levels of the day) only increased the need for institutions to mitigate uncertainty.

Succession in modern authoritarian states

This book has dealt with the problem of succession in a bygone era, in which ordinary people had little involvement in politics, state administrations were rudimentary, and monarchs ruled by the grace of God. Do our findings have any relevance in the modern world? We think so, with some caveats.

Our findings place in relief what is arguably the key advantage of modern representative democracy, its ability to handle the problem of succession in a new and constructive way. By mandating regular rotation in office and introducing checks on the executive, the stakes of succession have been decreased. Contenders for power know that a failed attempt will not result in loss of life and that they will get another chance, later on. As Joseph Schumpeter (1973[1942]) long ago observed, stripped to the core, democracy is a non-violent mechanism for designating a successor; in the words of Karl Popper, it is the only regime 'in which it is possible to get rid of a government without bloodshed' (1999: 93). Modern democracy thus solves the problem of how to transfer power that has bedevilled virtually all other political regimes throughout history and which primogeniture only mitigates. Nonetheless, even in well-consolidated democracies leadership transitions can become moments fraught with uncertainty, as became all too evident after the US presidential election of 3 November 2020. For more than two months, the institutional guardrails of democratic power transfer were tested. They held firm but only after a turbulent period where the former president and his allies attempted to subvert the rules of the game.

However, a significant portion of the world's states are still non-democratic and according to recent scholarship there are even tendencies that democracy is losing its foothold in several places (Lührmann and Lindberg 2019; but see Skaaning 2020). And when one person is in charge, the problem of succession always looms large. Sooner or later, the person at the top of the pyramid must be replaced. As Nobel laureate and Soviet exile Joseph Brodsky (1987: 113) once ironically put it '[i]llness and death are, perhaps, the only thing that a tyrant has in common with his subjects.' Just as an ambitious nobleman in the thirteenth century had to secure the backing of key persons to make a bid for power, so must the aspiring authoritarian president today. It is only the titles of the key persons that have changed: duke, count, queen, cardinal, and royal steward back then; general, minister, first lady, business mogul, and party official now. Then as now, no one wants to be dragged into an uncertain and dangerous power struggle, but most of all, no one wants to back a loser. The game stays the same, even though the circumstances have changed.

A majority of authoritarian regimes do not survive the death or the departure of the first leader (Meng 2020: 97), showing the frailty of most undemocratic systems today. This means that questions of succession will continue to remain high on the political agenda for years to come. But what are the different ways authoritarian succession is handled today?

Modern-day monarchy

Monarchies—disregarding constitutional ones with democratic institutions, as in much of Western Europe—are today a small minority, but some still exist, most notably in the Middle East. Comparative research has found that among authoritarian states, monarchies are often more durable and less prone to experience civil war than military dictatorships and party-based regimes (Hadenius and Teorell 2007; Svolik 2012; Møller 2019), which could possibly be attributed to the mechanisms regulating succession. However, primogeniture is not always the norm in these monarchies. In Saudi Arabia, succession has for long followed the principle of agnatic seniority, the throne passing between the sons of the founder Ibn Saud. As the remaining sons are now very old, this practice is becoming unsustainable, and in June 2017, King Salman appointed his 32-year-old son Mohammed bin Salman as crown prince. There was much opposition against this in the royal family and the decision had to be enforced by a de facto purge within the family. This heavy-handed attempt to solve the problem of succession has not ended the speculation about who will eventually replace King Salman. In March 2019, there were even reports that the aging king was afraid that Mohammed bin Salman would unseat him ahead of time (*The Guardian* 2019). Whatever the truth of these rumours, such fears would not be unfounded given that King Salman has had two different designated successors before Mohammed bin Salman. The crown prince problem is on full display—with his status as designated successor, Mohammed bin Salman is now often referred to as the real power behind the throne, but he cannot be certain that he will inherit and therefore has an incentive to hasten the succession.

Michael Herb (1999) has argued that the ambiguity of the succession rules is a cause of the longevity of the Saudi Arabian monarchy. Because the principle has been largely undefined and subject to negotiation between different branches of the sprawling royal family, it necessitates compromising and compensating rivals. Needless to say, we disagree with Herb's assessment. A regime that manages to survive despite regular succession crises might be durable but only because there are other factors that ensure its survival. If we subject many units to a stress test, those which do not break are indeed the strongest, but this is not a causal effect of the stress test; it is only a filtering mechanism. We need to look at general patterns in the whole sample. Moreover, it is dubious whether Saudi Arabia can really be seen as a success story with respect to succession: of the seven monarchs that have held power since the state's founding, two have been deposed. Looking at the entire region, the monarchies that have practiced primogeniture have seen fewer depositions (Kokkonen and Sundell 2014), which might be a reason for the Sultanate of Oman's recent adoption of primogeniture as the principle of succession, a transition from a system of designation by the reigning sultan (Reuters 2021).

Hereditary succession in non-monarchies

Some non-monarchic states have attempted, and succeeded, to transfer power from father to son. Notable examples include the Assads in Syria, the Duvaliers in Haiti, and the Kims in North Korea (Brownlee 2007). However, this kind of modern-day de facto hereditary succession cannot be expected to have the same effects as in the medieval and early modern monarchies we have studied in this book. States are no longer seen as property that can be inherited and liberal ideas of equality and impartiality have decreased the validity of blood relation as a legitimate claim to power. Furthermore, our primary argument for why primogeniture increased political stability is that it was predictable, almost mechanic. When father-to-son succession is neither enshrined in the constitution nor widely seen as legitimate, it remains unpredictable and unlikely to solve the coordination problem.

For instance, Kim Jong-un of North Korea allegedly had his half-brother assassinated and his uncle executed as part of his attempt to consolidate power. And there are many examples of failed attempts at hereditary succession: Egypt's dictator Hosni Mubarak was, for example, positioning his oldest son, Gamal, for the top job on the eve of the Arab Uprisings in 2011. However, his grooming effort ended in failure and according to many observers triggered the events that led to his downfall. Efforts to imitate primogeniture in the absence of monarchical institutions are a recipe for conflict, as Mubarak discovered.

This might sound strange considering evidence that a lot of hereditary grooming—promoting children of the ruler to positions of power—is still going on in today's autocracies. However, this is probably mainly for the reasons discussed in Chapter 8, namely that rulers feel more comfortable relying on family members in the exercise of power (see also Ambrosio and Tolstrup 2021). As emphasized earlier, the fact is that we find very few *successful* attempts to pass on the top job to children, at least outside of the few remaining monarchies.

So, why has genuine hereditary succession almost died out in modern autocracies? Brownlee (2007) has made the point that we do not see this kind of succession in regimes with strong ruling parties, but the absence of hereditary succession in contemporary autocracies is a much more general phenomenon. The main reason seems to be simpler, namely that after the advent and success of modern representative democracy this succession order is by and large illegitimate. Our book has emphasized a historical analogue to this, namely the opposition that kings in elective monarchies often encountered when trying to render elections void by placing their sons on the throne prematurely. The difference is of course that today the idea of dynastic rule is much more suspect, which makes it even harder to introduce a form of de facto hereditary succession order.

Constitutions

A marked difference between autocratic states of past and present is thus that the latter almost all bear many of the trappings of representative democracy, such as legislatures, recurring elections, and constitutions (Brooker 2011). These constitutions often stipulate term limits for the executive and sometimes also procedures for succession, and at first glance thus seem to be a solution to the uncertainty regarding the transfer of power. However, without credible checks and balances—or an equal power balance between rulers and ruled more generally—institutions such as a constitution can never be truly effective. Still, it has been argued that term limits could prove to be an obstacle for an authoritarian leader wishing to rule indefinitely as transgressions of them are easily observable and thus serve as a rallying point for the elite (Svolik 2013). The constitution itself is toothless but can help solve the coordination problem by providing 'a line in the sand' (Svolik 2012: 198).

A study of African states found that when constitutional rules regulating the succession were in place, leaders saw less frequent coups and the attempts that were made were less successful (Meng 2020: 198). Of course, an obvious threat to the stabilizing effect of constitutions is that they can be changed by the dictator. But, according to the same study, when amendments to the constitution regulating succession were created, three-fourths of the amendments were in fact allowed to remain in place (Meng 2020: 105). Constitutions in authoritarian states do not have the same power as in democracies but are apparently not completely meaningless, either.

However, there seems to be differences in the binding strength of different constitutional features. A survey of whether authoritarian leaders abide by term limits show that they are often transgressed but virtually never through outright rule-breaking. Instead, the constitution is amended to allow the ruler to prolong his tenure (Meng 2019). Notable recent examples include Vladimir Putin's amendment of the Russian constitution to allow for a third term and Xi Jinping's abolition of the term limits for the Chinese presidency. The Chinese case is especially interesting as it had until then been highlighted as an odd case where institutions had been able to constrain authoritarian leaders. Communist China seemed to have succeeded in devising a set of institutions that dealt efficiently with the problem of succession, in the form of a combination of term limits and a rotation system that had been in place since the days of Deng Xiaoping. Xi Jinping's break with the model demonstrates that in autocracies, even institutions that seem firmly established can quickly disintegrate.

Parties

During the twentieth century, parties became the dominant form of political organization in democracies as well as dictatorships (Brooker 2011). They fulfil many functions, both vis-à-vis the population and the elite. Parties provide a vehicle for mobilizing the population, as well as distributing goods to it and collecting information from it. In relation to the elite, parties provide arenas for cooperation and conflict-solving as well as recruitment and training of new political talent. Dictators who create parties after taking power therefore remain longer in power and their regimes survive longer (Geddes, Wright, and Frantz 2018: 124).

By formalizing and regulating political conflict within the regime, parties should also be well positioned to mitigate problems of succession. Two examples from the communist Soviet Union and communist China, where parties have been more powerful than anywhere else, speak both to their strengths and limitations in this regard. As mentioned earlier, since the time of Deng Xiaoping the Chinese Communist Party has been unusually successful in regulating leadership succession, but Xi Jinping's gradual accumulation of power has cast doubt on the future of the system. In the Soviet Union, in the wake of the death of Josef Stalin, several top party officials competed for power, with Nikita Khrushchev eventually coming out on top. The struggle was not an all-out war but conducted within the confines of party organization, by taking control of different party organs and securing support of different factions (Burling 1974: 218). Nevertheless, it was still a succession struggle and resulted in the execution of the perhaps most powerful contender for Stalin's throne, the minister of internal affairs and former head of the NKVD, Lavrentiy Beria. Stalin never let any man take the position as second in command, for fear of the crown prince problem (Burling 1974: 214).

If parties remain under the firm control of the ruler, they cannot act as a credible constraint. And for the most part, they are: 80 per cent of all parties in dictatorships are led by the dictator (Geddes, Wright, and Frantz 2018: 134), which is natural given that they often are founded by the dictator. Most of these parties do not even survive the death or the departure of their founder (Meng 2019), which shows their level of dependence on an individual leader. It has therefore been argued that only parties that predate the dictator's rise are able to regulate the succession (Brownlee 2007). Still, other evidence shows that regimes where the party predated the ruler's ascension are just as likely to fall when the leader dies in office as those where the ruler's coming to power predated the party, meaning that this is no guarantee, either (Geddes, Wright, and Frantz 2018: 205).

Anne Meng argues that the problem of succession necessitates institutionalization, and true institutionalization can only occur when the institutions change the underlying distribution of power so that the elite becomes able to check the dictator—for instance, by the ruler designating a successor or second in command and giving that person real authority (Meng 2020). However, it is difficult in practice to determine which actions will empower a potential crown prince. Taking the example of Côte d'Ivoire, Meng shows how President

Félix Houphouët-Boigny did in fact amend the constitution to name a successor, which according to the argument should empower the elite. But the constitution was then changed several times to name new successors, creating uncertainty about the future (Meng 2020: 79). It thus seems as if the dictator is often able to decide how much to empower the elite.

The perennial problem of authoritarian succession

The dilemma of succession—the coordination problem and the crown prince problem—are still on full display in today's world, especially in authoritarian systems. While there are cases where authoritarian succession has worked peacefully, for instance in Mexico during the long rule of the Pardido Revolucionario Institucional, or in China since the time of Deng Xiaoping, there can never be guarantees. A designated successor will always be a threat to the current leader, which is why they are so rare. Most dictators choose the coordination problem as the lesser of two evils, suppressing discussion of the succession until stepping down or dying in office, with the consequence that many regimes then fall (Kendall-Taylor and Frantz 2016). Scholarship on modern authoritarian states agree that succession in dictatorships involves 'high stakes and extreme dangers' (Geddes, Wright, and Frantz 2018: 216), is 'one of the most daunting challenges for authoritarian rulers' (Brownlee 2007: 598), a 'perennial source of authoritarian instability' (Svolik 2012: 198), and that peaceful leadership succession is 'the most critical regime outcome' (Meng 2020: 33). So long as this is the case, modern authoritarian and autocratic states cannot aspire to true longevity.

The root cause was identified already by Thomas Hobbes in *Leviathan*. To be a sovereign, the ruler must be unconstrained, including in the choice of successor. If someone else can choose the successor, then that person is the true sovereign:

> But if he have no power to elect his successor, then there is some other man, or assembly known, which after his decease may elect a new; or else the Commonwealth dieth, and dissolveth with him, and returneth to the condition of war. If it be known who have the power to give the sovereignty after his death, it is known also that the sovereignty was in them before: for none have right to give that which they have not right to possess, and keep to themselves, if they think good.
>
> (Hobbes 2006[1651])

We see the same problem repeated in today's autocracies, in the difficulty of establishing institutions that bind the dictator. Dictators sometimes follow the constitution or abide by the wishes of a party, but it is very difficult, a priori, to know when it will happen and when the constitution will bend to the dictator's will. The more power a leader accumulates, the larger the void is when he inevitably steps down or dies.

Absent planning for the succession, the leader must project an aura of immortality to stave off instability. In Chapter 2, we described how Elizabeth I of England, who stubbornly refused to marry, went to increasing lengths to put on a literal 'mask of youth' with elaborate dress and heavy makeup. In Russia, Vladimir Putin has secured the constitutional right to run for election to two more terms, which means that he could be president until the age of 84 (barring any further constitutional amendments, of course)—provided he stays healthy. If the common speculation that he has undergone cosmetic surgery (Lelly 2011) is true, it would be a direct parallel to Elizabeth's attempt to stave off biological decay, but it remains unconfirmed. What is undoubtedly true is that Putin goes to great pains to project a youthful and vital image, participating in annual hockey games and releasing official photos where he lifts weights, hunts, and does martial arts. A display of customary strongman machismo, perhaps, or an attempt to forestall any questions about his health.

However, as put by the medieval law jurist Bartolus de Saxferrato, 'Nothing in this world can be perpetual ... except by substitution' (quoted by Ernst Kantorowicz (1957: 308)). Hereditary succession through primogeniture proved to be an ingenious compromise that took the discretion in choosing the successor away from monarchs, without giving it to someone else, thereby making the succession more predictable—insofar as the monarch managed to produce an heir. Of course, succession practices could sometimes be changed away from primogeniture, but tradition and the power of the Church was an important counterweight that made this difficult in medieval and early modern European monarchies.

Today we might say that representative democracy constitutes the best solution to the problem of succession. But we must keep in mind that representative democracy still has a short track record compared to hereditary monarchy. Several of the states in the sample we have investigated here, such as France or Denmark, remained more or less intact for close to a millennium before the advent of democracy. It is far from certain that liberal democracy as a political system will accomplish the same feat. The main advantage of the principle of hereditary succession from parent to child is that successions are few and far between, and when power transfers do happen, they do so in predictable ways. In democracy, we instead have frequent successions and, if political competition works, what has been termed 'institutionalized uncertainty' (Przeworski et al. 2000). Ideally, both population and elite get used to this flux, learn to manage uncertainty, and lower the stakes of each election. But when political polarization rises, so do the stakes—as well as the tendency to dispute informal norms or even official rules that were taken for granted in more tranquil times.

Succession will thus continue to be an issue of the highest political importance in the future, especially in authoritarian states but also in democracies. It is unlikely that we will see a large-scale return of hereditary monarchy, even if dictators will continue to lean on relatives, and even if some might try to pass power to their children. But to be durable, what comes instead must be able to strike the same delicate balance that was achieved in the medieval and early modern hereditary monarchies: predictability, stability, sovereignty, and from the ruler's point of view, security. As mentioned earlier, Communist China for a while appeared to have come up with a model that seemed to transform this eternal issue to routine. By accumulating power and abolishing term limits, Xi Jinping has made the future more uncertain. When the time comes for Xi to hand over the reins, as he eventually must, the transfer might not be as smooth as in recent decades. As Europe's past shows, such moments of uncertainty can spiral out of control, with devastating consequences. Any authoritarian leader ignores the problem of succession at their own peril; it can at best be postponed, never avoided.

Bibliography

Abramson, Scott F. (2017). 'The Economic Origins of the Territorial State'. *International Organization* 71(1): 97–130.

Abramson, Scott F. and Carles Boix (2019). 'Endogenous Parliaments: The Domestic and International Roots of Long-Term Economic Growth and Executive Constraints in Europe'. *International Organization* 73(4): 793–837.

Abramson, Scott F. and Carlos Velasco Rivera (2016). 'Time Is Power: The Noninstitutional Sources of Stability in Autocracies'. *The Journal of Politics* 78(4): 1279–95.

Acemoglu, Daron, Georgy Egorov, and Konstantin Sonin (2008). 'Coalition Formation in Non-democracies'. *The Review of Economic Studies* 75(4): 987–1009.

Acemoglu, Daron, Simon Johnson, and James Robinson (2005). 'The Rise of Europe: Atlantic Trade, Institutional Change, and Economic Growth'. *American Economic Review* 95(3): 546–79.

Acemoglu, Daron and James Robinson (2019). *The Narrow Corridor: States, Societies, and the Fate of Liberty*. Princeton: Princeton University Press.

Acharya, Avidit and Alexander Lee (2019). 'Path Dependence in European Development: Medieval Politics, Conflict, and State-Building'. *Comparative Political Studies* 52(13–14): 2171–206.

Agnew, Hugh Lecaine (2004). *The Czechs and the Lands of the Bohemian Crown*. Stanford: Hoover Institution Press.

Alderson, Anthony Dolphin (1956). *The Structure of the Ottoman Dynasty*. Oxford: Clarendon Press.

Ambrosio, Thomas and Jakob Tolstrup (2021). 'Hereditary Grooming and Succession in Post-Soviet Autocracies'. Unpublished working paper.

Anderson, Matthew Smith (1995). *The War of Austrian Succession 1740–1748*. London: Routledge.

Arnold, Benjamin (2009). *Princes and Territories in Medieval Germany*. Cambridge: Cambridge University Press.

Barbero, A. and Loring, M.I. (2005). The Catholic Visigothic kingdom. In Paul Fouracre (Ed.) The New Cambridge Medieval History. Cambridge: Cambridge University Press: 346–370.

Barlow, Frank (1999). *The Feudal Kingdom of England, 1042–1216*. Harlow: Pearson Education.

Bartlett, Robert (1993). *The Making of Europe: Conquest, Colonization, and Cultural Change 950–1350*. Princeton: Princeton University Press.

Bartlett, Robert (2000). *England under the Norman and Angevin Kings: 1075–1225*. Oxford: Oxford University Press.

Bartlett, Robert (2020). *Blood Royal: Dynastic Politics in Medieval Europe*. Cambridge: Cambridge University Press.

Bendix, Reinhard. (1980). *Kings or people: Power and the Mandate to Rule*. Berkeley: University of California Press.

Bendor, Jonathan, Amihai Glazer, and Thomas Hammond (2001). 'Theories of Delegation'. *Annual Review of Political Science* 4(1): 235–69.
Benzell, Seth G. and Kevin Cooke (2021). 'A Network of Thrones: Kinship and Conflict in Europe, 1495–1918'. *American Economic Journal: Applied Economics* 13(3): 102–33.
Bérenger, Jean (1994). *A History of the Habsburg Empire, 1273–1700*. London: Longman.
Berman, Harold J. (1983). *Law and Revolution: The Formation of the Western Legal Tradition*. Cambridge, MA: Harvard University Press.
Bertocchi, Graziella (2006). 'The Law of Primogeniture and the Transition from Landed Aristocracy to Industrial Democracy'. *Journal of Economic Growth* 11(1): 43–70.
Besley, Timothy, Jose G. Montalvo, and Marta Reynal-Querol (2011). 'Do Educated Leaders Matter?' *The Economic Journal* 121(554): F205–27.
Betts, Russell R. (1955). 'Social and Constitutional Development in Bohemia in the Hussite Period'. *Past & Present* 7: 37–54.
Beverly Smith, Jenkyn (1986). 'Dynastic Succession in Medieval Wales'. *The Bulletin Board of Celtic Studies* 33: 199–232.
Biggs, Frederick M. (2005). 'The Politics of Succession in "Beowulf" and Anglo-Saxon England'. *Speculum* 80(3): 709–41.
Bisson, Thomas N. (1979). *Conservation of Coinage: Monetary Exploitation and its Restraint in France, Catalonia, and Aragon (c. AD 1000–c. 1225)*. Oxford: Clarendon Press.
Bisson, Thomas N. (1986). *The Medieval Crown of Aragon: A Short History*. Oxford: Oxford University Press.
Bisson, Thomas N. (2009). *The Crisis of the Twelfth Century: Power, Lordship, and the Origins of European Government*. Princeton: Princeton University Press.
Blake, Judith (1981). 'Family Size and the Quality of Children'. *Demography* 18(4): 421–42.
Blanning, Tim (2007). *The Pursuit of Glory: The Five Revolutions that Made Modern Europe: 1648–1815*. London: Penguin.
Blattman, Christopher and Edward Miguel (2010). 'Civil War'. *Journal of Economic Literature* 48(1): 3–57.
Blau, Peter Michael (1977). *Inequality and Heterogeneity: A Primitive Theory of Social Structure*. New York: Free Press New York.
Blaydes, Lisa and Eric Chaney (2013). 'The Feudal Revolution and Europe's Rise: Political Divergence of the Christian West and the Muslim World before 1500 CE'. *American Political Science Review* 107(1): 16–34.
Blaydes, Lisa and Christopher Paik (2016). 'The Impact of Holy Land Crusades on State Formation: War Mobilization, Trade Integration, and Political Development in Medieval Europe'. *International Organization* 70(3): 551–86.
Blaydes, Lisa and Christopher Paik (2021). 'Muslim Trade and City Growth before the Nineteenth Century: Comparative Urbanization in Europe, the Middle East and Central Asia'. *British Journal of Political Science* 51(2): 845–68.
Bloch, Marc (1971[1939]). *Feudal Society*. London: Routledge.
Bodin, Jean (1967[1575]). *Six Books of the Commonwealth*. Oxford: Basil Blackwell.
Boix, Carles (2015). *Political Order and Inequality*. Cambridge: Cambridge University Press.
Boix, Carles and Milan Svolik (2013). 'The Foundations of Limited Authoritarian Government: Institutions, Commitment, and Power-sharing in Dictatorships'. *The Journal of Politics* 75(2): 300–16.
Bosker, Maarten, Eltjo Buringh, and Jan Luiten Van Zanden (2013). 'From Baghdad to London: Unraveling Urban Development in Europe, the Middle East, and North Africa, 800–1800'. *Review of Economics and Statistics* 95(4): 1418–37.

Boucoyannis, Deborah (2015). 'No Taxation of Elites, No Representation: State Capacity and the Origins of Representation'. *Politics and Society* 43(3): 303–32.
Boyle, Alexander (1977). 'Matrilineal succession in the Pictish monarchy'. *Scottish Historical Review*, 56: 1–10.
Brodsky, Joseph (1987). *Less Than One: Selected Essays*. Reading: Penguin Books.
Broms, Rasmus and Andrej Kokkonen (2019). 'Inheritance Regimes: Medieval Family Structures and Current Institutional Quality'. *Governance* 32(4): 619–37.
Brooker, Paul (2011). 'Authoritarian Regimes'. In Daniele Caramani (ed.), *Comparative Politics*, 3rd edition. Oxford: Oxford University Press: 96–110.
Brougham, Henry (1845). 'Lord Brougham's Political Philosophy'. *The Edinburgh Review* 81(1–2).
Brown, Elizabeth A. R. (1974). 'The Tyranny of a Construct: Feudalism and Historians of Medieval Europe'. *The American Historical Review*, 79(4): 1063–88.
Brown, Peter (1997). *The Rise of Western Christendom*. Oxford: Blackwell.
Brownlee, Jason (2007). 'Hereditary Succession in Modern Autocracies'. *World Politics* 59(4): 595–628.
Bueno De Mesquita, Bruce et al. (2005). *The Logic of Political Survival*. Cambridge, MA: MIT Press.
Bueno De Mesquita, Bruce and Alastair Smith (2010). 'Leader Survival, Revolutions, and the Nature of Government Finance'. *American Journal of Political Science* 54(4): 936–50.
Burling, Robbins (1974). *The Passage of Power: Studies in Political Succession*. New York: Academic Press.
Burton-Chellew, Maxwell and Robin Dunbar (2011). 'Are Affines Treated as Biological Kin? A Test of Hughes' Hypothesis'. *Current Anthropology* 52(5): 741–6.
Capoccia, Giovanni and Daniel Kelemen (2007). 'The Study of Critical Junctures: Theory, Narrative, and Counterfactuals in Historical Institutionalism'. *World Politics* 59(3): 341–69.
Carnes, Nicholas and Noam Lupu (2016). 'What Good Is a College Degree? Education and Leader Quality Reconsidered'. *The Journal of Politics* 78(1): 35–49.
Carpenter, David A. (1990). *The Minority of Henry III*. Berkeley, CA: University of California Press.
Carpenter, David A. (1999). 'The Plantagenet Kings'. In David Abulafia (ed.), *The New Cambridge Medieval History V*. Cambridge: Cambridge University Press: 314–57.
Cawley, John (2006). Medieval Lands database, accessed 10 January 2019, http://fmg.ac/Projects/MedLands/index.htm
Centeno, Miguel Angel (2003). *Blood and Debt: War and the Nation-state in Latin America*. University Park: Penn State University Press.
Cheibub, José Antonio, Jennifer Gandhi, and James Raymond Vreeland (2010). 'Democracy and Dictatorship Revisited'. *Public Choice* 143(1–2): 67–101.
Chiozza, Giacomo and Hein E. Goemans (2003). 'Peace through Insecurity: Tenure and International Conflict'. *Journal of Conflict Resolution* 47(4): 443–67.
Chiozza, Giacomo and Hein E. Goemans (2004). 'Avoiding Diversionary Targets'. *Journal of Peace Research* 41(4): 423–43.
Chiozza, Giacomo and Hein E. Goemans (2011). *Leaders and International Conflict*. Cambridge: Cambridge University Press.
Cohn, Samuel Kline (2006). *Lust for Liberty: The Politics of Social Revolt in Medieval Europe, 1200–1425*. Cambridge, MA: Harvard University Press.
Collier, Paul and Anke Hoeffler (2004). 'Greed and Grievance in Civil War'. *Oxford Economic Papers* 56(4): 563–95.

Cowdrey, Herbert Edward John (1998). *Pope Gregory VII, 1073–1085*. Oxford: Oxford University Press.
Cowdrey, Herbert Edward John (2000). *Popes and Church Reform in the 11th Century*. Farnham: Ashgate.
Cox, Eugene L. (1974). *The Eagles of Savoy: The House of Savoy in Thirteenth-century Europe*. Princeton: Princeton University Press.
Cox, Gary W. (2009). 'Authoritarian Elections and Leadership Succession, 1975–2004'. *APSA 2009 Toronto Meeting Paper*. URL: https://www.haas.berkeley.edu/wp-content/uploads/cox_20071119.pdf.
Cox, Gary W. and Barry R. Weingast (2018). 'Executive Constraint, Political Stability, and Economic Growth'. *Comparative Political Studies* 51(3): 279–303.
Croco, Sarah E. (2011). 'The Decider's Dilemma: Leader Culpability, War Outcomes, and Domestic Punishment'. *American Political Science Review* 105(3): 457–77.
Crouch, Jace T. (1994). 'Isidore of Seville and the Evolution of Kingship in Visigothic Spain'. *Mediterranean Studies* 4: 9–26.
Dahl, Robert A. (1971). *Polyarchy: Participation and Opposition*. New Haven: Yale University Press.
Daly, Martin and Margo Wilson (1988). 'Evolutionary Social Psychology and Family Homicide'. *Science* 242(4878): 519–24.
Davies, Norman (1997). *Europe: A History*. London: Pimlico.
Davies, Norman (2005). *God's Playground: A History of Poland, Vol. 1: The Origins to 1795*. Oxford: Oxford University Press.
De Montesquieu, Charles (2011[1750]). *The Spirit of the Laws*. New York: Cosimo Classics.
De Tocqueville, Alexis (1955[1856]). *The Old Regime and the French Revolution*. New York: Doubleday.
De Tocqueville, Alexis (1984[1835/1840]). *Democracy in America*. New York: Penguin Books.
Diehl, Daniel and Mark P. Donnelly (2006). *Tales from the Tower of London*. Stroud: The History Press.
Dincecco, Mark and Massimiliano Gaetano Onorato (2018). *From Warfare to Wealth*. Cambridge: Cambridge University Press.
Doucette, Jonathan Stavnskær (2021). 'Autocratic Succession and Urban Regime Change'. Unpublished working paper.
Douglas, David C. (1964). *William the Conqueror: The Norman Impact upon England*. Berkeley: University of California Press.
Downing, Brian (1992). *The Military Revolution and Political Change: Origins of Democracy and Autocracy in Early Modern Europe*. Princeton: Princeton University Press.
Dube, Oeindrila and S. P. Harish (2020). 'Queens'. *Journal of Political Economy* 128(7): 2579–652.
Duby, Georges (1984). *The Knight, the Lady and the Priest: The Making of Modern Marriage in Medieval France*. Chicago: University of Chicago Press.
Duindam, Jeroen (2016). *Dynasties: A Global History of Power, 1300–1800*. Cambridge: Cambridge University Press.
Dunbar, Robin I. M., Amanda Clark, and Nicola L. Hurst (1995). 'Conflict and Cooperation among the Vikings: Contingent Behavioral Decisions'. *Ethology and Sociobiology* 16(3): 233–46.
Dvornik, Francis (1962). *The Slavs in European History and Civilization*. New Brunswick: Rutgers University Press.

Earenfight, Theresa (2007). 'Without the Persona of the Prince: Kings, Queens and the Idea of Monarchy in Late Medieval Europe'. *Gender and History* 19(1): 1–21.
Earenfight, Theresa (2017). 'Medieval Queenship'. *History Compass* 15(3): 1–9.
Edbury, Peter W. (1991). *The Kingdom of Cyprus and the Crusades, 1191–1374*. Cambridge: Cambridge University Press.
Egorov, Georgy and Konstantin Sonin (2011). 'Dictators and their Viziers: Endogenizing the Loyalty–Competence Trade-off'. *Journal of the European Economic Association* 9(5): 903–30.
Egorov, Georgy and Konstantin Sonin (2015). 'The Killing Game: A Theory of Non-democratic Succession'. *Research in Economics* 69(3): 398–411.
Eisner, Manuel (2003). 'Long-term Historical Trends in Violent Crime'. *Crime and Justice* 30: 83–142.
Eisner, Manuel (2011). 'Killing Kings: Patterns of Regicide in Europe, AD 600–1800'. *The British Journal of Criminology* 51(3): 556–77.
Engel, Pál (2001). *The Realm of St Stephen: A History of Medieval Hungary, 895–1526*. London: IB Tauris.
Ertman, Thomas (1997). *Birth of the Leviathan: Building States and Regimes in Medieval and Early Modern Europe*. Cambridge: Cambridge University Press.
Esders, Stefan (2019). 'Chindasvinth, the "Gothic Disease", and the Monothelite Crisis'. *Millennium* 16(1): 175–212.
Essock-Vitale, Susan M. and Michael T. McGuire (1985). 'Women's Lives Viewed from an Evolutionary Perspective, II: Patterns of Helping'. *Ethology and Sociobiology* 6(3): 155–73.
Fearon, James D. (1995). 'Rationalist Explanations for War'. *International Organization* 49(3): 379–414.
Fearon, James D. and David D. Laitin (2003). 'Ethnicity, Insurgency, and Civil War'. *American Political Science Review* 97(1): 75–90.
Fernández-Armesto, Felipe (1995). *Millenium: A History of the Last Thousand Years*. New York: Simon & Schuster.
Fichtner, Paula Sutter (1976). 'Dynastic Marriage in Sixteenth-century Habsburg Diplomacy and Statecraft: An Interdisciplinary Approach'. *The American Historical Review* 81(2): 243–65.
Fichtner, Paula Sutter (1989). *Protestantism and Primogeniture in Early Modern Germany*. New Haven: Yale University Press.
Fine, John V. A. (1986). *The Late Medieval Balkans: A Critical Survey from the Late Twelfth Century to the Ottoman Conquest*. Ann Arbor: University of Michigan Press.
Finer, Samuel E. (1996). *The History of Government from the Earliest Times, Vol. I: Ancient Monarchies and Empires*. New York: Oxford University Press.
Finer, Samuel E. (1997a). *The History of Government from the Earliest Times, Vol. II: The Intermediate Ages*. New York: Oxford University Press.
Finer, Samuel E. (1997b). *The History of Government, Vol. III: Empires, Monarchies, and the Modern State*. Oxford: Oxford University Press.
Fischlin, Daniel (1997). 'Political Allegory, Absolutist Ideology, and the "Rainbow Portrait" of Queen Elizabeth I'. *Renaissance Quarterly* 50(1): 175–206.
Fletcher, Joseph (1979). 'Turco-Mongolian Monarchic Tradition in the Ottoman Empire'. *Harvard Ukrainian Studies* 3: 236–51.
Frantz, Erica and Elizabeth A. Stein (2017). 'Countering Coups: Leadership Succession Rules in Dictatorships'. *Comparative Political Studies* 50(7): 935–62.
Fried, Johannes (2015). *The Middle Ages*. Cambridge, MA: Harvard University Press.

Fukuyama, Francis (2011). *The Origins of Political Order: From Prehuman Times to the French Revolution.* New York: Farrar, Straus and Giroux.
Fukuyama, Francis (2014). *Political Order and Political Decay: From the Industrial Revolution to the Globalization of Democracy.* New York: Farrar, Straus and Giroux.
Fukuyama, Francis (2015). 'Comment on Møller: The Importance of Equality'. *Journal of Democracy* 26(3), 124–128.
Gandhi, Jennifer and Adam Przeworski (2006). 'Cooperation, Cooptation, and Rebellion under Dictatorships'. *Economics and Politics* 18(1): 1–26.
Gandhi, Jennifer and Adam Przeworski (2007). 'Authoritarian Institutions and the Survival of Autocrats'. *Comparative Political Studies* 40(11): 1279–301.
Garnett, George (2007). *Conquered England: Kingship, Succession, and Tenure 1066–1166.* Oxford: Oxford University Press.
Gaubatz, Kurt Taylor (1991). 'Election Cycles and War'. *Journal of Conflict Resolution* 35(2): 212–44.
Geddes, Barbara, Joseph Wright, and Erica Frantz (2014). 'Autocratic Breakdown and Regime Transitions: A New Data Set'. *Perspectives on Politics* 12(2): 313–31.
Geddes, Barbara, Joseph Wright, and Erica Frantz (2018). *How Dictatorships Work: Power, Personalization, and Collapse.* Cambridge: Cambridge University Press.
Gelpi, Christopher and Joseph M. Grieco (2001). 'Attracting Trouble: Democracy, Leadership Tenure, and the Targeting of Militarized Challenges, 1918–1992'. *Journal of Conflict Resolution* 45(6): 794–817.
Gerring, John, Tore Wig, Wouter Veenendaal, Daniel Weitzel, Jan Teorell, and K. Kikuta (2021). 'Why Monarchy? The Rise and Demise of a Regime Type'. *Comparative Political Studies* 54(3–4): 585–622.
Gillingham, John (1991). 'Elective Kingship and the Unity of Medieval Germany'. *German History* 9(2): 124–36.
Goody, Jack (1966). *Succession to High Office.* Cambridge: Cambridge University Press.
Goody, Jack (1983). *The Development of the Family and Marriage in Europe.* Cambridge: Cambridge University Press.
Goody, Jack (2000). *The European Family.* Hoboken: Wiley-Blackwell.
Gorski, Philip and Vivek Swaroop Sharma (2017). 'Beyond the Tilly Thesis: "Family Values" and State Formation in Latin Christendom'. In Lars Bo Kaspersen and Jeppe Strandsbjerg (eds), *Does War Make States?: Investigations of Charles Tilly's Historical Sociology.* Cambridge: Cambridge Univer sity Press: 98–124.
Grant, Jeanne E. (2015). *For the Common Good: The Bohemian Land Law and the Beginning of the Hussite Revolution.* Leiden: Brill.
Green, David (2007). *Edward the Black Prince: Power in Medieval Europe.* Harlow: Pearson Education.
Greengrass, Mark (2014). *Christendom Destroyed: Europe 1517–1648.* London: Allen Lane.
Gregory, Timothy E. (2005). *A History of Byzantium.* Hoboken: John Wiley & Sons.
Greif, Avner (2006). *Institutions and the Path to the Modern Economy: Lessons from Medieval Trade.* Cambridge: Cambridge University Press.
Grierson, Philip (1941). 'Election and Inheritance in Early Germanic Kingship'. *Cambridge Historical Journal* 7(1): 1–22.
Gustafsson, Harald (1998). 'The Conglomerate State: A Perspective on State Formation in Early Modern Europe'. *Scandinavian Journal of History* 23(3–4): 189–213.
Hadenius, Axel and Jan Teorell (2007). 'Pathways from Authoritarianism'. *Journal of Democracy* 18(1): 143–57.

Haldén, Peter (2020). *Family Power: Kinship, War and Political Orders in Eurasia, 500–2018.* Cambridge: Cambridge University Press.

Hall, John A. (1985). *Powers and Liberties: The Causes and Consequences of the Rise of the West.* Oxford: Basil Blackwell.

Hamilton, William D. (1964). 'The Genetical Evolution of Social Behaviour, II'. *Journal of Theoretical Biology* 7(1): 17–52.

Harris, Barbara (1976). 'The Trial of the Third Duke of Buckingham—A Revisionist View'. *The American Journal of Legal History* 20(1): 15–26.

Helle, Knut (1973). *Konge og gode menn i norsk riksstyring ca. 1150–1319.* Oslo: Universitetsforlaget.

Helle, Knut (1981). 'Norway in the High Middle Ages: Recent Views on the Structure of Society'. *Scandinavian Journal of History* 6(1–4): 161–89.

Helle, Knut (1995). 'Under kirke og kongemakt 1130–1350'. *Aschehougs Norges Historie* 3.

Helle, Knut (2003). 'The Norwegian Kingdom: Succession Disputes and Consolidation'. In Knut Helle (ed.), *The Cambridge History of Scandinavi, Vol. 1: Prehistory to 1520.* Cambridge: Cambridge University Press: 369–91.

Henrich, Joseph (2020). *The Weirdest People in the World: How the West Became Psychologically Peculiar and Particularly Prosperous.* New York: Farrar, Straus and Giroux.

Herb, Michael (1999). *All in the Family: Absolutism, Revolution, and Democracy in Middle Eastern Monarchies.* Albany: Suny Press.

Herbst, Jeffrey (2000). *States and Power in Africa: Comparative Lessons in Authority and Control.* Princeton: Princeton University Press.

Herz, John H. (1952). 'The Problem of Successorship in Dictatorial Regimes: A Study in Comparative Law and Institutions'. *The Journal of Politics* 14(1): 19–40.

Hintze, Otto (1975[1906]). 'Military Organization and the Organization of the State'. In Felix Gilbert (ed.), *The Historical Essays of Otto Hintze.* New York: Oxford University Press: 178–215.

Hobbes, Thomas (2006[1651]). *Leviathan.* London: A&C Black.

Holt, James C. (1997). *Colonial England 1066–1215.* London: Hambledon Press.

Horowitz, Michael C., Allan C. Stam, and Cali M. Ellis (2015). *Why Leaders Fight.* Cambridge: Cambridge University Press.

Howe, John C. (2016). *Before the Gregorian Reform: The Latin Church as the Turn of the First Millennium.* New York: Cornell University Press.

Huber, John D. and Charles R. Shipan (2006). 'Politics, Delegation, and Bureaucracy'. In Donald A. Wittman and Barry R. Weingast (eds), *The Oxford Handbook of Political Economy.* New York: Oxford University Press: 256–72.

Imber, Colin (2009). *The Ottoman Empire, 1300–1650: The Structure of Power.* London: Palgrave Macmillan.

Ives, Eric William (2008). 'Tudor Dynastic Problems Revisited'. *Historical Research* 81(212): 255–79.

Iyigun, Murat (2013). 'Lessons from the Ottoman Harem on Culture, Religion, and Wars'. *Economic Development and Cultural Change* 61(4): 693–730.

Jaski, Bart (2000). *Early Irish Kingship and Succession.* Dublin: Four Courts Press.

Johnson, Steven B. and Ronald C. Johnson (1991). 'Support and Conflict of Kinsmen in Norse Earldoms, Icelandic Families, and the English Royalty'. *Ethology and Sociobiology* 12(3): 211–20.

Jones, Benjamin F. and Benjamin A. Olken (2005). 'Do Leaders Matter? National Leadership and Growth since World War II'. *The Quarterly Journal of Economics* 120(3): 835–64.

Jones, Benjamin F. and Benjamin A. Olken (2009). 'Hit or Miss? The Effect of Assassinations on Institutions and War'. *American Economic Journal: Macroeconomics* 1(2): 55–87.
Jones, Eric L. (2008[1981]). *The European Miracle. Environments, Economies and Geopolitics in the History of Europe and Asia*. Cambridge: Cambridge University Press.
Jordan, William Chester (2001). *Europe in the High Middle Ages*. London: Penguin.
Kagay, Donald J. (1981). *The Development of the Cortes in the Crown of Aragon, 1064–1327*. ETD Collection for Fordham University.
Kagay, Donald J. (1997). 'Rebellion on Trial: The Aragonese Unión and its Uneasy Connection to Royal Law, 1265–1301'. *The Journal of Legal History* 18(3): 30–43.
Kaldellis, Anthony (2015). *The Byzantine Republic: People and Power in New Rome*. Cambridge, MA: Harvard University Press.
Kamen, Henry (2001). *Philip V of Spain: The King Who Reigned Twice*. New Haven: Yale University Press.
Kann, Robert A. (1974). *A History of the Habsburg Empire, 1526–1918*. Berkeley: University of California Press.
Kannowski, Bernd (2007). 'The Impact of Lineage and Family Connections on Succession in Medieval Germany's Elective Kingdom'. In Fabrice Lachaud and Michael Penman (eds), *Making and Breaking the Rules: Succession in Medieval Europe c.1000–c.1600*. Turnhout: Brepols Publishers: 13–22.
Kantorowicz, Ernst (1957). *The King's Two Bodies: A Study in Medieval Political Theology*. Princeton: Princeton University Press.
Kapelle, William E. (1979). *The Norman Conquest of the North: The Region and its Transformation 1000–1135*. Raleigh-Durham: University of North Carolina Press.
Kendall-Taylor, Andrea and Erica Frantz (2016). 'When Dictators Die'. *Journal of Democracy* 27(4): 159–71.
Kern, Fritz (1948[1914]). *Kingship and Law in the Middle Ages*. Oxford: Oxford University Press.
Kershaw, Stephen P. (2013). *A Brief History of the Roman Empire*. London: Hachette.
Kulikowski, Michael (2020). 'How to End a Dynasty'. *London Review of Books* 19 March: 25–6.
Khaldūn, Ibn (1958[1377]). *The Muqaddimah: An Introduction to History; in Three Volumes*. Princeton: Princeton University Press.
King, Edmund (1994). 'Introduction'. In Edmund King (ed.), *The Anarchy of King Stephen's Reign*. Oxford: Clarendon Press: 1–35.
King, Paul David (1972). *Law and Society in the Visigothic Kingdom*. Cambridge: Cambridge University Press.
Kokkonen, Andrej and Jørgen Møller (2020). 'Succession, Power-sharing, and the Development of Representative Institutions in Medieval Europe' *European Journal of Political Research* 59(4): 954–75.
Kokkonen, Andrej and Anders Sundell (2014). 'Delivering Stability—Primogeniture and Autocratic Survival in European Monarchies 1000–1800'. *American Political Science Review* 108(2): 438–53.
Kokkonen, Andrej and Anders Sundell (2020). 'Leader Succession and Civil War'. *Comparative Political Studies* 53(3–4): 434–68.
Kollman, Nancy Shields (1990). 'Collateral Succession in Kievan Rus'. *Harvard Ukrainian Studies* 14(3/4): 377–87.
Konrad, Kai A. and Vai-Lam Mui (2017). 'The Prince—Or Better No Prince? The Strategic Value of Appointing a Successor'. *Journal of Conflict Resolution* 61(10): 2158–82.

Kristo, Gyula and Ferenc Makk (1996). *Az Arpad-haz uralkodoi [Rulers of the House of Arpad]*. Budapest: I.P.C. Könyvek.

Kurrild-Klitgaard, Peter (2000). 'The Constitutional Economics of Autocratic Succession'. *Public Choice* 103(1): 63–84.

Landes, David (1998). The Wealth and Poverty of Nations. Why Some Are So Rich and Some So Poor. New York: W.W. Norton.

Le Patourel, John (1971). 'The Norman Succession, 996–1135'. *The English Historical Review* 86(339): 225–50.

Lelly, Kathy (2011). 'Botox Buzz Surrounds Putin'. *Washington Post*. URL: https://www.washingtonpost.com/world/middle-east/putin-botox-rumor-hums-online/2011/09/30/gIQA82ISAL_story.html.

Lewis, Andrew W. (1981). *Royal Succession in Capetian France: Studies on Familial Order and the State*. Cambridge, MA: Harvard University Press.

Lieberman, Max (2010). 'The Medieval "Marches" of Normandy and Wales'. *The English Historical Review* 125(517): 1357–81.

Lieven, Dominic (2006). 'The Elites'. In Dominic Lieven (ed.), *The Cambridge History of Russia, Vol. II: Imperial Russia, 1689–1971*. Cambridge: Cambridge University Press: 227–44.

Lindkvist, Thomas. (2003). Kings and Provinces in Sweden. In Helle, K. (editor) (2003) *The Cambridge History of Scandinavia Volume 1: Prehistory to 1520*. Cambridge: Cambridge University Press, 221–234.

Lönnroth, Erik (1934). *Sverige och Kalmarunionen 1397–1457*. Doctoral thesis: University of Gothenburg.

Lührmann, Anna and Staffan I. Lindberg (2019). 'A Third Wave of Autocratization Is Here: What Is New about it?' *Democratization* 26(7): 1095–113.

Lustick, Ian S. (1996). 'History, Historiography, and Political Science: Multiple Historical Records and the Problem of Selection Bias'. *American Political Science Review* 90(3): 605–18.

Lynn, John (1999). *The Wars of Louis XIV, 1667–1714*. London: Routledge.

MacCulloch, Diarmaid (2009). *A History of Christianity: The First Three Thousand Years*. London: Allen Lane.

MacDonald, Alasdair (2003). 'Princely Culture in Scotland under James III and James IV'. In Martin Gosman, Alasdair Macdonald, and Arjo Vanderjagt (eds), *Princes and Princely Culture 1450–1650*. Leiden: Brill: 147–71.

MacDonald, Robert A (1965). 'Alfonso the Learned and Succession: A Father's Dilemma'. *Speculum* 40(4): 647–53.

Machiavelli, Niccolo (1988[1532]). *The Prince*. Cambridge: Cambridge University Press.

Maddicott, John Robert (2010). *The Origins of the English Parliament, 924–1327*. Oxford: Oxford University Press.

Madelung, Wilferd (1997). *The Succession to Muhammad: A Study of the Early Caliphate*. Cambridge: Cambridge University Press.

Madsen, Elainie A. et al. (2007). 'Kinship and Altruism: A Cross-cultural Experimental Study'. *British Journal of Psychology* 98(2): 339–59.

Magaloni, Beatriz (2008). 'Credible Power-sharing and the Longevity of Authoritarian Rule'. *Comparative Political Studies* 41(4–5): 715–41.

Mahoney, James (2000). 'Path Dependence in Historical Sociology'. *Theory and Society* 29(4): 507–48.

Mahoney, James (2003). 'Strategies of Causal Assessment in Comparative Historical Analysis'. In J. Mahoney and D. Rueschemeyer (eds), *Comparative Historical Analysis in the Social Sciences*. Cambridge: Cambridge University Press: 337–72.
Mahoney, James and Kathleen Thelen (2010). *Explaining Institutional Change: Ambiguity, Agency, and Power*. New York: Cambridge University Press.
Mann, Michael (1986). *The Sources of Social Power*. Cambridge: Cambridge University Press.
Mantel, Hilary (2009). *Wolf Hall*. London: Fourth Estate.
Marafioti, Nicole (2014). *The King's Body: Burial and Succession in Late Anglo-Saxon England*. Toronto: University of Toronto Press.
Marongiu, Antonio (1968). *Medieval Parliaments: A Comparative Study*. London: Eyre & Spottiswoode.
Marsham, Andrew (2009). *Rituals of Islamic Monarchy: Accession and Succession in the First Muslim Empire*. Edinburgh: Edinburgh University Press.
Martin, Janet (1995). *Medieval Russia 980–1584*. Cambridge: Cambridge University Press.
Martin, Russel E. (2019). 'Anticipatory Association of the Heir in Early Modern Russia.' In Elena Woodacre et al. (eds), *The Routledge History of Monarchy*. London: Routledge: 420–42.
Mason, Roger (1987). 'Kingship, Tyranny and the Right to Resist in Fifteenth-century Scotland'. *The Scottish Historical Review* 66(182): 125–51.
McFarlane, Kenneth Bruce (1981). *The Nobility of Later Medieval England*. Oxford: Oxford University Press.
McNeill, William H. (1982). 'A Defence of World History: The Prothero Lecture'. *Transactions of the Royal Historical Society* 32: 75–89.
Melville, Gert (2016). *The World of Medieval Monasticism: Its History and Forms of Life*. Collegeville: Cistercian Publications.
Meng, Anne (2019). 'Accessing the State: Executive Constraints and Credible Commitment in Dictatorship'. *Journal of Theoretical Politics* 31(4): 568–99.
Meng, Anne (2020). *Constraining Dictatorship: From Personalized Rule to Institutionalized Regimes*. Cambridge: Cambridge University Press.
Meng Anne (2021). 'Winning the Game of Thrones: Leadership Succession in Modern Autocracies'. *Journal of Conflict Resolution* 65(5): 950–81.
Merrills, Andrew H. (2010). 'The Secret of my Succession: Dynasty and Crisis in Vandal North Africa'. *Early Medieval Europe* 18(2): 135–59.
Møller, Fenja Søndergaard (2019). 'Blue Blood or True Blood: Why Are Levels of Intrastate Armed Conflict So Low in Middle Eastern Monarchies?' *Conflict Management and Peace Science* 36(5): 517–44.
Møller, Jørgen (2014). 'Why Europe Avoided Hegemony: A Historical Perspective on the Balance of Power'. *International Studies Quarterly* 58(4): 660–70.
Møller, Jørgen (2017). 'The Birth of Representative Institutions: The Case of the Crown of Aragon'. *Social Science History* 41(2): 175–200.
Møller, Jørgen (2018). 'The Ecclesiastical Roots of Representation and Consent'. *Perspectives on Politics* 16(4): 1075–84.
Møller, Jørgen and Svend-Erik Skaaning (2021). 'The Ulysses Principle: A Criterial Framework for Reducing Bias When Enlisting the Work of Historians'. *Sociological Methods & Research* 50(1): 103–34.
Møller, Jørgen and Jonathan Stavnskær Doucette (2022). *The Catholic Church and European State Formation, AD 1000–1500*. Oxford: Oxford University Press.

Moore, Barrington (1991[1966]). *Social Origins of Dictatorship and Democracy: Lord and Peasant in the Making of the Modern World*. London: Penguin.
Moore, Robert Ian (2000). *The First European Revolution: 97—1215*. New Jersey: Wiley-Blackwell.
Morris, Colin (1989). *The Papal Monarchy: The Western Church from 1050 to 1250*. Oxford: Clarendon Press.
Morris, Ian (2014). *War! What Is It Good For? Conflict and the Progress of Civilization from Primates to Robots*. New York: Farrar, Straus and Giroux.
Mote, Frederick W. (1999). *Imperial China 900–1800*. Cambridge, MA: Harvard University Press.
Murray, Alan V. (1988). 'Monarchy and Nobility in the Latin Kingdom of Jerusalem, 1099-113: Establishment and Origins'. PhD thesis, University of St Andrews.
Nelson, Janet (2008a). 'Kingship and Royal Government'. In Rosamond McKitterick (ed.), *The New Cambridge Medieval History, Part II: Government and Institutions*. Cambridge: Cambridge University Press: 381–430.
Nelson, Janet (2008b). 'The Frankish Kingdoms, 814-898: The West'. In Rosamond McKitterick (ed.), *The New Cambridge Medieval History, Part I: Political Development*. Cambridge: Cambridge University Press: 110–41.
Nexon, Daniel H. (2009). *The Struggle for Power in Early Modern Europe: Religious Conflict, Dynastic Empires, and International Change*. Princeton: Princeton University Press.
North, Douglass C., John Joseph Wallis, and Barry R. Weingast (2009). *Violence and Social Orders: A Conceptual Framework for Interpreting Recorded Human History*. Cambridge: Cambridge University Press.
O'Callaghan, Joseph F. (1975). *A History of Medieval Spain*. Ithaca and London: Cornell University Press.
O'Callaghan, Joseph F. (1989). *The Cortes of Castile-León: 1188-1350*. Philadelphia: University of Pennsylvania Press.
Oakley, Francis (2010). *Empty Bottles of Gentilism: Kingship and the Divine in Late Antiquity and the Early Middle Ages (to 1050)*. New Haven and London: Yale University Press.
Oakley, Francis (2012). *The Mortgage of the Past: Reshaping the Ancient Political Inheritance (1050-1300)*. New Haven and London: Yale University Press.
Oleson, Tryggvi J. (1957). 'Edward the Confessor's Promise of the Throne to Duke William of Normandy'. *The English Historical Review* 72(283): 221–8.
Olson, Mancur (1993). 'Dictatorship, Democracy, and Development'. *American Political Science Review* 87(3): 567–76.
Orme, Nicholas (1984). *From Childhood to Chivalry: The Education of the English Kings and Aristocracy, 1066-1530*. London: Routledge.
Orning, Hans Jacob (2008). *Unpredictability and Presence: Norwegian Kingship in the High Middle Ages*. Leiden: Brill Publishers.
Oskarsson, Sven, C. T. Dawes, K. O. Lindgren, and R. Öhrvall (2021). 'Big Brother Sees You, But Does He Rule You? The Relationship between Birth Order and Political Candidacy'. *Journal of Politics* 83(3): 1158–62.
Paine, Thomas (1986[1776]). *Common Sense*. New York: Penguin.
Painter, Sidney (2001[1933]). *William Marshall, Knight-Errant, Baron and Regent of England*. Toronto: University of Toronto Press.
Palmer, Alan (1970). *The Lands Between. A History of East-Central Europe since the Congress of Vienna*. New York: The Macmillan Company.

Palmer, John (1998). 'War and Domesday Waster'. In Matthew Strickland (ed.), *Armies, Chivalry and Warfare in Medieval Britain and France*. Paul Watkins: 256–78.
Palmstierna, Markel et al. (2017). 'Family Counts: Deciding When to Murder among the Icelandic Vikings'. *Evolution and Human Behavior* 38(2): 175–80.
Parker, Geoffrey (1996[1988]). *The Military Revolution: Military Innovation and the Rise of the West, 1500–1800*. Cambridge: Cambridge University Press.
Peirce, Leslie (2003). *Morality Tales: Law and Gender in the Ottoman Court of Aintab*. Berkeley: University of California Press.
Penman, Michael (2007). 'Diffinicione successionis ad regnum Scottorum: Royal Succession in Scotland in the Later Middle Ages'. In Fabrice Lachaud and Michael Penman (eds), *Making and Breaking the Rules: Succession in Medieval Europe c.1000–c.1600*. Turnhout: Brepols: 43–60.
Phillips, Charles and Alan Axelrod (2005). *Encyclopedia of Wars*. New York: Facts on File.
Philpott, Daniel (2001). *Revolutions in Sovereignty: How Ideas Shaped Modern International Relations*. Princeton: Princeton University Press.
Pierson, Paul (2000). 'Increasing Returns, Path Dependence, and the Study of Politics'. *American Political Science Review* 94(2): 251–67.
Podany, Amanda H. (2014). *The Ancient Near East: A Very Short Introduction*. Oxford: Oxford University Press.
Poggi, Gianfranco (1978). *The Development of the Modern State: A Sociological Introduction*. Stanford: Stanford University Press.
Popper, Karl R (1999). *All Life is Problem Solving*. London: Routledge.
Prestwich, Michael (1997). *Edward I*. New Haven: Yale University Press.
Prestwich, Michael (2003). *The Three Edwards: War and State in England 1272–1377*. London: Routledge.
Previté-Orton, Charles William (1912). *The Early History of the House of Savoy 1000–1233*. Cambridge: Cambridge University Press.
Price, Neil (2020). *Children of Ash and Elm: A History of the Vikings*. London: Allen Lane.
Procter, Evelyn S. (1980). *Curia and Cortes in León and Castile 1072–1295*. Cambridge: Cambridge University Press.
Przeworski, Adam et al. (2000). *Democracy and Development: Political Institutions and Well-being in the World, 1950–1990*. Cambridge: Cambridge University Press.
Putnam, Bertha H. (1908). *The Enforcement of the Statutes of Labourers*. New York: Columbia University and Longmans.
Quataert, Donald (2005). *The Ottoman Empire, 1700–1922*. Cambridge: Cambridge University Press.
Rawski, Evelyn S. (1998). *The Last Emperors: A Social History of Qing Imperial Institutions*. Berkeley: University of California Press.
Reuters (2021). 'New Oman Succession Law: From Ruler to Eldest Son'. *Khaleej Times*. URL: https://www.khaleejtimes.com/region/mena/new-oman-succession-law-from-ruler-to-eldest-son.
Reynolds, Susan (1994). *Fiefs and Vassals: The Medieval Evidence Reinterpreted*. Oxford: Clarendon Press.
Riché, Pierre (1993). *The Carolingians: A Family Who Forged Europe*. Philadelphia: University of Pennsylvania Press.
Riehl, Anna (2010). *The Face of Queenship: Early Modern Representations of Elizabeth I*. New York: Palgrave Macmillan.
Riley-Smith, Jonathan (1973). *Feudal Nobility and the Kingdom of Jerusalem, 1174–1277*. London: Macmillan.

Rokkan, Stein (1975). 'Dimensions of State Formation and Nation Building: A Possible Paradigm for Research om Variations within Europe'. In Charles Tilly (ed.), *The Formation of National States in Western Europe*. Princeton: Princeton University Press: 562–600.
Rossabi, Morris (2012). *The Mongols: A Very Short Introduction*. Oxford: Oxford University Press.
Rousseau, Jean-Jacques (1920[1762]). *The Social Contract: & Discourses*. London: JM Dent & Sons.
Rowe, John H. (2006). 'The Inca Civil War and the Establishment of Spanish Power in Peru'. *Nawpa Pacha* 28(1): 1–9.
Ruiz, Teofilo (2004). *From Heaven to Earth: The Reordering of Castilian Society, 1150–1350*. Oxford: Oxford University Press.
Sartori, Giovanni (1984). *Social Science Concepts: A Systematic Analysis*. London: Sage Publications.
Schedler, Andreas (2013). *The Politics of Uncertainty: Sustaining and Subverting Electoral Authoritarianism*. Oxford: Oxford University Press.
Scheidel, Walter (2019). *Escape from Rome: The Failure of Empire and the Road to Prosperity*. Princeton: Princeton University Press.
Schmidt Voges, Inken and Ana Solana Crespo (2017). 'Introduction'. In Inken Schmidt Voges and Ana Solana Crespo (eds), *New Worlds? Transformations in the Culture of International Relations around the Peace of Utrecht*. London: Routledge: 1–18.
Schück, Herman (1984). 'Sweden as an Aristocratic Republic'. *Scandinavian Journal of History* 9(1): 65–72.
Schück, Herman (2003). 'The Political System'. In Knut Helle (ed.), *The Cambridge History of Scandinavia, Vol. 1: Prehistory to 1520*. Cambridge: Cambridge University Press: 679–709.
Schulz, Jonathan F. et al. (2019). 'The Church, Intensive Kinship, and Global Psychological Variation'. *Science* 366: 1–12.
Schumpeter, Joseph A. (1974 [1942]). *Capitalism, Socialism and Democracy*. London: Unwin University Books.
Scott, James C. (2017). *Against the Grain: A Deep History of the Earliest States*. New Haven: Yale University Press.
Sedlar, Jean W. (1994). *East Central Europe in the Middle Ages, 1000–1500*. Seattle: University of Washington Press.
Sharma, Vivek Swaroop (2015). 'Kinship, Property, and Authority: European Territorial Consolidation Reconsidered'. *Politics and Society* 43(2): 151–80.
Sharma, Vivek Swaroop (2017). 'War, Conflict and the State Reconsidered'. In Lars Bo Kaspersen and Jeppe Strandsbjerg (eds), *Does War Make State? Investigations of Charles Tilly's Historical Sociology*. Cambridge: Cambridge University Press: 181–217.
Shaw, R. Dykes (1906). 'The Fall of the Visigothic Power in Spain'. *The English Historical Review* 21(82): 209–28.
Shih, Victor (2010). *The Autocratic Difference: Information Paucity*. Mimeo: Northwestern University.
Siedentop, Larry (2014). *Inventing the Individual*. Cambridge, MA: Harvard University Press.
Silverstein, Adam J. (2010). *Islamic History: A Very Short Introduction*. Oxford: Oxford University Press.
Skaaning, Svend-Erik (2020). 'Waves of Autocratization and Democratization: A Critical Note on Conceptualization and Measurement'. *Democratization* 27(8): 1533–42.

Skovgaard-Petersen, Inge (2003). 'The Making of the Danish Kingdom'. In Knut Helle (ed.), *The Cambridge History of Scandinavia, Vol. 1: Prehistory to 1520.* Cambridge: Cambridge University Press: 168–83.
Southern, Richard (1956). *The Making of the Middle Ages.* London: Hutchinson & Co.
Southern, Richard (1970). *Western Society and the Church in the Middle Ages.* New York: Penguin Books.
Spruyt, Hendrik (1994). *The Sovereign State and its Competitors: An Analysis of Systems Change.* Princeton: Princeton University Press.
Spruyt, Hendrik (2017). 'War and State Formation: Amending the Bellicist Theory of State Making'. In Lars Bo Kaspersen and Jeppe Strandsbjerg (eds), *Does War Make States?: Investigations of Charles Tilly's Historical Sociology.* Cambridge: Cambridge University Press: 73–97.
Starr, Paul (2019). *Entrenchment: Wealth, Power and the Constitution of Democratic Societies.* New Haven: Yale University Press.
Stasavage, David (2010). 'When Distance Mattered: Geographic Scale and the Development of European Representative Assemblies'. *American Political Science Review* 104(4): 625–43.
Stasavage, David (2016). 'Representation and Consent: Why They Arose in Europe and Not Elsewhere'. *Annual Review of Political Science* 19: 145–62.
Stasavage, David (2020). *The Decline and Rise of Democracy.* Princeton: Princeton University Press.
Stephenson, John Home (1927). 'The Law of the Throne: Tanistry and the Introduction of the Law of Primogeniture: A Note on the Succession of the Kings of Scotland from Kenneth MacAlpin to Robert Bruce'. *The Scottish Historical Review* 25(97): 1–12.
Stokes, Antony Derek (1970). 'The System of Succession to the Thrones of Russia: 1054–1113'. In Robert Auty, Lucian Ryszard Lewitter, and Alexis Peter Vlasto (eds), *Gorski Vijenats: A Garland of Essays Offered to Professor Elizabeth Mary Hill.* Cambridge: Modern Humanities Research Association: 268–75.
Stone, Daniel (2001). *The Polish-Lithuanian State 1386–1795.* Seattle: University of Washington Press.
Strayer, Joseph (1987[1965]). *Feudalism.* Malabar: Krieger Publishing Company.
Sumption, Jonathan (1999). *The Hundred Years War, Vol. 1: Trial by Battle.* Philadelphia: University of Pennsylvania Press.
Sutton, John L. (1980). *The King's Honor and the King's Cardinal: The War of the Polish Succession.* Lexington: University Press of Kentucky.
Svolik, Milan (2012). *The Politics of Authoritarian Rule.* New York: Cambridge University Press.
Svolik, Milan (2013). 'Incentives, Institutions, and the Challenges to Research on Authoritarian Politics'. *APSA Comparative Democratization Newsletter.*
Taylor, Craig (2001). 'The Salic Law and the Valois Succession to the French Crown'. *French History* 15(4): 358–77.
The Guardian (2019). 'Rumours grow of rift between Saudi king and crown prince'. URL: https://www.theguardian.com/world/2019/mar/05/fears-grow-of-rift-between-saudi-king-salman-and-crown-prince-mohammed-bin-salman.
Thomas, Hugh M. (2003). 'The Significance and Fate of the Native English Landholders of 1086'. *The English Historical Review* 118(476): 303–33.
Thorpe, Lewis (1974). *Gregory of Tours: The History of the Franks.* London: Penguin Books.

Tierney, Brian (1988). *The Crisis of Church and State, 1050–1300*. Toronto: University of Washington Press.
Tilly, Charles (1975). *The Formation of National States in Western Europe*. Princeton: Princeton University Press.
Tilly, Charles (1992). *Coercion, Capital, and European States, AD 990–1990*. Oxford: Blackwell.
Tullock, Gordon (1987). *Autocracy*. Berlin: Springer Science & Business Media.
Turner, Ralph V. and Richard R. Heiser (2013). *The Reign of Richard Lionheart: Ruler of the Angevin Empire 1189–99*. London: Routledge.
Ullmann, Walter (1970[1955]). *The Growth of Papal Government in the Middle Ages: A Study in the Ideological Relation of Clerical to Lay Power*. London: Methuen.
Van Dam, Raymond (2008). 'Merovingian Gaul and the Frankish Conquests'. In Paul Foracre (ed.), *The New Cambridge Medieval History, Part I: The Sixth Century*. Cambridge: Cambridge University Press: 193–231.
Van Nimwegen, Olaf. (2010). 'The Transformation of Army Organisation in Early-modern Western Europe, c.1500–1789. In Frank Tallett and D. J. B. Trim (eds), *European Warfare 1350–1750*, Cambridge: Cambridge University Press: 159–80.
Van Tricht, Filip (2017). 'Claiming the Basileia ton Rhomaion: A Latin Imperial Dynasty in Byzantium (1204–1261)'. *The Medieval History Journal* 20(2): 248–87.
Van Zanden, Jan Luiten, Eltjo Buringh, and Maarten Bosker (2012). 'The Rise and Decline of European Parliaments, 1188–1789'. *The Economic History Review* 65(3): 835–61.
Vaughan, Richard (1973). Charles the Bold: The Last Valois Duke of Burgundy. London: Longman.
Verbrugge, Lois M. (1977). 'The Structure of Adult Friendship Choices'. *Social Forces* 56(2): 576–97.
Vincent, Nicholas (2012). *Magna Carta: A Very Short Introduction*. Oxford: Oxford University Press.
Wang, Yuhua (2018). 'Sons and Lovers: Political Stability in China and Europe before the Great Divergence'. URL: https://papers.ssrn.com/sol3/papers.cfm?abstract_id=3058065.
Wang, Yuhua (2019). 'Elite Kinship Network and State Building: Theory and Evidence from Imperial China'. URL: https://papers.ssrn.com/sol3/papers.cfm?abstract_id=3355692.
Ward, John O. (1985). 'Feudalism: Interpretative Category or Framework of Life in the Medieval West?' In Ronald Leach, Soumyendra Nath Mukherjee, and John O. Ward (eds), *Feudalism: Comparative Studies*. Sydney: The Sydney Association for Studies in Society and Culture: 40–67.
Warren, Wilfred Lewis (1973). *Henry II*. Berkeley: University of California Press.
Waterfield, Robin (2012). *Dividing the Spoils: The War for Alexander the Great's Empire*. Oxford: Oxford University Press.
Watson, Andrew John (1992). *Economic Reform and Social Change in China*. London: Routledge.
Weber, Max (1948). *From Max Weber: Essays in Sociology*. London: Routledge.
Weber, Max (1968). *Economy and Society*. New York: University of California Press.
Weber, Max (2019). *Economy and Society: A New Translation*. Cambridge: Harvard University Press.
Weiler, Björn (2007). 'Suitability and Right: Imperial Succession and the Norms of Politics in Early Staufen Germany'. In Fabrice Lachaud and Michael Penman (eds), *Making and Breaking the Rules: Succession in Medieval Europe c.1000–c.1600*. Turnhout: Brepols Publishers: 71–88.

Weiler, Björn (2013). 'Describing Rituals of Succession and the Legitimation of Kingship in the West, ca. 1000–ca. 1150'. In Alexander Beihammer, Stavroula Constantinou, and Maria G. Parani (eds), *Court Ceremonies and Rituals of Power in Byzantium and the Medieval Mediterranean*. Leiden: Brill: 113–40.
West, Charles (2019). 'Plenty of Puff'. London Review of Books, 19 December.
Whaley, Joachim (2012). *Germany and the Holy Roman Empire*. Oxford: Oxford University Press.
Wheatcroft, Andrew (1995). *The Habsburgs: Embodying Empire*. London: Penguin Books.
Whittaker, Cynthia Hyla (2001). 'Chosen by All the Russian People—The Idea of an Elected Monarch in the 18th Century Russia'. *Acta Slavica Iaponica* 18: 1–18.
Wickham, Chris (2005). *Framing the Early Middle Ages: Europe and the Mediterranean, 400–800*. Oxford: Oxford University Press.
Wickham, Chris (2009). *The Inheritance of Rome: A History of Europe from 400 to 1000*. London: Penguin.
Wickham, Chris (2015). *Sleepwalking into a New World: The Emergence of Italian City Communes in the Twelfth Century*. Princeton: Princeton University Press.
Wickham, Chris (2016). *Medieval Europe*. New Haven: Yale University Press.
Wilson, Peter (2009). *Europe's Tragedy: A New History of the Thirty Years War*. Cambridge: Harvard University Press.
Wilson, Peter (2016). *Heart of Europe: A History of the Holy Roman Empire*. Cambridge: Harvard University Press.
Winch, Donald (2013). *Malthus: A Very Short Introduction*. Oxford: Oxford University Press.
Wolford, Scott (2007). 'The Turnover Trap: New Leaders, Reputation, and International Conflict'. *American Journal of Political Science* 51(4): 772–88.
Wong, Roy Bin (1997). *China Transformed: Historical Change and the Limits of European Experience*. Ithaca: Cornell University Press.
Wright, Joseph (2008). 'Do Authoritarian Institutions Constrain? How Legislatures Affect Economic Growth and Investment'. *American Journal of Political Science* 52(2): 322–43.
Zagorin, Perez (1982). *Rebels and Rulers, 1500–1600, Vol. 1: Agrarian and Urban Rebellions: Society, States, and Early Modern Revolution*. Cambridge: Cambridge University Press.

General Index

Tables and figures are indicated by an italic *t* and *f*, following the page number.

Abbasid caliphate 133, 189, 211
absence of successor vi, 10, 16, 20, 40, 87, 106, 111, 214
   civil wars and 106
   depositions 171
   as problematic for the regime and the ruler himself 24
   see also heir
African states 219
agnatic seniority
   benefits of 33
   coordination problem 32–3, 91
   crown prince problem 33
   dataset 56
   depositions 17, 120, 124, 124*t*, 130, 131*t*, 132*f*
   East-Central Europe 79
   family and dynasty 160
   Imperial China 198, 203, 213
   monarchs' age 119, 119*t*
   monarchs' relationship to their predecessors 118, 118*t*
   Ottoman Empire 190
   Poland 178
   political instability 57, 58, 160
   Russian Empire 80
   Saudi Arabia 216
   as succession order 13, 31, 32–3
   succession wars 17, 91, 101
   successors' age 118
   winning coalition and 34
anarchy 8, 21, 39, 88, 205, 207
Arpad dynasty 79
authoritarian/autocratic regime 16
   authoritarian politics as unruly 47
   autocratic successions and elite members 20, 206
   crown prince, competence aspect 26–7
   family/kinship ties 49
   institutions 22, 47–8, 58, 206
   leadership succession vi
   people, the 46
   power transfer in 20, 206
   problem of succession 4, 205–6, 216
   secrecy 22, 48, 89
   violence 4, 47, 58, 205
authoritarian/autocratic regime (modern) 29, 58
   absence of hereditary succession 218
   constitutions 218–19, 221
   coordination problem 221
   crown prince problem 217, 220, 221
   hereditary succession in non-monarchies 217–18
   modern-day monarchy 216–17
   parties 219–21
   perennial problem of authoritarian succession 18, 216, 221–3
   succession in modern states 215–21
   see also dictatorship

Bjälbo dynasty 78
Bohemia 6, 52, 53, 56, 79, 80
Brut Chronicle 55
Burgundy 50, 62
Byzantine Empire
   civil wars 18, 185
   depositions 186, 189, 214
   elective monarchy 31, 80
   hereditary emperorship 84, 185
   Islam and 185
   Latin west/Byzantine Empire comparison 71, 82–4, 86–7, 203, 211
   Mandate of Heaven 84, 186, 195
   Ottoman conquest of 26, 53, 80
   political instability 185–6, 195
   primogeniture 16, 84, 86
   problem of succession 15, 18, 20, 84, 184, 185–6, 203

GENERAL INDEX 241

succession based on military strength 25, 186
usurpation 18, 185, 186, 212
violence 185, 186

Capetian dynasty 207-9, 214-15
'accursed kings' 215
Capetian kings 10, 14, 50, 73, 185
elective monarchy 31, 73, 208
end of 215
primogeniture 56, 73-4, 76, 87, 207-8, 210
capitalized coercion 40
Carolingian Empire 1, 206
decline of 11
split into three kingdoms 1, 2, 38, 207, 209-10
succession wars 38, 186, 187
Treaty of Verdun 1, 207
Carolingian Renaissance 14, 64
Carolingians 14, 68, 73
breakdown of public order 71-2, 87, 186-7
'Carolingian wonder' 69, 186
divorce 64
marriage 64
monogamy 64, 68
partible inheritance 13, 36, 38, 68, 69, 207
primogeniture 2, 11, 68-9, 86
state-building success 207
Catholic Church
314 Council of Neocaesaria 62
517 Council of Epaon, Burgundy 62
1095 Council of Clermont 67
1620 Battle of the White Mountain 26
Catholic/Orthodox Churches comparison 82-4
church-state relations 65, 71-3
clerical celibacy 66, 72
Cluniac reform 65-6, 72
divorce 61, 62, 64, 66, 67, 86, 106
elite and 64
Europe, exposure to the Catholic Church 64, 65f
family structures, transformation of 10, 16, 38, 60, 61-8, 72, 82, 86, 191, 212
Gregorian/papal reforms 66, 72, 86, 212

heirship practices forbidden by the Church in late antiquity 61-3
marriage 41, 61-3, 64, 66-7, 72, 86, 212
papacy crisis 65
primogeniture, origins and spread 10, 16, 38, 60-4, 69, 70-3, 81, 86, 87, 191, 212
'cellular structure for politics' 14
China *see* communist China; Imperial China
civil wars 96-7, 97f
Byzantine Empire 18, 185
depositions and 99-100, 100f
destructive consequences 41, 110
England 9, 109
heirs and 106-8, 106t, 107f
Imperial China 197, 198
Islamic states 188, 189
Mongols 202
natural death of rulers and 16-17, 99-100, 99t, 100f, 101t, 102-3, 102f, 106-8, 106t, 107f, 109, 210
Norway 88
Ottoman Empire 23, 190
primogeniture and 89, 90, 92, 101-3, 101t, 106t, 107-8, 107f, 110, 127, 210
succession as cause of 17, 20, 23, 42, 88, 89-92, 99, 99t, 100f, 101t, 102-3, 102f, 209
see also succession wars
communist China 18, 219, 220, 221, 223
Chinese Communist Party 220
constitutions 80, 116, 218-19, 221, 222
coordination problem 21-4, 42, 57, 90-1, 206, 210
agnatic seniority 32-3, 91
autocratic regime (modern) 221
constitutions 219
depositions 127-9, 128t, 129t, 132
elective monarchy 31-2
Imperial China 199
partible inheritance 37, 38
primogeniture 35, 88-9, 91, 92, 106, 127, 210
risk of war 98
Côte d'Ivoire 220-1
coup 47, 89, 114, 127
African states 219
crown prince problem 24

242 GENERAL INDEX

crown prince 24, 90
    'barrier effect' 24, 113
    landed wealth 30, 32, 33, 119
    mortality 25, 163
    primogeniture 13, 90
    Saudi Arabia 216–17
    son as crown prince 163
    see also heir
crown prince problem 12, 21, 24–30, 42, 57, 115, 117, 206, 210
    age aspect 25
    agnatic seniority 33
    autocratic regime and 26–7
    autocratic regime (modern) 217, 220, 221
    competence aspect 25–9, 90–1
    depositions 129–30, 132
    Henry, German crown prince 165
    Imperial China 127, 199, 213
    partible inheritance 37
    primogeniture 34, 35, 210
    resource aspect 29–30, 91, 119–20
    Saudi Arabia 217
    succession wars 90, 110
    ultimogeniture 35, 36

democracy 45, 47, 111–12, 215–16
    2020 US presidential election 215
    'institutionalized uncertainty' 223
    peaceful transfer of power 4, 215
    problem of succession 223
    succession order 20
    see also representative democracy
Denmark 10, 85, 78, 97
depositions 2, 4, 121, 132–3, 205
    agnatic seniority 17, 120, 124, 124*t*, 130, 131*t*, 132*f*
    Byzantine Empire 186, 189, 214
    childless monarchs 171
    civil wars and 99–100, 100*f*
    coordination problem 127–9, 128*t*, 129*t*, 132
    crown prince problem 129–30, 132
    descriptive statistics 120–2, 122*f*
    elective monarchy 17, 111, 120, 124, 124*t*, 131*t*, 132*f*
    family and dynasty 18, 160, 162–3, 167, 171–2, 171*f*, 172*f*, 173–5, 174*t*, 175*f*, 181

Imperial China 127, 183, 199, 200*t*, 202
international wars 99
Islamic states 189
monarchs' age at ascension 130–2, 132*f*
monarchs deposed, depending on principle of succession and son 128, 128*t*
partible inheritance 37–8
primogeniture and 17, 35, 120, 122, 124–7, 124*t*, 125*f*, 126*f*, 128, 128*t*, 129, 130–1, 131*t*, 132, 132*f*, 133, 167, 178, 210, 217
Saudi Arabia 217
succession principles and leader survival 112–20
succession wars 42, 99–100, 99*t*, 100*f*, 105
trends in leader tenure and depositions 122, 123*f*
uncertainty of the succession 17, 112, 113, 132, 133
violence 111
Visigothic monarchy 111, 112
Yuan dynasty 200, 200*t*, 201–2
dictatorship 45, 46, 49, 116, 219, 221–2
    parties in 219–20
divorce 61, 67–8, 67*f*, 86
    ban on 61, 62, 66, 85, 86
    Carolingians 64
    Catholic Church 61, 62, 64, 66, 67, 86, 106
    Henry VIII, King of England 106, 159
    Orthodox Church 83
    Protestant churches 85
Doomsday Book 95, 109
dynastic politics 7, 13, 49, 85, 158, 166, 209
    dynastic stability 13, 18
    dynastic succession 4, 7
    primogeniture 11, 18, 158
    see also family and dynasty

East-Central Europe 79–80
    agnatic seniority 79
East Francia 1, 72, 207
Egypt 218
    Mamluk Sultanate 18, 190, 191, 212
elective monarchy 27, 45
    advantages 31
    coordination problem 31–2

crusader states in the Middle East 192
dataset 56
depositions 17, 111, 120, 124, 124t, 131t, 132f
elected co-kings 56, 73
end of 211
family and dynasty 160, 167, 177–8
international wars 94
monarchs' age 119, 119t
monarchs' male children precedence in succession order 106
parliaments and 153–4, 154f, 155, 156
pitfalls 9, 31, 32, 209
political instability 57, 58, 160
pool of candidates 31
'premature' elections 56, 218
relationship to their predecessors 118, 118t
succession by appointment 31–2, 75
as succession order 13, 31–2
succession wars 17, 91, 94, 101, 110, 127
winning coalition and 34
women in 13
elective monarchy: specific cases
　Byzantine Empire 31, 80
　Capetians 31, 73, 208
　crusader states in the Middle East 192
　England 31, 74
　France 31, 56, 208
　Holy Roman Empire 31, 72–3, 77, 208
　Imperial China 198, 203, 213
　Poland 2, 39, 79–80, 92
　Scandinavia 78, 160
elite 45–6
　autocratic regime and 21–2
　Catholic Church and 64
　competition within 21–2
　contested succession 21
　crown prince, competence aspect 27–8
　parliaments and 141, 146, 148
　parties and 219–20
　political power as based on landed wealth 30
　royal minorities and 119, 137
　succession and 12–13, 19, 20, 22–3, 42, 89–90, 136, 205, 206
　see also coordination problem; ruler–elite relations; winning coalition

England 211
　1066 Norman Conquest of 7, 26, 32, 74, 88
　1066 Battle of Hastings 32, 109
　1069–1070 Harrying of the North 95
　Anarchy in 88
　Anglo-Saxon England 31, 74, 192
　army 29
　civil wars 9, 109
　elective monarchy 31, 74
　hereditary monarchy 72, 75
　Magna Carta/Great Charter 48, 134, 136, 138, 152
　Norman-English succession 74–5
　Parliament 134, 139, 141, 144, 152, 156–7, 159
　primogeniture 40, 74, 75, 85, 210
　Protestantism 85, 159
　state-formation 6
　Succession Acts 144
　succession by appointment 32, 74, 75
　ultimogeniture 35
　Wars of the Roses 88, 164
　Witenagemot 74
Eurasia 15, 31, 212, 214
　political instability 203, 212
　primogeniture 15, 60, 87
　see also Byzantine Empire; Imperial China; Islamic states

family and dynasty 17–18, 48–9, 158–60, 163, 180–2
　agnatic seniority 160
　conflicts within 23, 26, 159, 167, 190, 216, 218
　daughters, sisters, female relatives 17, 18, 165–6, 172–3, 175, 176–7
　depositions 18, 160, 162–3, 167, 171–2, 171f, 172f, 173–5, 174t, 175f, 181
　descriptive statistics on royal families 167–71
　dynastic solidarity as self-reinforcing institution 117, 163
　elective monarchy 160, 167, 177–8
　functions performed by family 163–7
　Imperial China 164
　kin as trusted agents 161, 164–5, 167

family and dynasty (*Continued*)
  larger families as secure shield for monarchs 163, 166, 171–3, 174–5, 180–1
  length of dynasties 177–9, 178*f*, 179*f*, 181
  living brothers and sisters over a monarch's lifetime 168–9, 169*f*
  longer-lasting dynasties 160, 167, 210
  marriage alliances 17, 165–6, 167, 172, 175–7, 176*t*, 177*f*, 181
  noble houses and royal spouses 175–6, 176*t*
  North Korea 218
  primogeniture 159, 160, 166, 167, 173, 178, 178*f*, 179*f*, 181, 210
  primogeniture, partible inheritance, and size of states 167, 179–80, 180*t*, 182
  relationship of monarchs to their predecessors and successors 117–18, 118*t*, 159
  Saudi Arabia 216
  solidarity with the lineage 159–60
  sons, brothers, male relatives 17, 18, 164–5, 167, 172–3, 176–7, 181
  uncles and aunts 169, 170*f*, 173–5
  why trust kin? 161–3, 166, 171, 218
  see also marriage; royal children
family structure
  adoption 61, 62–3, 86, 106
  agnatic family 61, 62, 82
  Catholic Church and transformation of 10, 16, 38, 60, 61–8, 72, 82, 86, 191, 212
  offspring of clerics as illegitimate 72
  offspring out of wedlock as illegitimate 61, 63–4, 66, 68, 106, 163
  see also divorce; marriage
female inheritance 41, 108, 115, 211
  Latin west 43
  marriage alliance 13, 40–1, 166
  'Pragmatic Sanction' 93
  state-formation and 42
  widows 61, 62
  see also women
fragmentation of power 46
  Europe/Imperial China comparison 41
  Latin west 14, 16
  partible inheritance 37, 40

France 211
  1346 Crecy battle 26
  1415 Agincourt battle 26
  army 29
  elective monarchy 31, 56, 208
  fall of Francia and birth of France 206–9
  parliament 140
  primogeniture 40, 210
  Salic Law 98
  state-formation 6
  strengthening of 6–7
Franks 68, 186
  church–state relations 65, 73
  expansionism 9–10
  Heerbanns 145
  partible inheritance 36, 207
  primogeniture 9, 70, 194, 214

German Empire
  'Great Interregnum' 7
  state-formation 6
  weakening of 6–7
  see also Holy Roman Empire
Germany 207

Habsburg dynasty 7, 53, 77, 80, 160
  'Habsburg jaw' 176
  marriage politics 165–6
  'Pragmatic Sanction' 53, 93, 144
  royal spouses from 176, 176*t*
  Spanish War of Succession 92, 93, 94
Haiti 217
Han dynasties 196, 197, 199–200, 203, 204
heir
  age 118–19, 119*t*
  civil wars and 106–8, 106*t*, 107*f*
  designating an heir 12
  heiress 166
  Imperial China, abundance of male heirs 10, 195, 196, 212
  incompetence as leaders 9, 27, 28
  monogamy, undersupply of legitimate male heirs 195, 213
  polygamy, abundance of male heirs 10, 195, 212
  primogeniture 17
  relation to the ruler 17, 117
  sons as heirs 25, 37, 106, 163
  see also absence of successor; crown prince; royal children

heirship practices
  Catholic Church and 61–3, 72, 82, 86, 212
  gradual spread of new heirship practices 63–5
  see also agnatic seniority; hereditary monarchy/succession; primogeniture; primogeniture: origins and spread
Heraclian dynasty 185
hereditary grooming 33, 35, 218
hereditary monarchy/succession 2, 181–2
  absence of hereditary succession in contemporary autocracies 218
  advantages of 8, 9, 13, 20, 39, 116, 133, 222–3
  disadvantages 9, 28, 209–10
  England 72, 75
  Gregory VII, Pope 66, 72
  Islamic states 188–9, 191
  Mongols 201
  normative argument for 9
  as personal and biological 5, 116
  political stability 39
  primogeniture 2, 4, 8–9, 39, 116
  Scandinavia 72
  sovereignty 8, 223
  state-formation 5
  see also monarchy; primogeniture
Holy Roman Empire 72, 77
  1212 Golden Bull 79
  1356 Golden Bull 53, 69, 77, 79, 191
  absence of successor 87
  elective monarchy 31, 72–3, 77, 208
  Hoftage 145
  partible inheritance 36, 38, 77, 86, 191–2
  primogeniture 77, 79, 85–6, 191–2
  Protestantism 85–6
  see also German Empire
Hundred Years' War 50, 88, 98, 164, 215
Hungary 53, 56, 79, 80, 157

Iberian Peninsula 36–7, 74, 75–6
  Aragon 152, 153, 157
  Castile 139–40
  primogeniture 69, 72, 75–6, 191
  ruler duration 193*t*, 194
  Siete Partidas 56, 76, 144
  see also Spain

Imperial China 18, 20, 194–202
  abundance of male heirs 10, 195, 196, 212
  agnatic seniority 198, 203, 213
  civil wars 197, 198
  concubinage 196
  Confucianism 196, 212
  coordination problem 199
  crown princes 127, 199, 213
  depositions 127, 183, 199, 200*t*, 202
  election/acclamation 198, 203, 213
  Europe/China comparison 41, 183, 196, 204, 211, 213–14
  family and dynasty 164
  'father-to-son' succession 183, 186, 195–6, 197, 198, 199–200, 203, 212, 213
  Mandate of Heaven 186, 195, 197, 198
  'native'/Han dynasties/succession practices 197, 199–200, 203, 204, 212–13
  nomad dynasties 197–200, 200*t*, 202, 203, 213
  patriarchy and ancestor worship 196
  political instability 196, 197–9
  political stability 183, 195–6, 197, 204, 212–13
  polygyny 10, 195, 196, 212
  primogeniture 60, 87, 164, 196, 202, 203, 212
  'secret succession' 199
  strong state and bureaucracy 195, 213
  succession crises 198–9, 203
  taxes 29, 195
  usurpation 197
  zu [lineage] leadership based on primogeniture 196
  see also Mongols
Inca Empire 203
institutions 44, 51, 215
  autocratic regime 22, 47–8, 58, 206
  'bounded change'/'conversion' 141
  communist China 219
  as coordination devices 116
  dynastic solidarity as self-reinforcing institution 163
  formalization of succession rules through institutions 116
  orderly power transfer and 214

institutions (*Continued*)
  path-dependency 140
  power-sharing institutions 135–6, 139, 205, 213
  state-building and 214
  see also Catholic Church; constitutions; parliaments
international wars 17, 26, 42, 96–7, 97*f*
  defensive/offensive wars 103–4, 103*t*, 105, 105*t*
  depositions and 99
  elective monarchy 94
  natural deaths of rulers 99*t*, 103, 104–5, 104*f*, 109
  positive consequences 41
  primogeniture and 94, 95, 103–5
  succession as cause of 90, 92–5, 99, 99*t*, 103–5, 103*t*, 105*t*
  see also succession wars
interregnum vii, 7, 201
Islamic states 20, 187–94
  Abbasid Caliphate 133, 189, 211
  al-Andalus Caliphate, Cordoba 189–90
  civil war/*fitna* 188, 189
  depositions 189
  early Islam 187–9, 190–1
  hereditary succession 188–9, 191
  Islamic rule in Southern Spain 64, 69
  Mamluk Sultanate 18, 190, 191, 212
  Muhammed's succession 187–8
  non-hereditary caliphates 188
  political instability 194
  polygyny 194
  succession problem 189, 190–1, 203
  Sunni/Shia Muslims divide 187
  Sunni theory of succession 188, 189
  Umayyad Caliphate 188–9, 190
  see also Middle East; Ottoman Empire
Islamic states/Western Europe comparison 191, 211, 214
  gap in ruler tenures 194, 214
  Holy Roman Empire 191–2
  Iberian Peninsula 193*t*, 194
  partible inheritance 191–2
  primogeniture 191, 193–4, 203, 214
  ruler duration 193, 193*t*
Italian Peninsula 76–7, 191
  southern Italy 9, 26, 69, 70, 76

Jagiellonian dynasty 56, 80
Jin/Jurchen Jin dynasty 198, 200, 200*t*, 203

Kalmar Union 53, 78, 96–7, 121

landed wealth 30
  Catholic Church 72
  crown lands 30, 50
  crown prince 30, 32, 33, 119
  primogeniture 72, 91, 120
  see also partible inheritance
Latin Christendom 10, 14, 84, 85
Latin west
  female inheritance 43
  fragmentation of power 14, 16
  institutions 48
  Latin west/Byzantine Empire comparison 71, 82–4, 86–7, 203, 211
  primogeniture: origins and spread 15, 16, 43, 60, 68–71, 70*f*, 81, 87
Liao dynasty (Khitan Empire) 197–8, 200, 200*t*, 203

Macedonian empire/dynasty 1, 185, 211
Malthusian Trap vi
Mamluk Sultanate 18, 190, 191, 212
Mandate of Heaven
  Byzantine Empire 84, 186, 195
  Imperial China 186, 195, 197, 198
marriage
  Catholic Church 41, 61–3, 64, 66–7, 72, 86, 212
  Charlemagne 68, 83
  concubinage 38, 61, 63, 66, 78, 83, 86, 196
  female inheritance 13
  'in-marriage'/cousin marriage 61, 62, 63, 64, 66, 67, 82, 86, 176
  levirate 61, 62, 63
  marriage alliance 7, 13, 17, 40–1, 80, 165–6, 167, 172, 175–7, 176*t*, 177*f*, 181, 209, 211–12
  monarchs married over the course of their lifetime 169, 170*f*
  noble houses and royal spouses 175–6, 176*t*
  Orthodox Church 82–3, 84
  'out-marriage'/exogamy 41, 61

GENERAL INDEX 247

remarriage 61, 62, 63, 66, 67, 83
  see also divorce; family structure; monogamy; polygamy/polygyny
Merovingians 63, 71, 207
  concubinage 38
  partible inheritance 13, 36, 38, 68, 186, 207
  political instability 186
  polygamy 38, 63, 68, 186
Mexico 221
Middle East 15, 18, 187, 203
  crusader states in 191, 192
  elective monarchy 192
  modern-day monarchy 216
  testamentary succession 192
  see also Islamic states
Middle Francia 1, 207
Ming dynasty 195, 196–7, 200*t*
monarch
  age under different principles of succession 119, 119*t*
  dataset 53–5
  homicide/battle death rates 121
  'the king is dead, long live the king' vii, 8
  king's *body natural/body politic* distinction 8
  mortality 19, 20, 106, 135, 215
  natural death of rulers and civil wars 16–17, 99–100, 99*t*, 100*f*, 101*t*, 102–3, 102*f*, 106–8, 106*t*, 107*f*, 109, 210
  power of 30, 44–5
  relationship to their predecessors 117–18, 118*t*
  relationship to their successors 128–9, 129*t*
  trends in leader tenure 122, 123*f*
  youthful/healthy appearance 23–4, 222
  see also ruler
monarchy
  modern-day monarchy 216–17
  states of present-day Europe as descendants of monarchical states 40
  succession and 8–9
  succession order 20
  see also elective monarchy; hereditary monarchy/succession
Mongols 1, 15, 200–1
  Chagatai Khanate 201, 202, 203

civil wars 202
conquest of Baghdad by 189
Golden Horde 201, 202, 203
hereditary succession 201
il-Khanate, Iran 201, 202, 203
interregnum 201
polygyny 201
succession crises 201–2, 203
succession problem 201–2
ultimogeniture 35, 200, 201
see also Yuan dynasty
monogamy 68, 87, 163
  biological caveat 215
  Carolingians 64, 68
  late Roman Empire 61
  primogeniture 40, 212
  undersupply of legitimate male heirs 195, 213
mortality
  crown princes 25, 163
  monarchs 19, 20, 106, 135, 215
  royal children 27, 35, 148, 168

neo-Assyrian Empire 203
Netherlands, the 40
North Korea 217–18
Norway 78
  1260 Law of Succession 55, 144
  Civil War Era 88

Oman 217
orderly succession
  institutions and 214
  orderly partible inheritance 69, 70*f*, 81*f*, 191, 192
  political stability 2
  primogeniture 16, 159
Orthodox Church
  Catholic/Orthodox Churches comparison 82–4
  iconoclasm 83
  marriage 82–3, 84
  national churches 84
Ottoman Empire
  agnatic seniority 190
  Byzantine Empire, Ottoman conquest of 26, 53, 80
  civil wars 23, 190
  political instability 190, 194

Ottoman Empire (*Continued*)
  problem of succession 11, 15, 23, 190, 191
  rivalry between siblings 23, 26, 190
  succession based on military strength 25, 190

parliaments (parliament-like assemblies) 3, 155–7
  Aragon 152, 153, 157
  assembly politics 145
  Castile 139–40
  development of 17, 134, 145–6
  elective monarchies 153–4, 154f, 155, 156
  elites and 141, 146, 148
  England 134, 139, 141, 144, 152, 156–7, 159
  former monarch as deposed or killed 139
  France 140
  Franks: *Heerbanns* 145
  geographical factors 149, 151
  Holy Roman Empire: *Hoftage* 145
  institutional persistence 152–3, 156–7
  meeting frequency 146–7, 146f, 148t
  natural successions 148, 148t, 149, 150f, 151, 154–5, 155f
  placitum/placita 145
  political immediate effects of succession 136–8, 152, 153
  political long-term effects of succession 138–42, 152, 153
  as power-sharing institution 136, 145, 152–3, 156, 210
  'pre-parliaments' 135, 145–6
  primogeniture 17, 142–4, 153–5, 154f, 156, 210
  royal minorities 138, 139–40, 147, 148, 148t, 151, 151f, 152, 156
  succession 17, 135, 136, 145–55, 148t, 150f, 156
  troubled successions 17, 137, 148, 152–3, 156
partible inheritance 15
  coordination problem 37, 38
  crown prince problem 37
  depositions 37–8
  fragmentation of political power 37, 40
  orderly partible inheritance 69, 70f, 81f, 191, 192
  political instability 37, 38–9
  political stability 38–9, 57, 192
  primogeniture/partible inheritance distinction 37, 40, 160, 167, 182
  primogeniture, partible inheritance, and size of states 167, 179–80, 180t, 182
  reconsolidating of the realm 179–80
  state-formation 39f
  as succession order 31, 36–9, 179
  switch to primogeniture 13–14, 160, 179–80, 191–2
  uncertainty 38
  winning coalition 38
partible inheritance: specific cases
  Carolingians 13, 36, 38, 68, 69, 207
  Franks 36, 207
  Holy Roman Empire 36, 38, 77, 86, 191–2
  Iberian Peninsula 36–7
  Islamic states/Western Europe comparison 191–2
  Merovingians 13, 36, 38, 68, 186, 207
parties 219–21
patriarchy 172–3, 196
people, the 20, 46
Piast dynasty 79, 160, 176, 176t
  length of dynasty 178
Poland 41, 56, 79, 160
  agnatic seniority 178
  elective monarchy 2, 39, 79–80, 92
  Partitions of Poland 39–40
  primogeniture 79
  War of Succession 2, 92–3, 205
political instability
  agnatic seniority 57, 58, 160
  Byzantine Empire 185–6, 195
  elective monarchy 57, 58, 160
  Eurasia 203, 212
  Imperial China 196, 197–9
  Islamic states 194
  Mamluk Egypt 190
  Merovingians 186
  Ottoman Empire 190, 194
  partible inheritance 37, 38–9
  problem of succession 2, 9, 209, 210
  Roman Empire 184
  state-formation and 7

Visigoths 111, 112, 186
Yuan dynasty 183, 199, 200, 202, 203
political stability
 hereditary monarchy 39
 Imperial China 183, 195–6, 197, 204, 212–13
 importance of 5–7
 internal stability 39, 41
 orderly succession 2
 partible inheritance 38–9, 57, 192
 primogeniture vii, 2, 3, 4, 10, 13, 15, 17, 39, 41, 57, 108, 133, 158, 160, 211, 214
politics of succession vii, 2, 6, 7, 12–14
 AD 1000–1800 2–3, 212
 European state-formation and 11, 12
 neglected by scholarship 11
 see also succession
politics of succession: dataset 12, 16, 51–8
 monarchs 53–5
 states/polities 51–3, 54*t*, 55*f*
 succession arrangements 55–8
polygamy/polygyny 85, 186, 194–5, 201
 abundance of male heirs due to 10, 195, 212
 Imperial China 10, 195, 196, 212
 Islamic states 194
 Merovingians 38, 63, 68, 186
 Mongols 201
 Scandinavia 68
Portugal 67
Premyszslid dynasty 79
primogeniture
 AD 1000–1800 vii
 agnatic primogeniture/eldest son 33, 35–6
 biological caveat 17, 106, 120, 181, 214, 215
 codification in laws 143–4
 criticism and pitfalls vi, 34, 40, 41
 dataset 56–8
 de facto primogeniture 38, 56, 57, 69, 81*f*, 87
 de jure primogeniture 56, 57, 87
 dynasties and 158
 female inheritance 34
 hereditary monarchy 2, 4, 8–9, 39, 116
 landed wealth 72, 91, 120
 as law of nature 8, 42, 60
 male preference primogeniture 34, 40

monarchs' age 119, 119*t*
normative argument for 9
primogeniture/partible inheritance distinction 37, 40, 160, 167, 182
rarity outside Europe 212
royal minorities 142
as succession order 31, 33–6, 40
successors' age 118
winning coalition and 34, 35
primogeniture: benefits vii, 4, 8, 13–14, 34, 40, 69, 75, 120, 133, 222
 civil wars 89, 90, 92, 101–3, 101*t*, 106*t*, 107–8, 107*f*, 110, 127, 210
 coordination problem 35, 88–9, 91, 92, 106, 127, 210
 crown prince problem 34, 35, 210
 depositions 17, 35, 120, 122, 124–7, 124*t*, 125*f*, 126*f*, 128, 128*t*, 129, 130–1, 131*t*, 132, 132*f*, 133, 167, 178, 210, 217
 family and dynasty 159, 160, 166, 167, 173, 178, 178*f*, 179*f*, 181, 210
 international wars 94, 95, 103–5
 Islamic states/Western Europe comparison 191, 193–4, 203
 orderly succession 16, 159
 parliaments 17, 142–4, 153–5, 154*f*, 156, 210
 political stability vii, 2, 3, 4, 10, 13, 15, 17, 39, 41, 57, 108, 133, 158, 160, 211, 214
 primogeniture, partible inheritance, and size of states 167, 179–80, 180*t*, 182
 primogeniture as solution to succession problem 2, 3, 13, 15–16, 42, 210
 state-formation 9–10, 11, 13–14, 39, 39*f*, 42, 110, 204, 209–12, 214
 succession wars 17, 35, 85, 110
primogeniture: origins and spread 3, 10, 13, 15, 43, 86–7, 191
 agnatic family 61, 82
 Catholic Church 10, 16, 38, 60–4, 69, 70–3, 81, 86, 87, 191, 212
 family structures, transformation of 10, 16, 38, 60, 61–8, 72, 82, 86, 191, 212
 gradual adoption of 3, 68, 81–2, 194, 204, 210
 heirship practices, transformation of 10, 16, 38, 60, 61–5, 86, 212

primogeniture: origins and spread (*Continued*)
   Latin west 15, 16, 43, 60, 68–71, 70*f*, 81, 87
   Latin west/Byzantine Empire comparison 71, 87
   Orthodox Church 82–4, 86–7
   proliferation of primogeniture over time 81–2, 81*f*
   Protestant churches 85–6, 87
   as revolutionary heirship practice 60
   state weakness 61, 71–3, 87, 212
   switch from partible inheritance to primogeniture 13–14, 160, 179–80, 191–2
   West Francia 72, 208
   see also marriage
primogeniture: specific cases
   Byzantine Empire 16, 84, 86
   Capetians 56, 73–4, 76, 87, 207–8, 210
   Carolingians 2, 11, 68–9, 86
   England 40, 74, 75, 85, 210
   Eurasia 15, 60, 87
   France 40, 210
   Franks 9, 70, 194, 214
   Holy Roman Empire 77, 79, 85–6, 191–2
   Iberian Peninsula 69, 72, 75–6, 191
   Imperial China 60, 87, 164, 196, 202, 203, 212
   Poland 79
   Russian Empire 80–1, 117
   Scandinavia 78
   United States vi
   West Francia 72, 73, 74, 191, 208
problem of succession 4, 5, 9, 11, 203–4, 205
   authoritarian regime 4, 205–6, 216
   autocratic regime (modern) 18, 216, 221–3
   Byzantine Empire 15, 18, 20, 84, 184, 185–6, 203
   democracy and 223
   dilemma of succession 13, 16, 221
   as driver of conflict 2, 209
   institutionalization, need of 220–1
   Islamic states 189, 190–1, 203
   Mongols 201–2
   Ottoman Empire 11, 15, 23, 190, 191

political instability 2, 9, 209, 210
primogeniture as solution 2, 3, 13, 15–16, 42, 210
representative democracy as solution 4, 215, 222
Roman Empire 15, 184–5, 203
Russian Empire 15
Protestant churches/Reformation 85–6, 87
Prussia 93, 95, 157, 164–5

Qing dynasty 195, 199, 200*t*
Quraysh 187, 188, 189

representative democracy vi, 218
   as solution to problem of succession 4, 215, 222
'Rise of Europe' 214
Roman Empire 71
   five 'good' emperors 184
   political instability 184
   problem of succession 15, 184–5, 203
royal children
   education 28, 91
   legitimate children as only claimants to primogeniture 38
   living sons and daughters over a monarch's lifetime 168, 168*f*
   mortality 27, 35, 148, 168
   well prepared for ruling 29, 91
   see also family and dynasty; heir
royal minorities 27, 36, 49, 90–1, 118, 120, 137, 147, 147*f*
   Alfonso XI, King of Castile 139–40
   Edward VI, King of England 144, 159
   elite and 119, 137
   Henry III, King of England 138, 143, 152
   James the Conqueror, King of Aragon 152
   Louis XIV, King of France 140
   parliaments 138, 139–40, 147, 148, 148*t*, 151, 151*f*, 152, 156
   power-sharing concessions 139, 142
   primogeniture and 142
   regency 137–8, 139–40, 144, 147

ruler
    authoritarian/autocratic leaders 44
    definition 44–5
    see also monarch
ruler–elite relations 2, 12, 21–2, 46, 47, 50, 51, 58
    capitalized coercion 40
    delegation problem 161
    institutions 48
    loyalty-for-spoils contract 112, 160, 162
    parliaments and 101–2
    power-sharing concessions 140–1, 148, 152–3
    succession 12–13, 112, 113–14, 132, 213
Rurikid dynasty 57, 80, 160
Russia 18, 219, 222
Russian Empire
    agnatic seniority 80
    New Law of Succession 81
    primogeniture 80–1, 117
    problem of succession 15
    succession wars 80

Saudi Arabia 18, 216–17
Scandinavia 65, 77–8
    elective monarchy 78, 160
    hereditary monarchy 72
    polygamy 68
    primogeniture 78
    things 78
Scotland 75, 85
selectorate theory 22, 44
Song dynasty 197, 198
sovereignty 8, 53, 221, 223
Soviet Union 220
Spain
    al-Andalus Caliphate, Cordoba 189–90
    Islamic rule in Southern Spain 64, 69
    Northern Spain 72, 190, 203
    Reconquista 70, 190
    see also Iberian Peninsula
Spanish War of Succession 92, 93, 94, 95, 205
state 49–51
    church–state relations 71–3
    composite states 37–8, 51
    dataset: states/polities 51–3, 54*t*, 55*f*
    national state 40
    'nation states' 3, 211
    patrimonial state 48–9
    state weakness and origins of primogeniture 61, 71–3, 87, 212
    territorial boundaries 50–1
state-building 3–4
    Carolingians 207
    institutions and orderly power transfer 214
    state as 'perpetually lived organization' 4
state-formation (European) 3
    AD 1000–1800 14
    'bellicist' approach 3, 5, 6, 7, 11, 211
    endowment approach 3, 5–6, 11
    England 6
    France 6
    German Empire 6
    hereditary monarchy 5
    partible inheritance 39*f*
    patterns 6
    political instability and 7
    politics of succession 11, 12
    primogeniture 9–10, 11, 13–14, 39, 39*f*, 42, 110, 204, 209–12, 214
    succession and 2, 3, 10–11, 14–16, 39–42
succession 205
    'basic/fragile natural states' distinction 11
    dataset of succession arrangements 55–8
    difficulties of 20–1
    Europe before the introduction of primogeniture 183–7
    politicization of 12
    power-sharing arrangements 136
    scholarship on 8–12
    state-formation and 2, 3, 10–11, 14–16, 39–42
    see also politics of succession; problem of succession
succession by appointment 81, 209, 217
    elective monarchy 31–2, 75
    England 32, 74, 75
succession order 20–1, 209
    dataset 56
    succession orders in medieval Europe 30–6
    see also agnatic seniority; elective monarchy; partible inheritance; primogeniture

succession principles 112–20
   characteristics of the designated
      successor 117–20
   existence of a designated
      successor 113–15
   how easily can designations be
      changed? 116–17
succession rules 11, 13
   formalization of succession rules
      through institutions 116
   vague rules of succession 15, 58, 113,
      133, 143, 209, 217
succession wars 88, 97–100, 109–10, 215
   agnatic seniority 17, 91, 101
   crown prince problem 90, 110
   definition 97–9, 110
   depositions 42, 99–100, 99t, 100f, 105
   elective monarchy 17, 91, 94, 101, 110,
      127
   heirs and succession crises 106–8
   natural deaths of rulers 17, 99t, 108–9
   negative impact of 88, 109–10, 205
   primogeniture and 17, 35, 85, 110
   see also civil wars; international wars;
      war/warfare
Sweden 32, 52, 78, 210
Switzerland 40
Syria 217

Tang dynasty 202
taxes 29, 49
   Imperial China 29, 195
territorial agglomeration 13, 200, 211
testamentary succession 13, 26–7, 32, 192
Thirty Year's War 80, 86, 95
Treaty of Verdun 1, 207
Tudor dynasty 106, 158, 159

ultimogeniture 35–6
   England (Borough-English) 35
   Mongols 35, 200, 201
Umayyad Caliphate 188–9, 190
United Sates vi, 215
usurpation
   Byzantine Empire 18, 185, 186, 212
   Imperial China 197

Vikings 14, 187
violence 47
   authoritarian regime 4, 47, 58, 205

Byzantine Empire 185, 186
depositions 111
succession and 205, 210
see also succession wars; war/warfare
Visigoths 111, 112, 186

war/warfare
   'bellicist' approach to state-formation 3,
      5, 6, 7, 11–12, 211
   negative impact of 95
   war in medieval and early modern
      Europe 95–7, 96f, 97f
   see also civil wars; international wars;
      succession wars
West Francia 1–2, 14, 49, 207–8
   breakdown of public order 71–2, 87,
      186–7, 207
   Cluniac reform 66
   primogeniture 72, 73, 74, 191, 208
winning coalition 19–20, 42, 45–6
   agnatic seniority and 34
   commitment problems 22
   elective monarchy and 34
   partible inheritance 38
   primogeniture and 34, 35
   as self-enforcing 22
   sub-coalitions 22–3, 30, 89
   see also elite
Wittelsbach dynasty 176, 176t
women
   attrition rates among queens 169
   dowry 37, 166
   elective monarchy 13
   family and dynasty 17, 18, 165–6, 172–3,
      175, 176–7
   heiress 166
   queens: bearing children as main
      duty 167
   queens and countesses as royal or noble
      regents 166
   reigning queens 165
   see also female inheritance; marriage

Xi Xia dynasty 198–9, 200, 200t, 203

Yuan dynasty (Mongol) 183, 197, 201
   depositions 200, 200t, 201–2
   fall of 202
   political instability 183, 199, 200, 202,
      203

Index of Names

Abaoji, Khitan Khan 198
Abbas (Muhammed's paternal uncle) 189
Abramson, Scott F. 6, 52, 125, 131
Abu Bakr, First Caliph 188
Acemoglu, Daron 6, 22, 28, 41
Acharya, Avidit 10, 106, 108
Aguda, Emperor 198
Albrecht of Mecklenburg, King of Denmark and Norway 32
Alexander the Great 1, 27
Alfonsi, Petrus 21
Alfonso III, King of Portugal 67
Alfonso X, King of Castile 55, 144
Alfonso XI, King of Castile 139–40
Alfred the Great, King of England 74
Ali, Fourth Caliph 187–8
Alphonso III, King of Aragon 153
Amalric, King of the Visigoths 111
Andronikos II, Emperor 122
Arigh Böke Khan 202
Arrhideus/Phillip III, King of Macedonia 27
Arthur, Prince of Wales 158, 159
Arthur I, Duke of Brittany 75, 143
Augustus, Emperor 184
Augustus II, King of Poland 2, 92
Axelrod, Alan 105

Baldwin I of Boulogne, King of Jerusalem 192
Baldwin II of Bourcq, King of Jerusalem 192
Bartlett, Robert 9–10, 21, 38, 70, 94, 109, 113, 115, 163, 164, 165, 185, 214, 215
Bartolus de Saxferrato 222
Bei, Khitan Prince 198
Beria, Lavrentiy 220
Bernard, King of Italy 209
Bertrade de Montfort 67
Bisson, Thomas N. 14, 83
Blanning, Tim 15, 140
Blaydes, Lisa 191, 193–4, 214

Bodin, Jean 8, 9, 60, 94
Boix, Carles 6, 136, 139, 140, 152
Boleslaw III Drymouth, Duke of Poland 79
Börte (Chinggis's principal wife) 201
Bosker, Maarten 102
Brodsky, Joseph 216
Brougham, Henry 88
Brownlee, Jason 23, 218, 221
Bueno De Mesquita, Bruce 22, 44, 162
Burgundy, Dukes of 7, 50
Buringh, Eltjo 102
Burling, Robbins 21, 113

Carpenter, David A. 138–9
Catherine of Aragon, Queen of England 159
Chagatai Khan 201
Chaney, Eric 191, 193–4, 214
Charlemagne, Emperor 66, 72, 186, 187
 coronation 1, 206
 marriages 68, 83
Charles II, the Bald, King of West Francia 207
Charles II, King of Spain 92
Charles IV, King of France 98, 208
Charles V, Emperor 37–8, 164
Charles VI, Emperor 92, 93, 144
Charles VII, King of France 50
Charles XII, King of Sweden 144
Charles the Bold, Duke of Burgundy 7, 50
Charles Martel 63, 68
Chinggis Khan, Emperor 183, 200–1, 203
Christian II, King of Sweden 97
Christian IV, King of Denmark 121
Clodius Albinus, Emperor 184
Commodus, Emperor 184
Constantine the Great, Emperor 185

De Montesquieu, Charles 24
Deng Xiaoping 219, 220, 221
Desiderata, Langobard princess 68
De Tocqueville, Alexis vi, 209

INDEX OF NAMES

Didius Julianus, Emperor 184
Diocletian, Emperor 184, 185
Drinkwater, John 184
Dube, Oeindrila 106

Edward I, King of England 75, 152, 156
Edward III, King of England 98, 114, 164
Edward VI, King of England 144, 159
Edward the Black Prince 164
Edward the Confessor, King of England 32, 92, 109
Edward Stafford, Duke of Buckingham 114
Egorov, Georgy 22
Eisner, Manuel 120–1
Elizabeth I, Queen of England 23–4, 144, 159, 169, 222
Eric of Pomerania, King of Denmark, Norway, and Sweden 37, 78, 121

Fearon, James D. 96
Feodor I, Tsar of Russia 80
Ferdinand II, King of Bohemia 80
Fernando IV, King of Castile 139
Fichtner, Paula Sutter vii, 85–6, 164
Finer, Samuel P. 186, 189, 195, 211–12
  History of Government 13, 20, 202–3
Franklin, Benjamin vi, 163
Frantz, Erica 221
Fredegar 111
Frederick II, Emperor 7, 165, 191
Frederick V, Elector Palatine and King of Bohemia 80
Frederick Barbarossa, Emperor 191
Frederick the Great, King of Prussia 93, 164–5
Frederik III, King of Denmark 78
Fukuyama, Francis 11, 181
Fulk IV, Count of Anjou 67

Galba, Emperor 184
Geddes, Barbara 221
Gelasius I, Pope 66
Genghis Khan, Emperor 1, 15
Geoffrey II, Duke of Brittany 75, 143
Gerring, John 45
Ghazali, Abu Hamid Muhammad al- 28
Goody, Jack 61–2
Greengrass, Mark 172–3
Gregory VII, Pope 66, 72–3

Gregory, Bishop of Tours 111, 115
Gustav Vasa, King of Sweden 78, 85

Haakon IV, King of Norway 78
Harald Bluetooth, King of Denmark. 77–8
Harald Hardrada, King of Norway 92, 109
Harish, S. P. 106
Harold Godwinson, King of England 32, 74, 109
Henrich, Joseph 63
Henry I, King of England 74
Henry II, King of England 74, 88, 117, 180
Henry III, King of England 48, 75, 134, 141, 152, 152, 156
  accession 136–7, 138
  royal minority 138, 143, 152
Henry IV, Emperor 121–2
Henry VII, King of England 158
Henry VII, King of Germany 165
Henry VIII, King of England 106, 114–15, 158–9
  divorce 106, 159
  Succession Acts 144
Henry Louis, Prince of Prussia 165
Herb, Michael 217
Hertz, John 25
Hintze, Otto 5
Hobbes, Thomas 8, 9, 158, 221
Houphouët-Boigny, Félix 221
Hugh Capet, King of the Franks 51, 73, 207
Hugh of Die, papal legate 67
Hulagu Khan 201, 202

Ibn Khaldun 117, 161–2
Ibn Saud, King of Saudi Arabia 216
Ingeborg of Denmark 67
Innocent III, Pope 48, 67, 134

James I, King of Aragon 121
James II, King of Aragon 153
James III, King of Scotland 130
James IV, King of Scotland 130
James the Conqueror, King of Aragon 152, 153
Jochi Khan 201, 202
Jogaila/Wladyslaw II Jagiellon, Grand Duke of Lithuania and King of Poland 80

Index of Names

John Lackland, King of England 75, 136–7, 143, 180, 208
   death 54–5, 138–9
   Magna Carta 48, 134, 136
Johnson, Simon 6
Jordan, William Chester 9, 13, 28

Kangxi Emperor 199
Kantorowicz, Ernst 181, 222
Khrushchev, Nikita 220
Khubilai Khan, Emperor 183, 201, 202
Kim Jong-un 218
Kulikowski, Michael 184
Kurrild-Klitgaard, Peter 10

Laitin, David D. 96
Lee, Alexander 10, 106, 108
Leo I, Pope 66
Leo III, Emperor 62
Leo III, Pope 1
Leo VI, the Wise, Emperor 83
Leopold I, King of Hungary 80
Lewis, Andrew W. 73
Lothair I, King of Middle Francia 207
Lothar II, King of Francia 64
Louis I, King of Hungary 79
Louis II the German, King of East Francia 207
Louis VIII, King of France 134, 143, 208
Louis IX, King of France 74
Louis XIV, King of France (the Sun King) 2, 41, 121, 140
Louis XV, King of France 2
Louis XVI, King of France 51
Louis the Pious, Emperor 1, 68, 209–10
   death 1, 2, 38, 68, 186, 207

Machiavelli, Niccoló 163, 184
Maddicott, John Robert 137, 138, 139
Magnus III, King of Sweden 160
Magnus Eriksson, King of Sweden 27
Malthus, Thomas Robert vi
Mann, Michael 141
Mantel, Hilary 158
Margarethe, Queen of Denmark, Norway and Sweden 32, 78
Maria Theresa of Spain (House of Habsburg) 93, 94, 144
Marongiu, Antonio 135, 145–6

Marshall, William 134, 136
Mary, Queen of England 114, 144, 159
Mason, Roger 130
Mehmed II, Sultan 190
Mehmed III, Sultan 190
Meng, Anne 116, 220–1
Michael Romanov, Tsar of Russia 81, 117
Mohammed bin Salman, crown prince of Saudi Arabia 216–17
Möngke Khan, Emperor 201
Moore, Barrington vi
Moore, Robert Ian 9, 10, 15–16, 60, 72
Mote, Frederick W. 196
Muawiya, Umayyad Caliph of Damascus 188
Mubarak, Gamal 218
Mubarak, Hosni 218
Muhammed, Prophet 187–8

Napoleon, Emperor 1
Nero, Emperor 184
Nerva, Emperor 184
Nicholas I, Pope 64, 65
North, Douglas 4, 11

Ögödei Khan 201, 202
Olof I Tryggvason, King of Norway 78
Olson, Mancur 4, 28, 110, 133
Olympias (Alexander the Great's mother) 27
Otho, Emperor 184
Ottokar I, King of Bohemia 79

Paine, Thomas 9
Palmer, Alan 40
Paul I, Emperor 81
Pepin III, King of the Franks 68, 186
Pepin of Herstal 63
Pertinax, Emperor 184
Pescennius Niger, Emperor 184
Peter II, King of Aragon 152
Peter III, King of Aragon 153
Peter the Great, Emperor 15, 31, 81, 116–17
Philip I, King of France 66–7
Philip II, Habsburg King 37–8, 164
Philip II Augustus, King of France 56, 67, 73, 208
Philip III, King of France 73–4, 75

INDEX OF NAMES

Philip IV the Fair, King of France 215
Philip V, King of Spain 92
Philip VI, King of France 98
Philip the Good, Duke of Burgundy 50
Phillips, Charles 105
Pizarro, Francisco 203
Podany, Amanda H. 203
Popper, Karl 215
Putin, Vladimir 219, 222

Ralph of Coggeshall 55
Richard I (Lionheart), King of England 74–5, 117
Richard III, King of England 158, 173
Rivera, Carlos Velasco 125, 131
Robert Curthose, Duke of Normandy 74
Robert of Normandy, Count 64
Robinson, James 6, 28, 41
Rokkan, Stein 6
Rossabi, Morris 202
Rousseau, Jean-Jacques 9, 28
Rudolf I, King of Germany 7, 165–6

Salman Al Saud, King of Saudi Arabia 216–17
Sancho 'the Great', King of Pamplona and Navarre 75
Scheidel, Walter 11, 41
Schulz, Jonathan F. 64, 82
Schumpeter, Joseph 215
Septimius Severus, Emperor 184
Shakespeare, William 173
Sharma, Vivek 10–11, 58–9
Shunzi Emperor 199
Sigeric, Prince of Burgundy 115
Sigismund, King of the Burgundians 115
Sonin, Konstantin 22
Spruyt, Hendrik 11
Stalin, Josef 220
Stasavage, David 189–90, 194, 195
Stephen of Blois, King of England 74
Svend Estridsen, Danish King 65
Svolik, Milan 12–13, 46, 50, 116, 135–6, 139, 140, 152, 219, 221, 222

Tegüder, Sultan 202
Temür Khan 202
Thelen, Kathleen 140, 141
Theudoald 63
Theutberga 64
Thorpe, Lewis 111, 115
Tilly, Charles 3, 5, 40, 211
Tolui Khan 201
Tostig Godwinson, Anglo-Saxon Earl of Northumbria 109
Trajan, Emperor 184
Tullock, Gordon 10, 11, 25

Ulrika Eleonora, Queen of Sweden 144
Umar, Second Caliph 188
Urban II, Pope 66–7
Uthman, Third Caliph 188

Van Zanden, Jan Luiten 102
Vasily II, Grand Prince of Moscow 80
Vespasian, Emperor 184
Vitellius, Emperor 184

Wallis, John 4, 11
Wang, Yuhua 10, 164, 183, 195, 197, 213
Warren, Wilfred Lewis 117
Weber, Max 48, 51, 87, 133, 187
Weingast, Barry 4, 11
Wheatcroft, Andrew 160
Wickham, Chris 14, 64, 83, 145
William the Conqueror, King of England 32, 63–4, 74, 92, 109
   Harrying of the North 95
William Rufus, King of England 74
Wladyslaw I Lokietek, Kinf of Poland 79
Wolford, Scott 93–4
Wright, Joseph 221

Xi Jinping 219, 220, 223

Yaroslav the Wise, Grand Prince of Kiev 80
Yongzhen Emperor 199
Yury of Zvenigorod, Duke of Zvenigorod and Galich 80

Zoe Karvounopsina, Empress Consort 83